GOLD

advanced

teacher's book

Clementine Annabell
Rawdon Wyatt

CONTENTS

Rationale

Welcome to *Gold Advanced*, an innovative and engaging course for students preparing to sit Cambridge English: Advanced or working at C1 on the common European framework. *Gold Advanced* follows the same identity and approach as the previous *CAE Gold Plus*, but with all new content tailored to the 2015 exam specifications. Rich authentic texts, carefully chosen to appeal to adults and older teenagers, provide the basis for lessons that will captivate the interest of both students and teachers alike.

A well-prepared student will enter the exam confident both of their English level and the best strategies to approach each task. Students will finish the *Gold Advanced* course confident of what to expect in the exam from the detailed Exam focus section and tips for every practice task. In addition, there is an extensive Writing reference section with sample graded answers and comments, and useful language for each genre.

The *Gold Advanced* package combines a suite of printed and digital components that can be used individually or in a multitude of combinations to suit the learner's needs and the technology available. The table on page 5 gives an overview of how the components available with *Gold Advanced* fit together. The teaching notes include many ideas for how and when to integrate the different components to provide a seamlessly integrated and easy-to-use course package that both tech-savvy teachers and those using an interactive whiteboard for the first time will find invaluable.

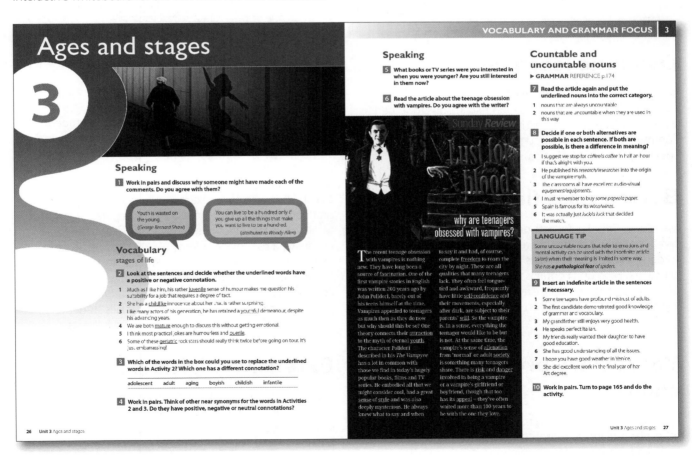

Main features of the course

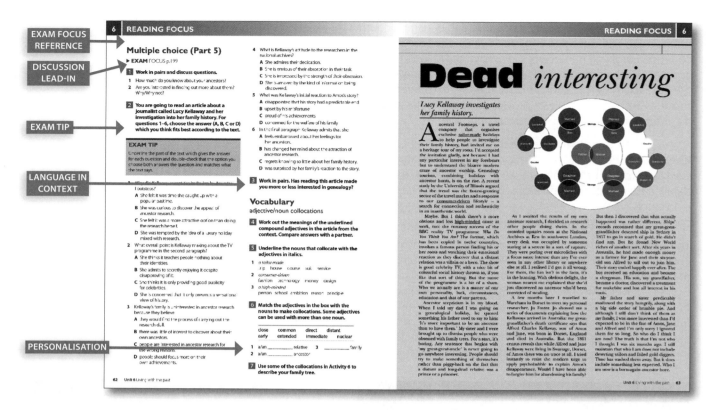

Dynamic learning

Using *Gold Advanced* makes it easy to teach light, fun classes with stimulating, discussion-rich lessons together with lots of personalisation. There is a strong emphasis on communicative practice and the development of natural speaking skills to develop student confidence.

Better class flow

Material in *Gold Advanced* is divided into lessons on spreads or pages so that there is a natural progression through a variety of activities including individual, pair- and classwork. Each unit contains practice for all four papers of the Cambridge English: Advanced exam and every lesson includes an integrated range of skills with plenty of discussion.

Vocabulary presented in chunks

In *Gold Advanced,* phrasal verbs, collocations, idioms and other vocabulary are presented and practised in context to help students understand and remember them better.

Comprehensive exam practice and support

Gold Advanced ensures that both teachers and students know what to expect in the 2015 exam and how to deal with each part effectively, thanks to the carefully staged exam tasks and comprehensive Exam focus section detailing strategies for every part of the exam, as well as extra tips with every exam task. Support levels are graduated through the book to help prepare students for tackling the tasks independently in the exam. The *Exam Maximiser* also provides plenty of revision, practice and extension, as well as a complete Practice test, additional Use of English sections and advice on how to avoid making common exam errors. *MyEnglishLab: Cambridge Advanced* provides further online practice of the skills students will need to excel in their exam as well as two full tests.

Extensive digital package

The *Gold Advanced* digital components provide an easy-to-use solution for teachers and schools who wish to incorporate technology to a greater extent in their classes to provide a more engaging student experience. Components include the *eText for students, eText IWB software for teachers, Online Testmaster* and *MyEnglishLab: Cambridge Advanced.* You will find many ideas of how and when to use these included in the *Teacher's Book* along with other suggestions for incorporating technology, and suggested web searches.

Gold *Advanced* Package Components

Component	Technology Required	Description
Coursebook		The *Gold Advanced Coursebook* includes fourteen engaging units integrating all skills and papers, authentic texts, exam-style practice and exam tips with every exam task. It also contains a useful Grammar reference, a detailed Exam focus section, and a comprehensive Writing reference including model answers for each text type.
Exam Maximiser	Internet connection for audio Download the Maximiser audio at: www.english.com/goldadvanced	The *Exam Maximiser* is an additional practice book providing extra work on exam tasks and language points. Activities follow on from but are not dependent on the *Coursebook* and include plenty of extra listening practice, with audio available online. There are seven additional Use of English spreads, as well as a complete Practice test. In the *Teacher's Book*, activities from the *Exam Maximiser* are suggested at the end of each lesson.
MyEnglishLab: Cambridge Advanced	Computers with internet connection Students' unique access codes are on the inside front cover of their *Coursebook with MyEnglishLab*. Arrange your teacher's access code through your local Pearson office: www.pearsonelt.com/worldwideoffices	*MyEnglishLab: Cambridge Advanced* is designed to be used alongside the *Gold Advanced* course. It includes comprehensive training in the subskills and areas of language that underpin the exam, video presentations of each part of the exam and two full practice tests. Most activities are automatically graded, giving students instant rich feedback and saving you time in the classroom. The gradebook allows you to track students' progress as a group or individually and, along with the Common Error Report, identify individuals or general areas for additional attention.
eText for students	Student netbooks/computers Students' unique access codes are printed on their eText Access Card.	The *Gold Advanced eText for students* is a digital version of the coursebook for students to use at home or on netbooks or computers in the classroom. It includes interactive activities and the full audio so they can listen as many times as they need to and read along with the audio script.
Teacher's Book	Photocopier for photocopiables	The *Gold Advanced Teacher's Book* is a complete guide to using all of the *Gold Advanced Components* in a blended classroom. You'll find lesson plans with answers, audio scripts and sample writing task answers. The teaching notes include references to all of the Gold components as well as supplementary ideas for warmers and extension activities, advice on using the digital components and other ideas for a blended classroom, including suggested web searches. The *Teacher's Book* also includes two photocopiable activities for each unit to provide extra communicative practice in class.
eText IWB software for teachers	Interactive Whiteboard/Projector	*Gold Advanced eText IWB software for teachers* can be used during class to display the course pages, play audio and do exercises. You can also bring up answers for all activities, watch a video of a mock speaking test and, of course, access all the essential IWB tools and add notes, links and documents. Each unit includes games practising key grammar points or vocabulary from the unit.
Online Testmaster	Computer with internet connection Access the Testmaster through your local Pearson office: www.pearsonelt.com/worldwideoffices	The *Online Testmaster* provides the teacher with customisable tests including placement tests, a unit test for each unit, five progress tests and an exit test.
Class Audio	Internet connection or CD player Access the online audio through your local Pearson office: www.pearsonelt.com/worldwideoffices	Class audio is available online for teaches who choose not to use the IWB software. Audio CDs are also available in some markets.

For details on how to order, please go to www.pearsonelt.com

Teaching strategies

The *Gold Advanced Online Testmaster* includes an entry test which may be used as an aid to establish whether a student is at an appropriate level for the *Gold Advanced* course. Even if two students were to attain an identical numerical score, no two learners are exactly the same and consequently it is natural that every teacher has to manage a degree of diversity in their class due to variation in prior knowledge, learning pace and style, and motivation.

A key aspect to successfully teaching a multi-level class is to know your learners.

Ideas to help you know your learners:

Student reflection

Ask students to reflect on and describe their own goals, strengths and weaknesses in their personal English-learning journey. This works well as an initial writing assignment for the first day's homework on the course.

Test to help you teach

The *Gold Advanced Online Testmaster* includes a range of assessment resources including entry and exit tests, fourteen unit tests and five progress tests. *MyEnglishLab: Cambridge Advanced* includes two full practice tests, which give feedback directly into students' gradebooks. Using these tests can help you focus your classes more precisely to your students' needs.

Make time to listen

During group discussions and pairwork, take the opportunity to circulate and listen. Make notes on what you hear, especially any areas that require targeted development to deal with later in the lesson or at a future point.

Read student writing regularly

Each *Gold Advanced* unit includes a writing assignment. By giving individual feedback, you will learn a lot about each student as a writer. Make sure you keep in mind what you notice to include in future teaching.

Try to be constructive in your feedback and give encouragement as well as suggestions. Consider using a consistent approach to marking, for example 'Things you did well'/'Things you could improve on next time'.

Tutorials

Some teachers find meeting with students individually in a tutorial beneficial for monitoring and discussing progress. You could allow 15 minutes once a month for this.

Record-keeping

Records could be as simple as a page for each student in the class register binder, or could be kept electronically in a document or spreadsheet. Having a place to keep notes on each student including goals, test scores and writing feedback makes it easier to remember the details of individuals as well as to write reports.

If you are using *MyEnglishLab: Cambridge Advanced*, you could store all of the information in your resources area within the platform.

Manage multi-level classes

Plenty of pairwork

Working in pairs and small groups gives students the opportunity to learn reciprocally. Discussing reasons for their answers in an activity can be particularly useful by providing both the challenge of articulating a reason effectively and the support of having someone else's thought process explained. The lesson plans in the *Gold Advanced Teacher's Book* include pairwork in every lesson.

Mix them up

The more diverse your class, the more important it is to change partners regularly to ensure students get a range of practice with people with different strengths. This is particularly important for preparation for the Speaking paper of Cambridge Advanced, where students will be paired with someone who may have a higher or lower level than themselves.

Repeating an exercise with a new partner is a useful strategy which gives students of all abilities the opportunity to improve on their first performance.

Offer choices

Many students respond well to choices that help them make a decision about their own learning. For example: 'OK, I'm going to offer you a choice here. For those of you who would like to look at the third conditional in more detail, I'm going to work through the Grammar reference now. If you feel you are already familiar with the third conditional, you are welcome to start the third conditional activity on page X.'

Have a plan for fast finishers

If your class is particularly diverse, there may be a significant variation in the time it takes for students to complete an exercise, especially during timed tests or writing activities. One option is to write the day's homework on the board before class, and let students know that if they finish class exercises early they are welcome to begin working on their homework. Another option for fast finishers in almost any lesson is for them to design a few extra questions/exercises on the lesson topic for the rest of the class. Some teachers like to have a basket of English newspapers/magazines/readers available.

Provide extra support

Some additional suggestions for students who are finding the course very challenging include:

- giving students the opportunity to rehearse before discussion activities, e.g. 'You're going to speak with your partner about the photos on page X. Take a minute now to look at them and think about what you're going to say. I'll let you know when to begin.'

- for writing activities, eliciting starters on the board which students may choose to use.

- encouraging students to listen to the audio from the lesson again after class.

See page 191 for some recommended additional resources.

Teaching with MyEnglishLab

MyEnglishLab: Cambridge Advanced complements *Gold Advanced* and allows you to provide students with a blended learning experience. Focusing on the subskills that underpin the Cambridge English: Advanced exam, *MyEnglishLab: Cambridge Advanced* includes interactive practice activities, video introductions to each part of the exam and two full practice tests. You and your students can access these materials wherever there is an internet connection.

Using *MyEnglishLab: Cambridge Advanced* allows you to spend less time marking exercises in class, which frees up classroom time for more communicative activities, project work, and so on, and students receive instant detailed feedback which is relevant to the answer they gave.

Introduce MyEnglishLab to your students

After you have registered and created your course, students can register using the unique access code from their Coursebook and your Teacher's course code. Students will feel more confident about accessing their online course activities if you demonstrate how in class.

Introducing the purpose of MyEnglishLab to your class is essential. You can discuss how you intend to use it and why it is beneficial: students can work in a digital format – perhaps they'll like this for variety and a sense of independence, or perhaps they are preparing for the computer-based test; they'll have access to additional practice of the key skills they'll need to excel in the exam; they can get instant feedback on their answers; they can track their progress very easily with the onscreen indicators.

Assign work regularly

You can make all of the material available for students to work through in their own time or assign specific activities as you go through your course. Suggestions for activities to assign with Gold Advanced are made in the Additional Practice sections of these teacher's notes. You can assign tasks to the whole class, to groups of students with different needs or to individual students. It's nice to send students an email about their assignments using the email function in the Messages tab.

Make the most of the gradebook

Check the gradebook regularly to see how your students are doing. If students are not completing activities, you can email them to find out why. You can export the gradebook as an Excel file to make life easy when you need to write student reports.

Common Error Report

The Common Error Report in the gradebook shows the frequency and types of errors students have made on an exercise. This makes it easy for you to identify areas for further remedial teaching.

Messages

MyEnglishLab: Cambridge Advanced enables you to send and keep track of messages to your students outside class. You can remind students about their homework, offer guidance, and have one-to-one exchanges with individual students. There is also a folder where you can upload documents for the class such as reading material, sample answers or notices.

Where we live

Speaking and Use of English focus ▶ CB p.6

Speaking

Aims
• to introduce the topic of 'where we live' • to provide spoken practice

Warmer: Introducing each other

If this is a new class, have students introduce a partner to the class. In pairs, ask students to find out their partner's name, home town and reasons for taking this course. Then each student introduces their partner, e.g. *This is Talia. She grew up in a small town not far from Moscow. She is planning on studying International Business and wants English for her career.*

1 Students discuss in pairs. Elicit a few answers to each question.

Alternative activity: Move around

If there is room in the classroom, students walk around answering one question with each person, before moving on to a new partner.

Interview (Part 1)
talking about yourself

Aims
• to introduce an exam-style speaking task (Speaking Part 1) • to practise giving personal information in an exam-style discussion

Tell students that the Speaking paper of the exam is divided into four parts. Part 1 consists of an interview which involves answering questions with personal information and opinions. For more detailed information and strategies for this section, refer students to the **Exam focus** on p.204 and turn to it on eText if you are using it.

2 Play the recording and elicit which question the examiner asks.

3 Ask students which of the candidates provides a response of an appropriate length. Focus students' attention on the **Exam tip** and elicit some other introductory phrases (e.g. *You know, I suppose, Let me see*).

4 For each response listed, elicit the question that was asked. Then ask students to think about how they would respond to each question with something longer and more interesting. Students take turns to ask and answer the questions in pairs.

5 Ask students to complete the task on p.152, alternating the roles of examiner and candidate.

6 Tell students that the Speaking paper is marked in bands, with Band 5 being the highest. Summarise the bands in the following way: Band 5: Speaks fluently and accurately, uses a wide range of complex language. Band 3: Speaks fairly fluently and mostly accurately, uses a range of language. Band 1: Speaks with some hesitation, uses mainly simple forms and vocabulary. For more detail, refer students to the **Marking guidelines** on p.207. Give students a moment to evaluate their own performance against the guidelines. Then give them a few minutes to discuss how they rated themselves and any suggestions they have for their partner to improve.

Teaching tip

Exam task videos
There is a video example of each exam task on the eText for you to show students.

Answers

2 What do you like most about the area where you grew up?

3 Karl

Multiple-choice cloze (Part 1)

Aim

- to complete an exam-style multiple-choice cloze task (Reading and Use of English Part 1)

Tell students that the Reading and Use of English paper of the exam is divided into eight parts. Part 1 is a multiple-choice cloze: a gapped text with a choice of four options for each gap. For more information, refer students to the **Exam focus** on p.197.

7 Focus students' attention on the title of the article. Elicit the meaning of the adjective *fairytale* (extremely happy, lucky, etc. in a way that usually only happens in children's stories, e.g. *a fairytale romance, a fairytale ending*). Read the **Exam tip** aloud with students and point out that knowledge of collocations is tested explicitly in the Reading and Use of English paper. Tell students not to read the article yet and elicit some other features that children might have included in their dream homes.

8 Emphasise that students should read the text quickly, without worrying about the gaps or unknown vocabulary at this stage. Elicit a few answers.

9 Give students a minute to match the reasons with the incorrect alternatives, then check as a class.

10 Students do the activity, then discuss their answers in pairs before you check as a class. For each answer, elicit reasons behind the choice (see Answers below).

11 Give students a moment to think about how the place they live now corresponds to their ideal home. Put students into small groups to share their thoughts.

Answers

9 1 C   2 A   3 D

10 1 B (*study* collocates with *revealed*)   2 C (*challenges* collocates with *conventional wisdom*; *challenges* can be followed by the preposition *to*, whereas *issues* is followed by *with/of* and *questions/tests* by *of*)
3 B (*express* collocates with *a desire*)   4 C (difference in meaning)   5 B (*ultimate* collocates with *dream*)
6 D (*opt* is the only option that can be followed by *for*; *choose/select* take a direct object without a preposition and *decide* is followed by *on* + direct object)
7 C (difference in meaning)   8 A (*rather* is followed by *than, instead* is followed by *of* and *between* does not fit semantically)

Additional activity: Collocations

Refer students back to the **Exam tip**. Ask them to reread the article and underline five collocations. Students share their answers in pairs and together write a sentence including three of the collocations. Elicit a few of the sentences with the class. To help, students could also use a dictionary such as the *Longman Exams Dictionary* or the *Longman Dictionary of Contemporary English*, which can be searched online at http://www.ldoceonline.com. Possible collocations include: *recent study, major challenges, challenge conventional wisdom, express a desire, ultimate dream house, indoor swimming pool, football pitch, bouncy castle, family home.*

ADDITIONAL PRACTICE | Maximiser p.6–7, Speaking 1, Use of English 1–2 | **MyEnglishLab: Cambridge Advanced**, Speaking 1: Giving good Part 1 answers, Speaking 2: What makes a good Part 1 answer, Speaking 3: Answering Part 1 questions about the future effectively, Use of English 18: Understanding the whole text.

Grammar focus ▶ CB p.8
Speaking

Aim
- to present perfect and continuous forms in context in preparation for revision of forms

1 Put students in pairs and ask them to think of at least three advantages and disadvantages of living in a small town. Then ask students for a show of hands to indicate whether they consider themselves a *city person* or a *small town person*. Invite a few students to give reasons for their choice.

2 Play the recording and elicit whether the speaker mentioned any of the things that were talked about in Activity 1. Elicit any other advantages or disadvantages she talked about.

Perfect and continuous forms

Aim
- to revise the use of perfect and continuous forms

3 Students choose the correct verb forms, then check their answers in pairs. Play the recording again for students to check which form the speaker uses in each case.

Additional activity: Think of …
Ask students to think of:
- two things they have done in the last month that have given them a sense of satisfaction.
- two things they hope they will have done by their next birthday.

Ask students to share their answers with a partner using some of the verb forms in Activity 3.

4 Students discuss the difference in meaning between each pair of sentences then compare ideas as a class.

5 Check students understand the terms *stative verb* (a verb that describes a state of being) and *dynamic verb* (a verb that describes an action). Ask them to divide the stative verbs into groups, then check as a class. Talk through the **Language tip** and see if students can think of any other examples of verbs with both stative and dynamic meanings (e.g. *have, be, think*).

Additional activity: Stative or dynamic?
Share the following examples and ask students, in pairs, to decide whether each verb is stative or dynamic.

I *have* coffee every morning. (dynamic) I *have* a dog. (stative) He *thinks* it's a great idea. (stative) She can't stop *thinking* about the issue. (dynamic) She *was* annoying. (dynamic) He *is* Korean. (stative)

Refer students to the **Grammar reference** on p.181 (Verb forms) and turn to it on eText if you are using it. Tell students that this provides a useful summary of verb forms and ask them to read it for homework.

6 Students complete the activity then compare their answers in pairs before you check as a class.

7 Give students a moment to think about the question and the verb forms. Share an example (e.g. *I've been living in my mansion for a year now. It's been wonderful having servants …*). For additional speaking practice, give students a few minutes to share their ideas in pairs first before they tell the class.

Answers

3 1 I'd been telling   2 I had, in fact, always been
3 both   4 both   5 both, have discovered
6 will have been

Forms used by speaker:
1 I'd been telling (past perfect continuous)
2 I had, in fact, always been (past perfect simple)
3 will have been living (future perfect)   4 I've been looking back … (present perfect continuous)   5 I've spent, have discovered (present perfect simple)   6 will have been (future perfect)

4 1 A They are still renovating. B They've finished renovating.
2 A The focus is on the total distance covered at the end of the journey. B The focus is on repeatedly covering the same distance every day.
3 A The focus is on completing the essay. B The focus is on the time spent writing it.

5 Emotions: care, like, love
Knowledge: believe, know, understand
Possession: belong, own, possess
Communication: agree, deny, promise
Senses: hear, smell, taste

6 1 think   2 am thinking   3 am seeing   4 see
5 am tasting   6 tastes

ADDITIONAL PRACTICE | **Maximiser** p.7, Grammar 1–5 |
MyEnglishLab: Cambridge Advanced, Use of English 10: Verb tenses |
Photocopiable p.142/171, 1A *Find the phrase*

Vocabulary focus ▶ CB p.9

Reading

Aim

● to present examples of figurative language in context

1 Focus attention on the picture and elicit what students can see. In pairs, students discuss which city noises they find irritating and which they like.

2 Ask students to read the article and see how many of the noises they discussed were mentioned.

Figurative language

Aim

● to extend students' knowledge of figurative language

Check students understand the heading *figurative language* and elicit the antonym *literal*. Explain that a figurative word or phrase is used in a different way from its usual meaning, to give you a particular idea or picture in your mind. The literal meaning is the basic or original meaning.

3 Ask students to look at the first underlined word in the text (*whine*) and ask what they think it means. Explain that the literal meaning of *whine* is 'to moan in a high-pitched voice', so in this case, it means that the scooters are making a high-pitched sound. Students complete the sentences with the correct form of the underlined words. Ask them to compare their answers in pairs before you check as a class.

Read the **Language tip** with the class and ask if students know of any other examples of animal sound verbs that we might use for human speech, e.g. *squeak* (mouse), *howl* (wolf), *growl* (dog).

4 Students work in pairs to decide which words in the box are associated with humans, animals or both. Go through the answers with the class, checking students understand each verb.

5 Students complete the activity, then compare answers in pairs before you check as a class.

6 Look at the first example with the class and elicit the answer (*clap*). Students choose the correct alternative in each sentence. Check answers as a class.

7 Students work in pairs to complete the activity on p.161. They take turns to use the verbs in Activities 4–6 to talk about one of the pictures and their partner guesses which picture they have chosen. Emphasise that they should avoid using specific nouns which would make it too obvious (e.g. they should say: *something is whining*, not *the ambulance is whining*).

Teaching tip

Recording vocabulary
Suggest students choose a place to record new vocabulary and collocations. Remind them that collocations are very important for Paper 1 and will also help with the other sections, as well as making their English sound more natural.

Answers

3 1 giggling 2 whining 3 sighed 4 wail
5 rumbling 6 buzzing

4 bark: A clap: H cough: B groan: H purr: A roar: B
shudder: B sigh: B stutter: H tremble: B

5 1 trembled 2 purrs 3 stuttered 4 groaned
5 clapped 6 roar 7 barks 8 cough 9 shudder
10 sigh

6 1 clap 2 roar 3 groaned, shudder 4 barked
5 coughed, stuttered 6 trembled

ADDITIONAL PRACTICE | **Maximiser** p.8, Vocabulary 1

Reading focus ▶ CB p.10

Speaking

Aims

● to introduce the topic of city navigation in preparation for the reading text
● to provide spoken practice

1 Students discuss the questions in pairs. Elicit a few ideas for each question. Then ask: *What jobs would require a good sense of direction?*

Multiple choice (Part 5)

Aim

● to complete an exam-style multiple-choice reading task (Reading and Use of English Part 5)

Tell students that Part 5 of the Reading and Use of English paper focuses on their ability to understand a long text in detail. It consists of a text with six multiple-choice questions. For more information, refer students to the **Exam focus** on p.199 and on eText if you are using it.

2 Give students a minute to read the title and first paragraph, then elicit a few predictions of what the whole article will be about. Give students five minutes to read the article quickly to check their predictions.

Teaching tip

Time limits

Set a time limit to encourage students to read quickly and gradually reduce the time during the course as students get used to reading quickly.

3 Read the **Exam tip** with the class. Ask students to read the questions and underline key words before rereading the text. Tell students that as they answer each question, they should find and mark the part of the text that each question relates to, then reread it in detail. After students have answered the questions, they compare their answers in pairs. As you go through the answers, elicit evidence for each one.

4 Students discuss the questions in pairs or small groups. Ask one student from each group to tell the class the most interesting story from their group.

Answers

3 **1** B (lines 1–5)

   2 B ('an intense intellectual ordeal'; 'two to four years to learn everything')

   3 A ('Incredible as it may seem')

   4 C ('undergo a change which makes them very different from those of mere mortals'; 'Among all of these groups, only the London cabbies, with their heightened spatial memories, have the change Maguire was looking for.')

   5 D ('Strange as it may seem, though, when researchers looked at drivers in these cities in a bid to replicate Maguire's London study, they found none of the same changes in brain structure.')

   6 B ('Believe these tales if you choose')

Vocabulary

working out meaning from context

Aim

- to practise working out meaning from context

5 Tell students that working out meaning from context is an important skill both in conversation and the exam. Brainstorm strategies for deducing the meaning of an unknown word, e.g. understand the context, read the whole sentence, work out the word class (is it a verb, noun, etc.?), have a good guess. Students match the underlined words with the meanings. They compare their answers in pairs, then as a class.

6 Tell students that they can change the form of the words if they need to (e.g. *frantic* → *frantically*). Allow students about ten minutes to write their sentences, then put them in pairs to compare.

Answers

5 **1** awe **2** somewhat **3** ordeal **4** baffled
   5 bewildering **6** feat **7** fare **8** frantic

ADDITIONAL PRACTICE | **Maximiser** p.8–9, Reading 1–4 |
MyEnglishLab: Cambridge Advanced, Reading 1: Predicting the text A

Listening focus ▶ CB p.12
Speaking

Aim

- to provide spoken practice

1 Check students understand the idea of a *floor plan* (a drawing of the shape of a building and the position of the things in it, as seen from above). Give students a couple of minutes to sketch a basic floor plan, then put them in pairs to discuss the questions.

Multiple matching (Part 4)

Aim

- to complete an exam-style multiple matching task (Listening Part 4)

Tell students that the Listening paper consists of four parts. Part 4 focuses on understanding informal speech and involves reading two tasks of eight statements each, then listening to five short monologues on a related topic and matching one statement from each task to one of the speakers. For more information, refer students to the **Exam focus** on p.203.

2 Ask students to follow Strategy 2 from the **Exam focus** (highlight key words or phrases). Elicit the meanings of *lack* (shortage), *be obliged* (have to do something), *claustrophobia* (fear of being enclosed in a small space) and *domestic chores* (small jobs in the home you have to do regularly). Students then tick the things they like least about the place where they currently live (Task 1), and tick the advantages it has (Task 2).

Teaching tip

eText pen tool
Use the pen tool on eText to model underlining key words in exam tasks.

3 Read the **Exam tip** with the class. Play the recording twice, pausing in between. Then check answers as a class.

4 Ask students to discuss in pairs what sort of person they think each speaker is, then elicit a few opinions about each.

Answers

3 Task 1 1 G   2 A   3 D   4 E   5 H
Task 2 6 D   7 C   8 B   9 F   10 G

Vocabulary

expressions with *space* and *room*

Aim

- to expand students' knowledge of expressions with *space* and *room*

5 Students complete the activity, then compare in pairs before you check as a class.

Additional activity: What's happening?

In pairs, ask students to take turns to guess who each speaker in Activity 5 might be talking to and what the situation is, e.g. *I think the first speaker might be talking to her partner or flatmate. Maybe they have a really cluttered flat and are having a big clean out.* Then ask each pair to choose one of the phrases and role-play the next part of the conversation. Invite pairs to share their conversations with the class.

6 Students turn to p.161 and work in pairs to ask and answer the questions using expressions with *space* and *room*. Elicit an answer to each question, along with the meaning of the words in italics: *room service, room temperature, no room to swing a cat, roomy, room and board* and *leg room*.

Answers

5 1 both   2 both   3 room   4 room   5 both
6 space   7 room   8 space

ADDITIONAL PRACTICE | **Maximiser** p.10, Listening 1–2 |
MyEnglishLab: Cambridge Advanced, Listening 7: Identifying opinion, Listening 13: Listening for main points and detail, Vocabulary 18: City vs country

Grammar focus ▶ CB p.13
Speaking

Aims

- to present emphasis with inversion in context
- to provide spoken practice

1 Put students in pairs or small groups to discuss the questions. If all students are from the same city, they could each choose another city they are familiar with to discuss.

2 Give students a few minutes to read the text and clarify any unknown vocabulary. Elicit the meaning of *a mecca* (a place that attracts a lot of people), *endowed* (with a good quality), *asset* (something that is useful), *slogan* (a short phrase used in advertisements) and *by-law* (a law which applies to a city or small area rather than the whole country).

Emphasis with inversion

Aim

- to revise emphasis with inversion

3 Check students understand that inversion in this case means 'changing the order of subject and verb in the sentence so that the verb comes first'. Read through the **Language tip** with the class and focus on the example: *Hardly had he arrived when Jo rushed in.* Ask students to identify the subject (*he*) and auxiliary verb (*had*) that have been inverted from the usual order in English. Elicit the sentence without inversion: *He had hardly arrived when Jo rushed in.* Explain that the effect of the inversion is to emphasise the adverb *hardly* by placing it first.

Elicit the answer to the question about the verb forms, then give students a few minutes to rewrite the sentences while you circulate to help as required. Ask students to turn to the **Grammar reference** on p.175 and read through it with the class, or on eText if you are using it. Check students understand everything. Leave it displayed on eText for students to refer to during Activity 4.

4 Point out that in some sentences (2, 4, 6, 7, 8), the adverb or adverbial phrase in the inverted sentence is different or in addition to the original; for example, in 2, *just* becomes *scarcely*. Students may refer back to the **Grammar reference** for help with phrases that are commonly inverted. Students complete the activity, compare answers in pairs, then check as a class.

5 Refer students back to the inverted sentence (1) in Activity 4: *Seldom has this city been in greater need of energy-efficient public transport than it is today.* Ask the class where you might expect to hear or read it, e.g. at a local council meeting, in a letter to the editor of a local paper, in a proposal for installing a tram. Remind students that they need to think of formal rather than informal settings. In pairs, students think of a few ideas for each of the other sentences in Activity 4. Elicit a few ideas for each sentence.

6 If students find this challenging, help by writing an auxiliary verb and subject on the board for each as a starter (e.g. *Seldom do I …, Scarcely had I …, Rarely do we …, Not only do I …, Under no circumstances should you …, No sooner had we …, At no time have I …, Hardly had we …*). Students compare their sentences with a partner. Consider collecting in the sentences to check that students are using inversion accurately.

Answers

3 The subject and verb are inverted.
They can not only boast lists as long as your arm of magnificent buildings, museums and galleries …
Visitors should not be led to believe a city can promise something it cannot deliver under any circumstances.

4 1 Seldom has this city been in greater need of energy-efficient public transport than it is today.

2 Scarcely had we ordered our meal when the waiter rudely asked us if we would mind paying the bill.

3 Rarely have I seen such a brilliant display of artistry and expertise.

4 Not only have you failed to hand in your essay on time, you have also copied several paragraphs directly from the internet.

5 Under no circumstances should you let people who don't respect the dress code into the club.

6 No sooner had she posted the letter than she began to regret what she had said.

7 At no time has my client ever revealed the contents of this document to the media.

8 Hardly had I finished the assignment when my boss asked me to do something else for her.

5 (Suggested answers)
1 editorial in a newspaper or political speech   2 letter of complaint or post on travellers' advice website   3 review of a performance or exhibition   4 teacher's comment on a student's essay   5 instructions given to bouncers at a club   6 story   7 lawyer giving evidence in court   8 letter to a friend

> **Additional activity:** City advertisement
> In pairs, students create a short advertisement to encourage people to visit an attraction in their city. It should contain at least two examples of inversion. Pairs take turns to read their advertisement aloud for the class (e.g. *Are you looking for a magnificent view? Come up the Sky Tower. Not only is it the tallest building in New Zealand, it also has 360-degree views of the city and harbour. Under no circumstances should you miss it!*)

ADDITIONAL PRACTICE | **Maximiser** p.10, Grammar 1–2 |
MyEnglishLab: Cambridge Advanced, Use of English 7: Word order |
Photocopiable p.143/171, 1B *Choose carefully*

Writing focus ▶ CB p.14

Listening

> **Aim**
> * to introduce the topic of neighbours
> * to provide listening practice

> **Warmer:** Discussion
> Students discuss the following question in pairs: *What do you think makes a good neighbour?*

1 Play the recording and elicit a few opinions on how people in students' neighbourhoods would react to such a scheme.

Essay (Part 1)
using the task input to help you plan

> **Aim**
> * to write an exam-style essay (Writing Part 1)

Tell students that the Writing paper consists of two parts. Part 1 is a compulsory essay; Part 2 is a choice of three tasks which could include an email or letter, a report or proposal, or a review. For more detail, refer students to the **Exam focus** on p.201.

2 Students work in pairs and follow the instructions. If you think they will find this difficult, brainstorm ideas as a class first.

3 Ask students to read the plans and decide which they think would produce a better essay. To help them decide, tell them to look at the checklist on p.185, or display it on eText. Elicit the answer.

4 Tell students to use Plan A in Activity 3 as a model as they plan the essay in Activity 2. Give them a few minutes to make their plan individually, then put them in small groups to compare.

5 Ask students to read the task input and underline key words before they begin their plan. Students write a plan while you circulate. Emphasise that the plan should follow the same structure as Plan A in Activity 3.

6 Read the **Exam tip** with the class. Set the essay as homework. Students should show their draft to two other students for advice and make changes before you collect the essays in to provide individual feedback. Focus especially on the structure of the essay in your feedback.

Answers

3 Plan A

6 Sample answer:

Too much traffic is a major headache for everyone in the city due to the noise, pollution and, of course, terrible delays during the rush hour. How can the government reduce traffic and dissuade people from driving their cars into the centre every day? In this essay, I will discuss two possible approaches to this pressing yet complex issue.

The first option to consider is an education campaign which could comprise of visual and radio advertising, presentations to businesses and special designated days such as 'Walk to Work Day'. Compared to the high cost of significantly upgrading our public transport system, advertising is relatively low-cost and straightforward to implement. On the other hand, it is difficult to gauge the effectiveness of such a campaign in advance because it relies on individuals changing their ingrained habits.

A second alternative would be to levy a tax on parking in the city. This could be applied both to businesses and directly to consumers. While it is true that this would have immediate gains in revenue and changed behaviour, taxes are unpopular and could also place unfair pressure on small businesses and individuals who do not have other transport options for work.

In my view, a multi-faceted education campaign would be the most effective starting point. In the future, a tax could be a possible option but it would be tolerated better once citizens are educated about the benefits of fewer cars and a more pedestrianised centre.

ADDITIONAL PRACTICE | **Maximiser** p.11, Writing 1–3 | **MyEnglishLab: Cambridge Advanced**, Writing 2: Giving an opinion in an essay, Writing 4: Useful language for essay writing

MyEnglishLab tip

Writing exercises
The MyEnglishLab writing exercises contain more useful language for essay writing, so suggest students complete them before they write their essay.

Review ▶ CB p.15

Aim
- to revise the structures, vocabulary and exam tasks covered in Unit 1

1 – **3** Ask students to complete the exercises, circulating to provide assistance. Ask students to check answers in pairs before checking as a class on eText. Alternatively, set as a homework activity and then go through the answers as a class, or on eText, to check.

Answers

1 1 did I manage to buy   2 only are the neighbours
3 no time should you   4 have been living here for/
have lived here for   5 no circumstances should you
6 sooner had I closed

2 1 smell   2 is tasting   3 am seeing   4 is smelling
5 are thinking   6 tastes

3 1 D 2 B 3 A 4 D 5 C 6 C 7 A 8 B

ADDITIONAL PRACTICE | **Testmaster** online and on **eText**, Unit 1 test

The art of conversation

2

Speaking and Use of English focus ▶ CB p.16

Long turn (Part 2)
giving opinions

Aim
- to complete an exam-style speaking task (Speaking Part 2)

Warmer: Discussion
Focus students' attention on the title of the unit and ask: *What is the art of conversation? Is it something you can learn or is it a natural ability?* Then put students in pairs to discuss the question: *What are the advantages of a text conversation compared to a call?* Elicit some ideas.

1 Students work in pairs to discuss what the worst thing would be about being stuck somewhere without a phone or internet access. Elicit a few ideas. Then ask the class: *Have you ever been stuck somewhere without a phone or internet access?*

2 Ask students to read the statements, then play the recording while they mark whether each speaker agrees or disagrees.

3 Play the recording again for students to write down the expressions for giving opinions that they hear. Allow students a few minutes to compare and check their answers on p.161.

4 Write up the expressions from Activity 3 on the board for students to refer to while they give their opinions. Keep these displayed while they do Activity 7 as well. For additional practice, students could discuss the statements again with a new partner, trying to use as many of the expressions as possible.

5 Tell students that in Part 2 of the Speaking paper, Individual long turn, the focus is on their fluency and their ability to organise their ideas and express themselves clearly. They will be in the exam with another candidate. They will be given three pictures and asked a question by the examiner, which they must answer by comparing two of the pictures. After the first candidate has compared the pictures, the second candidate will be asked a short question related to the topic. For more information, refer students to the **Exam focus** on p.204.

Focus students on the exam task. Ask them to underline the three things the examiner asks the candidate to do. If you are using eText, underline these on the eText page using the pen tool.

6 Ask students to read the questions, then play the recording for students to listen and answer the questions. Allow students a few minutes to compare, then check answers as a class.

7 Tell students that they are going to take turns to be the candidate and the examiner. Read the **Exam tip** on p.16 aloud, then ask them to turn to p.152 and p.158 and do the tasks. With weaker classes, check that the 'candidate' and 'examiner' have underlined the three things correctly before they begin their practice. The 'examiner' should check that the 'candidate' answers every part. Encourage students to use the phrases for giving opinions from Activity 3 in their answers.

Answers

2 1 A   2 D   3 A   4 D

3 1 I'm not saying … but …; generally speaking, …

2 That totally depends on the situation – I'm sure some people would argue that …; the way I see it, …; I don't have a problem …

3 I think that goes without saying.; … would even consider …

4 I wouldn't go that far but …; I think it's fair to say …

5 Look at the pictures. They show people using their phones. I'd like you to <u>compare two of the pictures</u> and <u>say why people might be communicating in this way</u> and <u>how effective this form of communication might be</u>.

6 1 no   2 no   3 no   4 yes

Word formation (Part 3)

Aim

- to complete an exam-style Use of English task (Reading and Use of English Part 3)

8 Tell students that Part 3 of the Reading and Use of English paper is a word formation task. They will be given a text with eight gaps. At the end of each line there will be a word in capitals, which students need to change to fit the gap, e.g. by adding a prefix/suffix or changing the word class. For more information, refer students to the **Exam focus** on p.198.

For question 1, elicit the part of speech missing (noun) and elicit how to change *COMMUNICATE* to a noun that fits here (*communicators*). The noun will be plural because it needs to agree with *politicians*. Students complete the remaining two gaps and then check their answers as a class before discussing the questions with a partner. Elicit a few ideas for each question.

9 Give students a minute to read through the text quickly and elicit what it is about (Kate Moore, US teenage texting champion). Look at the example (0) and ask: *How do we know that the missing word is an adverb?* (It comes after a subject and immediately before a verb.) Read the **Exam tip** with the class. Allow about ten minutes for students to complete the task.

10 Students compare answers with a partner using the questions as prompts, before checking as a class. If you are using eText, you can reveal the answers to the class.

11 Students ask their partner how well they would do in a texting competition.

> **Additional activity:** Text race
>
> As a bit of fun, ask students to swap mobile numbers with their partner if they are happy to do so. Write on the board: *I'll meet you outside the cinema at 8 p.m. See you soon!* When you say 'Go!', students have a race to see who can send the text the fastest without mistakes.

Answers

8 1 communicators (noun)   2 uncommunicative (adjective)   3 communication (noun)

9 1 finalists   2 completion   3 required   4 dismissive   5 sociable   6 astonishing   7 effectively   8 reference

ADDITIONAL PRACTICE | **Maximiser** p.12–13, Speaking 1, Use of English 1 | **MyEnglishLab: Cambridge Advanced**, Speaking 4: Strategies for dealing with Part 2 questions, Use of English 4: Word building

Listening focus ▶ CB p.18

Speaking

Aims

- to introduce vocabulary related to socialising
- to provide spoken practice

1 Focus students on the title of the quiz: *Are you an introvert?* Ask what students think *introvert* means (someone who is quiet and shy and likes a lot of time alone) and elicit the antonym: *extrovert*. Circulate while students complete the questionnaire. If necessary, pre-teach *to long* (to want to do something very much, especially when it seems unlikely). Put students in pairs to compare their answers, then refer them to p.162 to find out if they are an introvert. Make sure they realise that introversion/extroversion are not 'good' or 'bad', just different.

Multiple choice (Part 1)

Aim

- to complete an exam-style multiple-choice listening task (Listening Part 1)

Tell students that Part 1 of the Listening paper is a task which consists of listening to three short conversations and answering two multiple-choice questions about each one. It may test their understanding of the main idea, the purpose, the attitude or opinion of the speakers. For more detailed information and suggested strategies, refer students to the **Exam focus** on p.202.

2 Read the **Exam tip** with the class. Ask students to read the questions and options carefully and highlight the key words in each one before they listen (see Strategy 1 in the **Exam focus**). Play the recording once while students mark the answer they think is best. Then play the recording again for students to check their answers before checking as a class.

3 Play Extract One again while students listen for the paraphrases of *unsure*, *positive* and *relieved*, and the words which are summarised by *normal*. Elicit the answers as a class.

Teaching tip

eText audio script

If you are using eText, you can display the audio script. This can be useful if students find it difficult to hear the paraphrases in a task.

4 Students match the phrases A–E from the recording with the correct answers in Activity 2. Allow students time to compare their answers in pairs before you check as a class.

Answers

2 1 C 2 A 3 B 4 A 5 B 6 C

3 unsure = sceptical

relieved = reassuring

normal = absolutely nothing wrong with that at all

no paraphrase for 'positive'

4 A 3 B 2 C 5 D 6 E 4

Additional Activity: Discussion

Students discuss the following questions in small groups: *Do you have any friends that you have met online? What privacy advice would you give to a family member who is new to social networking? Have you ever tried to stay offline for a period of time? Would you like to?*

ADDITIONAL PRACTICE | **Maximiser** p.13, Listening 1 | **MyEnglishLab: Cambridge Advanced**, Listening 1: Speaker purpose, Listening 8: Identifying attitudes

Grammar focus ▶ CB p.19

Articles

definite, indefinite and zero articles

Aim

- to review the use of articles

Warmer: Discussion

Ask students to discuss the following questions in pairs: *Do you consider yourself a competitive person? In what situations is competitiveness a positive or negative trait?* Focus students' attention on the title of the article and ask: *What do you think a competitive conversation is?*

1 Ask students to read the paragraph and choose the best summary. Elicit the answer.

2 Check students are familiar with the terms *definite article* (*the*), *indefinite article* (*a/an*) and *zero article* (no article). Ask students to choose the correct articles in the paragraph and compare their answers in pairs before you check as a class. Read the **Language tip** with the class and elicit a few more examples (e.g. *the British*, *the hungry*, *the middle class*).

3 Give students a few minutes to answer the questions and find examples from the paragraph in Activity 1, then go through the answers as a class. Ask students to turn to the **Grammar reference** on p.171 and read through it with the class, on eText if you are using it. Check that students understand everything. If you are using eText, leave the **Grammar reference** displayed while students complete Activity 4.

4 Students complete the article, then compare their answers in pairs before you check as a class.

Answers

1 2

2 1 - 2 - 3 - 4 the 5 the 6 a 7 the 8 a
9 a 10 -

3 1 A: (7) the group; B: (4) the world; C: (5) the night
2 (6) a group, (8) a choir, (9) a sour note
3 A: (1) friends, (10) conversations; B: (2) happiness,
(3) human beings

4 1 the 2 - 3 the 4 the 5 the 6 a 7 a
8 the 9 an 10 a

Speaking

Aim

● to provide spoken practice

5 Put students in pairs to discuss the questions, then
elicit a few ideas for each.

Additional activity: Support response

Write on the board: *I'm thinking of …* and tell students
they should think of something they are considering at
the moment to complete the phrase (e.g. *I'm thinking of
going to the cinema this weekend.*). Students then work
in pairs. The first student shares their phrase and their
partner offers support responses of the type suggested
in the article in Activity 4, i.e. by asking a question (e.g.
Cool! What are you planning to see?). The pair should try
to keep the conversation going for a couple of minutes
before changing roles.

ADDITIONAL PRACTICE | **Maximiser** p.14, Grammar 1 |
Photocopiable p.144/172, 2A *Let's risk it!* | **MyEnglishLab: Cambridge
Advanced**, Use of English 3: Articles

Reading focus ▶ CB p.20
Gapped text (Part 7)

Aim

● to complete an exam-style reading task (Reading and
Use of English Part 7)

1 Allow students a couple of minutes to discuss their
answers. To support a weaker class, first elicit some of
the phrases from the Long turn Activity 3 earlier in this
unit (p.16) for giving opinions.

2 Tell students that Part 7 of the Reading and Use of
English paper is a task which involves reading a text
from which six paragraphs have been removed and
jumbled, then deciding where each of the paragraphs
fits. There is one extra paragraph that is not used.
For more detailed information and strategies, refer
students to **Exam focus** on p.200 or turn to it on eText
if you are using it.

Give students about two minutes to read the article
on p.21 quickly to find out what the writer thought of
the conversation class. Emphasise that students should
not worry about the missing paragraphs at this stage
and not use dictionaries for unknown vocabulary, as
this will be dealt with later in the lesson. Elicit what the
writer thought of the conversation class.

3 Ask students to read the first two paragraphs and
answer the question, then compare their answer with
a partner.

4 Read the **Exam tip** through with the class, then ask
students to read A–G to select the correct paragraph.
Elicit the answer.

5 Students complete the activity individually, then
compare their answers in pairs. Go through the
answers as a class, discussing the justification for each
one (see Answers below).

6 Remind students that working out meaning from
context is important for the exam and in real life. Give
students a few minutes to work out the meanings
of the underlined words and then compare with a
partner. Check answers with the class.

Answers

2 The writer thought the course was too theoretical rather
than practical.

3 2

4 G

5 1 G (*this* (paragraph G, line 1) refers to the topic 'How to
have a conversation' in the first paragraph.)
2 E (The second paragraph talks about people's views
on the negative effect of technology on conversation
with two quotes. Paragraph E continues this topic with
an additional quote.)
3 A (The topic of the third paragraph is people's reasons
for attendance. *These aims* (line 1) in paragraph A refers
to the classmates' reasons in the third paragraph.)
4 D (*Then* (paragraph D, line 1) links the fourth
paragraph to *After an enjoyable ten minutes spent
chatting to my classmates.* The fifth paragraph refers to
the discussion described in D.)

5 B (*these ideas* (in the sixth paragraph) refers to 1–6 in paragraph B. Paragraph G has similar content to B, however *this* in *the basics of this* has nothing to refer to.)

6 F (*this enjoyable burst of role play* (paragraph F) is described in the sixth paragraph: *try out ideas for unusual openings*.)

6 witty: clever and funny

empathise: understand the feelings of others

eloquence: the ability to express yourself articulately

banter: friendly, teasing conversation

unease: feeling of discomfort

dwindle: fade, grow weaker

Speaking

Aim

- to provide spoken practice

7 Students discuss the questions in pairs.

ADDITIONAL PRACTICE | **Maximiser** p.14–15, Reading 1–4 | **Photocopiable** p.145/173, 2B *Ten perfect pairs* | **MyEnglishLab: Cambridge Advanced**, Reading 3: Skimming for gist A

Vocabulary focus ▶ CB p.22

Speaking

Aim

- to provide spoken practice

1 Students discuss the statements in pairs.

Alternative activity: Rank it

Students rank the statements 1 (the one they agree with most strongly) to 4. They then compare and discuss their answers in small groups and try to agree a joint ranking. Groups can then report back to the class and discuss their differences.

Communication collocations

Aim

- to expand students' knowledge of collocations related to ways of communicating

2 Students match the collocations, then compare answers in pairs before checking as a class. To extend in a strong class, give students a few minutes to try, in their pairs, and think of two more collocations related to communication with the verbs *make, have, give* or *hold* (e.g. *make a phone call, make excuses, make enquiries, hold/have/give an interview, hold/give a tour, hold/have/give a demonstration, give an introduction*).

3 Students choose the correct alternatives, then compare answers in pairs before checking as a class.

Answers

2 make: conversation (no article), a speech

have: a chat, a conversation, a debate, a discussion, a gossip, a talk

give: a presentation, a speech, a talk

hold: a debate, a discussion

3 1 speech   2 conversation   3 talk   4 discussion
5 debate   6 conversation   7 debate
8 conversation

Adjectives: ways of speaking

Aim

- to use a range of adjectives to describe ways of speaking

4 Ask students to read questions 1–5 and if necessary, pre-teach *trustworthy* and *authoritative*. Play the recording while students answer the questions. Students compare their answers with a partner.

5 If possible, make dictionaries available for this activity. Students work in pairs to complete the activity.

6 Students discuss the questions in pairs.

7 Students complete the sentences, then compare answers in pairs before checking as a class.

8 Students complete the activity. Check answers as a class.

Answers

5 **1** positive: deep, husky, lively, mellow, soft, soothing, warm; negative: flat, harsh, high-pitched, monotonous, nasal, squeaky, wobbly

2 mellow, soft, soothing, warm; squeaky, wobbly; flat, monotonous

7 **1** soothing **2** nasal **3** husky **4** wobbly **5** flat **6** harsh

8 **1** deep, mellow, soft, soothing, warm **2** flat, harsh, monotonous, soft **3** deep, lively, mellow, soft, warm **4** flat, lively, monotonous

Additional activity: Guess the word

Students work in pairs. Student A from each pair closes their eyes. Choose a word or collocation from the lesson to write on the board for Student B to see, then erase it. Student B describes the meaning of the word to Student A, who has to guess the word. Then swap roles so that Student A describes the next word. Some example words/collocations to use are: *monotonous, nasal, soothing, deep in conversation, husky, have a debate, raise your voice, gossip.*

ADDITIONAL PRACTICE | Maximiser p.16, Vocabulary 1–3 |
MyEnglishLab: Cambridge Advanced, Vocabulary 2: Noun collocations with *political*, Vocabulary 4: Collocations with *social*

Grammar focus ▶ CB p.23

Defining and non-defining relative clauses

Aim

- to review defining and non-defining relative clauses

1 Students discuss the question in pairs.

2 Students read the article and choose the correct alternatives. They then compare their answers in pairs before checking as a class.

Additional activity: Relative pronouns review

If students have found this challenging, review relative pronouns with the following exercise. Tell students that relative pronouns are used to give information about the subject or object of a sentence. The most common relative pronouns are: *who, which, that, whose, when* and *where*. Write the pronouns above and the uses 1–6 below on the board. Working in pairs, ask students to match each pronoun with its use, then check as a class.

1 to refer to things
2 to refer to people
3 to refer to people or things
4 used after nouns referring to a place
5 used after nouns referring to a time
6 used to show possession

Answers: **1** which **2** who **3** that **4** where **5** when **6** whose

3 Students match the sentences with the meanings. Ask them to compare answers in pairs before checking as a class.

4 Students select the answer. Check as a class. Ask students to turn to the **Grammar reference** on p.178 and read through it with the class, on eText if you are using it. Check that students understand everything. Leave it displayed on eText for students to refer to during Activity 5.

5 Students complete the activity, then compare answers in pairs before you check as a class. Go through the **Language tip** with the class. Share or elicit a few more examples (e.g. *All that you need …, Everything that I planned …, Something that I'd like to see …, Somewhere that I'd like to visit …*).

6 Go through the activity with the class, eliciting the answers.

Answers

2 **1** which **2** where **3** who **4** whose **5** which **6** when **7** which **8** why

3 **1** A **2** B

4 1

5–6 **1** who/that (D) **2** where (D) **3** whom (D) **4** whose (D) **5** that (D) **6** which (ND) **7** when (D) **8** which (ND)

The relative pronoun can be omitted in sentence 5.

ADDITIONAL PRACTICE | Maximiser p.16, Grammar 1–4 |
MyEnglishLab: Cambridge Advanced, Use of English 12:
Relative clauses and relative pronouns

Writing focus ▶ CB p.24

Proposal (Part 2)

organising your ideas

Aims

- to review the structure of a proposal
- to write an exam-style proposal (Writing Part 2)

Warmer: They do what?

Elicit a few ideas to answer the following questions: *What methods of communication can be used in the workplace? What sorts of communication problems can you imagine occurring in a work setting?*

Write the following sentences on the board and tell students that they are from people who have a problem related to workplace communication. Working in pairs, students discuss with their partner what sort of advice they would give to each person. Elicit a few ideas for each scenario.

1 I receive a huge volume of emails every day and most are from people who work in the same office!

2 My colleague talks so quietly I can never hear him properly.

3 My colleague constantly interrupts and talks over me.

4 My boss never seems to say anything positive – it's always complaints.

Alternatively, put students in four groups and assign each group one scenario. The group brainstorms advice, then selects their three top pieces of advice to share with the class.

Remind students that the Writing paper is divided into two parts. Part 1 is a compulsory essay and Part 2 is a choice of three tasks which could include an email or letter, a report or proposal, or a review. For more detailed information on the exam tasks and strategies, refer students to the **Exam focus** on p.201.

1 Read through the two statements with the class and elicit which one refers to a proposal and which one refers to a report.

2 Give students a few minutes to look at the exam task, the tips for writing a proposal and the candidate's answer. Then elicit which of the tips the candidate has not followed.

3 Read the **Exam tip** aloud. Then ask students to look at the exam task and follow the steps to prepare to write. If you have a weaker class, students could do steps 1–2 with a partner. Refer students to the **Writing reference** on p.193 for more useful language for proposals. Set step 3 (writing the first draft) as a homework activity, then collect to provide individual feedback, with a focus on structure.

Answers

1 1 proposal 2 report

2 The candidate has not followed tip 5. There is no final sentence summarising the candidate's opinion.

3 Sample answer:

Helping with student presentations: a proposal

Introduction

In this proposal I will describe some of the difficulties students at this school have with preparing their final presentations, present the key needs to be addressed and conclude by making a series of recommendations on how teachers at the school could assist students with overcoming the obstacles to giving a successful presentation confidently.

Current situation

Following discussion among the students, it has become clear that many students are feeling very nervous about the upcoming presentations. A number of students are struggling to select an appropriate topic, while others are unsure about appropriate structure. Comments made suggest that students lack previous experience in public speaking and would like opportunities to practise before the final assessment.

Key needs to be addressed

Students require additional help with topic selection and presentation structure, and opportunities need to be provided for students to gain experience speaking in front of others.

Recommendations

I would suggest the following actions to teachers at the school:

- Provide students with a list of possible presentation topics.
- There should be a lesson or workshop on structuring a presentation for those who are interested.
- I recommend that students are given time during class to practise their presentations in small groups.
- Additional upfront speaking opportunities should be incorporated into classes including plays and games.

If these suggestions are implemented, it will lead to increased student confidence and performance for the final presentations.

ADDITIONAL PRACTICE | **Maximiser** p.17, Writing 1–4 |
MyEnglishLab: Cambridge Advanced, Writing 14: Choosing appropriate headings in a proposal

MyEnglishLab tip

Gradebook
The MyEnglishLab exercises are marked automatically so that students can have immediate feedback. Log on to and check the gradebook to see their progress.

Review ▶ CB p.25

Aim

- to revise the structures, vocabulary and exam tasks covered in Unit 2

1 – **4** Ask students to complete the exercises, circulating to provide assistance. Ask students to check answers in pairs before checking as a class on eText. Alternatively, set as a homework activity and then go through the answers as a class, or on eText, to check.

Answers

1 1 including 2 administrative 3 addiction
 4 Indecision 5 distinctive 6 interactive
 7 communicator 8 dismissal

2 1 a 2 - 3 - 4 a 5 the 6 - 7 the 8 a
 9 an 10 the

3 1 who/that 2 which 3 whose 4 which/that
 5 who/that

4 1 monotonous 2 soft 3 husky 4 squeaky
 5 warm 6 nasal

ADDITIONAL PRACTICE | **Maximiser** p.18–19, Use of English 1 |
Testmaster online and on **eText**, Unit 2 test

Ages and stages

Vocabulary and Grammar focus ▶ CB p.26

Speaking

Aims

- to introduce the topic of life stages
- to provide spoken practice

Warmer: Ages and stages brainstorm

Focus students' attention on the image on p.26. Ask: *What do you think the image is trying to say?* Elicit some ideas. Then brainstorm with the class any life stages they can think of and write these on the board. If they have not been mentioned, elicit *infancy, childhood, adolescence, young adulthood, middle age* and *old age*. Ask students to work in pairs to put the brainstormed words in order from the earliest to latest stage, then check as a class. With a partner, students choose one of the life stages and make a list of five characteristics they think are typical of someone at that life stage. Ask each group to read their list without revealing the life stage they have chosen and have the other students guess which one they were discussing.

1 Invite two students to read the quotes aloud. Students discuss whether they agree or disagree with each one in pairs. Elicit a few opinions about each one.

Additional activity: Quotes I like

See if students can think of any quotes or sayings about ages or stages in their own language and ask them to explain what they mean to a small group. For homework, ask students to look up some quotes or jokes on the internet about youth or aging (in English). Each student could choose one to share with the class (or a small group) and explain why it appeals to them.

Vocabulary

stages of life

Aim

- to expand students' vocabulary related to life stages

2 Check students understand *connotation* (a quality or an idea that a word makes you think of that is more than its basic meaning, e.g. the word *professional* has connotations of skill and excellence). Students complete the activity, then compare their answers in pairs before you check as a class. If necessary, elicit the meanings of *juvenile* (silly and typical of a child rather than an adult), *puerile* (childish, silly and stupid) and *geriatric* (too old to work well).

3 Students complete the activity and then discuss their answers as a class.

4 In pairs, students brainstorm any other synonyms they know for the words in Activities 2 and 3 and discuss the connotations. Elicit some ideas.

Additional activity: More notes

Point out that *puerile* is usually used in more formal contexts and is always negative, whereas *geriatric* and *juvenile* also have neutral meanings. For example, *juvenile* can mean 'relating to young people who are not yet adults', e.g. *juvenile court, juvenile crime*; and *geriatric* can be used to talk about medical care or treatment of old people, e.g. *geriatric medicine, geriatric facility*.

Answers

2 1 negative **2** positive **3** positive **4** positive
5 negative **6** negative

3 1 adolescent (negative), childish (negative), infantile (negative) **3** boyish (positive) **4** adult (positive) **5** childish (negative), infantile (negative) **6** aging (neutral)

4 (Suggested answers)

1 immature (negative) **2** naive (neutral) **3** fresh-faced (positive) **4** grown-up (positive) **5** immature (negative) **6** elderly (neutral); ancient (usually neutral, but negative in this context)

Speaking

Aims

● to provide spoken practice
● to present a range of countable and uncountable nouns in context

5 Students discuss the questions. Elicit some ideas from the class to see if any general patterns emerge.

6 Focus students' attention on the picture and title. Elicit any popular books, films or television shows students have heard of featuring vampires (e.g. *Twilight, True Blood*). Give students a moment to read the article. Ask: *How does the writer explain the teenage obsession with vampires?* (Teenagers admire their style, confidence and freedom to do as they like at night; teenagers relate to their being different from mainstream society; they enjoy the risk or danger of the idea of romance with a vampire.) Ask students whether they agree with the writer's explanation and elicit any alternative ideas students have.

Additional activity: Discussion

Students discuss the following question in pairs: *Do vampire-themed books/media appeal to you? Why/Why not? What sorts of characters do you think appeal to people at different stages of life?*

Countable and uncountable nouns

Aim

● to review common countable and uncountable nouns

7 Students put the underlined nouns into the correct category. Check the answers as a class.

8 Look at the first item as a class. Read the sentence with each alternative: *I suggest we stop for coffee.; I suggest we stop for a coffee.* Ask students whether both alternatives are possible (yes) and whether there is a difference in meaning (no). Students work through the rest of the activity in pairs. Then discuss each example as a class.

9 Read the **Language tip** aloud. Point out that *fear* is usually uncountable but because it has been limited in this case to the *fear of spiders*, it is used as a countable noun with the indefinite article *a*. Share/ Elicit another example with *fear* (e.g. *He has a fear of heights.*). Students complete the activity, then compare their answers in pairs before checking as a class. Refer students to the **Grammar reference** on p.174 and ask them to read it for homework. This includes lists of common nouns which are uncountable or both countable and uncountable.

10 Students turn to p.165 and work in pairs to identify the countable and uncountable nouns in each of the quotations. Check answers as a class. Students then discuss whether they agree with each quotation or not and why.

Answers

7 1 self-confidence, alienation 2 fascination, attraction, youth, sense, style, freedom, will, society, risk, danger, appeal

8 1 both – no difference in meaning 2 research 3 equipment 4 both – with a difference in meaning (second meaning is *newspaper*) 5 both – with a possible difference in meaning (*wine* = all wines in general; *wines* = different varieties of wine) 6 luck

9 1 **a** profound mistrust 2 **a** good knowledge 3 no article 4 no article 5 **a** good education 6 **a** good understanding 7 no article 8 no article

10 Countable nouns: answer, parents, friends
Uncountable nouns: advice, chance, choice, data, information, knowledge, understanding, wisdom

ADDITIONAL PRACTICE | Maximiser p.22, Vocabulary 1–2, Grammar 1 | **MyEnglishLab: Cambridge Advanced**, Vocabulary 3: Vocabulary collocations with *significant*, Use of English 2: Plural or singular

Reading focus ▶ CB p.28

Speaking

Aims
- to introduce the topic of diaries
- to provide spoken practice

1 Students discuss the questions about blogs and diaries in pairs. Elicit a few responses to each question.

Cross-text multiple matching (Part 6)

Aim
- to complete an exam-style cross-text multiple matching task (Reading and Use of English Part 6)

Tell students that Part 6 of the Reading and Use of English paper consists of reading four short texts on a related topic by different writers and answering four multiple matching questions. The questions test their ability to identify where the writers may have similar or different opinions to each other about a specific issue. For more detailed information and strategies, refer students to the **Exam focus** on p.200.

2 Give students a few minutes to read the extracts and then elicit which extracts talk about the risks of keeping a diary.

3 Focus attention on the questions and ask students to underline the main ideas. Underline them on eText if you are using it. Emphasise that students are not answering questions 1–4 at this stage.

Suggested underlining:
shares a similar opinion to columnist A about the risks of keeping a diary?
regards diaries as superior to social networking sites for a different reason to columnist D?
has a similar view to columnist B about teenagers' contradictory behaviour?
has a different attitude to columnist D about the reaction older people have to reading teenage diaries?

4 Students read the extracts again to complete the table. Check answers as a class.

5 Ask a student to read the **Exam tip** aloud. Then ask students to answer questions 1–4 in Activity 3.

6 Look at the first sentence with the class. Ask students to choose one of the underlined words/phrases in the text that fits in the gap semantically (*made fun*) and then elicit how the words need to change to fit the sentence: *making fun*. Students complete the rest of the activity, then compare their answers in pairs before you check as a class.

7 In pairs, students discuss which of the opinions in the extracts they agree with.

Additional activity: Compound verbs with *out*

Focus students' attention on this question from the text and elicit the meaning of *outgrown*.

Why, I wonder, when they are nothing more than records of the childish hopes and ambitions we've now outgrown?

See if students can think of any other compound verbs with *out*. Write the following verbs on the board, which can be combined with *out* to form a compound verb with a new meaning: *shine, weigh, live, play, smart, grow*. Then write sentences 1–6 below on the board and ask students to form a compound verb with *out* and one of the verbs above to complete each sentence. They will need to make sure it is also in the correct form.

1 The benefits of the scheme _____ the disadvantages.

2 He was simply _____ in the match by his highly skilled opponent.

3 My grandmother _____ all her siblings by more than ten years.

4 She _____ the rest of the cast with her brilliant performance in the play.

5 The criminals managed to _____ the police by hiding the stolen goods in safe houses all over the city.

6 She kept a lot of her old toys until one day she realised she had somehow _____ them.

Answers: **1** outweighed/outweigh **2** outplayed
3 outlived/has outlived **4** outshone/outshines
5 outsmart **6** outgrown

Answers

2 A and B

3 Questions 1 and 3 ask for the same opinions. Questions 2 and 4 ask for different opinions.

4 1 A, B 2 A, D 3 B, D 4 A, D

5 1 B (A: 'younger siblings can, and do, often find them [diaries] a huge temptation'; B: 'the prospect of somebody finding and reading a secret diary is enough to put many teenagers off the idea of keeping one')

2 A (D: 'They [social networking sites] are not safe places for baring one's soul … diaries are truly private places'; A: 'a conventional diary is wonderfully impermanent. It can be quickly and completely destroyed if the writer so chooses, something that does not hold true for digital media.')

3 D (B: 'Though they're perfectly happy to post all sorts of details about their personal lives on Facebook, the prospect of somebody finding and reading a secret diary is enough to put many teenagers off the idea of keeping one.'; D: 'Diaries with locks and keys have retained their popularity among teenage girls, despite the fact that they happily keep what amounts to digital diaries through posts on Facebook, Twitter or Tumblr.')

4 A (D: 'People who reread their teenage diaries are understandably appalled to discover how little space they gave to what really matters and how much time they dedicated to the boy or girl on the bus who might or might not have fancied them.'; A: 'Even as adults, though we might pretend to feeling nothing more than mild amusement on rereading our teenage diaries, more often than not we secretly cringe with embarrassment over their raw emotion and trivial content.')

6 1 making fun 2 cringe 3 irksome 4 appalling
5 prospect 6 downplay

ADDITIONAL PRACTICE | Maximiser p.20–21, Reading 1–2 |
MyEnglishLab: Cambridge Advanced, Reading 12: Inferring meaning A, Reading 19: Recognising paraphrase A

Grammar focus ▶ CB p.30

Reading

Aim

● to provide examples of the introductory *it* in context

1 Ask students not to open their books yet. Put students in small groups and ask them to make a list of five things they think all adults should be able to do. Ask a volunteer from each group to share their list with the class. Alternatively, if you have a very large class, ask each group to share their list with another group.

2 Ask students to open their books on p.30 and read the similar list in Activity 2 to see if they mentioned any of the same things. Check students understand *CPR* (cardiopulmonary resuscitation – when you press repeatedly on someone's chest in order to make them breathe again and make their heart start beating again after it has stopped) and *the Heimlich Manoeuvre* (when you help someone who is choking by putting your arms around their waist and jerking upwards strongly). Students tick the things they can already do and choose two more items to add. Ask students to compare their answers in pairs and discuss which of the skills they would most like to learn.

Introductory *it*

Aim

● to review the use of the introductory *it*

3 Read through the four uses of the introductory *it* with the class, then elicit another example for each use from the list in Activity 2. To extend in a strong class, elicit an additional original example for each use. Ask students to turn to the **Grammar reference** on p.176 and read through it with the class, on eText if you are using it. Check that students understand everything. Leave it displayed on eText for students to refer to during Activity 4. Focus students' attention on the **Language tip** and read through it with the class.

4 Students rewrite the sentences while you circulate providing help as necessary.

5 Give students a few minutes to write their sentences using *it*. Then ask students to compare their sentences with a partner while you circulate, listening to check the introductory *it* is being used appropriately.

Additional activity: It's all about me

Write the following sentence starters on the board: *I can't stand it when …, I hate it when …, I love it when …, I find it important to …, It's always good to …, It's definitely worth …, It's a lot of fun to …, It's astonishing how …*. Ask students to complete the sentences so that they are true for them. Students then take turns to share their ideas with a partner. Circulate and listen to check that students are using the introductory *it* correctly.

Answers

3 1 It's no fun being in debt.   2 One day it may be your partner or child who needs your help.   3 It's amazing how many people don't know how to find their most beguiling smile.   4 I find it appalling that so many young people live on pot noodles and toast.

4 1 It's sad that we have become so disconnected from the natural environment.   2 It's vital for school children to learn some basic first aid skills.   3 It worries me how dependent people have become on mobile phones.   4 It's likely that you were bitten by an insect of some kind.   5 It was difficult for me to make new friends.   6 It is vital for people to contact a member of staff first.   7 It makes good sense not to throw away letters with your name and address on them.   8 It's common knowledge that you should never tell anyone your password.

ADDITIONAL PRACTICE | **Maximiser** p.22–23, Grammar 2–4

Speaking focus ▶ CB p.31

Collaborative task and discussion (Parts 3 and 4)

Aim

- to practise responding to and expanding on a partner's ideas in an exam-style speaking task (Speaking Parts 3 and 4)

Warmer: Mature

Students look at the word map on p.31. Elicit the meaning of *mature* (*fully grown and developed*; *behaving in a sensible and reasonable way*). Ask students to discuss in pairs how each of the experiences listed on the word map would help someone to become more mature.

Tell students that the collaborative task (Part 3) in the Speaking paper tests their ability to negotiate with a partner to reach a decision. Explain that the task has two parts. First, students will be given a word map with five prompts and a question to discuss for two minutes. They will then be asked another question which they will need to reach a decision on. For more detailed information and strategies for Part 3, refer students to the **Exam focus** on p.205 and turn to it on eText if you are using it. Read through it with students, making sure they understand everything.

1 Play the recording and elicit the answer to the question. Read the **Exam tip** aloud. Point out that knowing strategies for responding will help students in social and work situations, as well as in the exam.

2 Play the recording again and ask students to underline the phrases that Daniela uses to respond to and expand on what Martin says. Check as a class. Remember that if you are using eText, you can display the included answers.

3 Read the first idea aloud with the class and elicit some possible ways to expand on this. Give students a minute to read the ideas and think about what they are going to say. Then put students in pairs to act out the conversations. Invite a few pairs to share one of their conversations with the class.

4 Tell students that the discussion task (Part 4) in the Speaking paper lasts about four minutes and involves the examiner asking both candidates some discussion questions related to the topic in Part 3. The idea is for students to respond and add to what the other candidate has said. For more detailed information and strategies for Part 4, refer students to the **Exam focus** on p.205 and turn to it on eText if you are using it.

Ask students to read the questions in Activity 4, then play the recording. Elicit the answers.

5 Tell students that they are now going to practise doing Parts 3 and 4 in groups of three, taking turns to be the examiner and the two candidates. It would be useful for each group to have a timer or watch with a second hand for the 'examiner' to use. Students turn to the activity on p.156, and follow the instructions. Encourage the 'candidates' to use the useful phrases from Activity 2 during the task, and the 'examiners' to give feedback on how well the 'candidates' responded to each other and expanded on each other's points.

Answers

1 Daniela

2 <u>You mean,</u> because you're having to ask your parents for money and possibly also having to justify what you spend it on?

<u>There's a lot to be said for that argument.</u> <u>In many cases, I think</u> it does make people less able to take responsibility for their own decisions and it often creates tensions in a family.

<u>Yes,</u> you're forced to mature by having to make sacrifices and by being responsible for other people, <u>aren't you?</u>

ADDITIONAL PRACTICE | **Maximiser** p.23, Speaking 1–4 | **Photocopiable** p.146/173, 3A *A good answer* | **MyEnglishLab: Cambridge Advanced**, Speaking 9: Strategies for dealing with the first part of a Part 3 task, Speaking 11: Responding appropriately to your partner in Part 3

MyEnglishLab tip

There are video introductions to all of the exam papers in MyEnglishLab which students may find useful to watch for homework.

Use of English focus

▶ CB p.32

Multiple-choice cloze (Part 1)

Aim

- to complete an exam-style multiple-choice cloze task (Reading and Use of English Part 1)

1 Ask students to read the questions, then elicit the difference between *life expectancy* (the length of time a person or animal is expected to live), and *longevity* (long life). Students discuss the questions in pairs. Elicit a few responses to each.

2 Elicit what students remember about the multiple-choice cloze task (Reading and Use of English Part 1) and refer them to the **Exam focus** on p.197 to check their ideas. Turn to it on eText if you are using it. Read through it with the students, making sure they understand everything. Leave it displayed on eText as a reference so students can follow the strategy as they do the task. Students read the article and discuss the question in pairs. Emphasise that they are not filling out the gaps yet.

3 Focus students' attention on the first sentence and demonstrate using Strategies 3 and 4 from the **Exam focus** on p.197 to help students choose the correct answer (*3 Look at the options for each gap carefully. Try putting each of the options in the gap to see which one fits best. 4 Check the words on either side of the gap to see if the option you have chosen goes with these.*).

4 Refer students to the **Exam tip**. Students discuss the question in pairs. Check as a class.

5 Students do the task, then compare their answers in pairs before you check as a class.

Teaching tip

Pairs
Comparing answers in pairs encourages students to think more carefully about the reasons for their choices.

Answers

3 1 B   2 C

4 3

5 1 A (difference in meaning)   2 D (*determine* collocates with *factors*)   3 C (difference in meaning)   4 D (*life* collocates with *expectancy*)   5 A (*reach a birthday/age* is a collocation)   6 B (difference in meaning)   7 A (difference in meaning)   8 A (*result* is the only option that can be followed by *in*; *lead* is followed by *to* and *produce/make* take a direct object without a preposition)

Speaking

Aim

- to provide spoken practice

6 Give students a minute to think about their answers to the questions. Then put students in small groups to discuss their answers.

Answers

6 1 The people live in homes that encourage physical activity, they avoid overeating, have purposeful lives and are surrounded by others who value and appreciate them.

ADDITIONAL PRACTICE | **Maximiser** p.24, Use of English 1 | **Photocopiable** p.147/174, 3B *Word exchange* | **MyEnglishLab: Cambridge Advanced**, Use of English 8: Phrasal verbs and common expressions

Listening focus ► CB p.33

Speaking

Aims

- to introduce the topic of longevity
- to provide spoken practice

Warmer: Agree/Disagree phrase competition

Divide the class into two groups and ask each group to select a person to write down their ideas. Give the groups two minutes to make a list of good phrases to use when agreeing and disagreeing. One group should brainstorm the phrases for agreeing and the other the phrases for disagreeing. The groups take turns to read one of their phrases. The group that has the most phrases wins.

1 Students discuss each statement in pairs. Tell students to try and use different phrases to agree/disagree each time (using the phrases from the Warmer to help). Elicit a few opinions about each statement.

Multiple choice (Part 3)

Aim

- to complete an exam-style multiple-choice listening task (Listening Part 3)

2 Tell students that Part 3 of the Listening paper involves listening to a conversation or interview and answering six multiple-choice questions focusing on the opinions and attitudes of the speakers. Ask students to turn to the **Exam focus** on p.203 and display it on eText if you are using it. Work through the strategies with the class: Read Strategy 1, then ask students to read the task. Elicit who the speakers are and what they will talk about. Refer students to Strategy 2 and give them a minute to underline key words. Refer them to Strategy 3, then play the recording. Refer them to Strategy 4 before playing the recording a second time. Go through the answers as a class.

3 Students discuss the questions in pairs. Elicit any longevity factors which students found surprising in the interview.

Answers

2 1 C   2 C   3 A   4 D   5 B   6 C

Vocabulary

working out meaning from context

Aim

- to practise working out meaning from context

4 Students discuss the meanings in pairs, then check as a class.

Answers

4 1 believing what you want to happen will happen even though it is impossible   2 stupid and reckless   3 used when you admit that something is true   4 relaxed and easy-going   5 change direction suddenly   6 when the situation is the opposite of what it was before

Additional activity: Vocabulary

Write the following on the board: *A sure, B easy-going, C if it is vice versa, D go, E reckless, F naive optimism*. Each of these can be used to replace the underlined words/phrases in Activity 4 with a similar meaning. Ask students to match them up, then compare their answers in pairs before you check as a class.

Answers: A 3   B 4   C 6   D 5   E 2   F 1

ADDITIONAL PRACTICE | **Maximiser** p.24, Listening 1 | **MyEnglishLab: Cambridge Advanced**, Listening 10: Listening for gist, Listening 18: Listening for stated opinions, attitudes and inferred ideas

Writing focus ► CB p.34

Speaking

Aim

- to provide spoken practice

1 Students discuss the questions in pairs. Elicit a few ideas for each question.

Report (Part 2)

dos and don'ts

Aims

- to identify dos and don'ts for writing an exam-style report
- to practise writing an exam-style report

Remind students that the Writing paper consists of a compulsory essay (Part 1) and a choice of three tasks in Part 2, one of which might be a report.

2 Ask students to look at the exam task and write a plan individually or in pairs.

3 Students look at the plans and answer the questions. Elicit the answers.

4 Students read the advice for writing reports and identify which piece of advice should start with *Don't*. Elicit the answer.

5 Refer students to the model report on p.192 to read, then elicit the answer.

6 Read through the useful language for report writing on p.193. Ask students to select a few expressions to use for the task in Activity 2.

7 Set the draft as homework and remind students to use the advice from Activity 4. During the next lesson, students share their work in pairs and make any improvements. Collect in to offer individual feedback.

Answers

3 **2** Plans A and B do not include a recommendation section.

5 Item 7 should start with *Don't*. Plan C is the most similar to the structure of the model report.

7 Sample answer:

Introduction

The main objectives of this report are to describe how young people in Canterbury feel about elderly people in their area and aging themselves. I will present results of a survey I conducted with a random selection of 200 young people at the local high school and in the final section I will include recommendations as to how attitudes could be improved.

Attitudes to older people

According to my survey, a significant proportion of young people never or hardly ever spend time with someone aged over 65. Reasons that respondents gave for this included: they have nothing in common, the elderly don't like teenagers and lack of time. More promisingly, nearly three quarters of those surveyed (74 percent) agreed that they could probably 'learn something' from older people.

Attitudes to aging

Those responding to the survey were almost equally split between preferring to think about it as little as possible and those who never thought about it. For those who did think about it, the prime concerns were loneliness, poor health and boredom.

Recommendations

Clearly more could be done to bridge the gap between young and old in our community. I would make the following recommendations:

- Set up volunteer tutoring opportunities for elderly citizens to help younger people at the high school with academic work or practical skills.
- Invite young people to tutor old people in technology use, e.g. how to text/send emails in return for a donation to be used for social events.

Hopefully, increased contact between the groups will lead to greater understanding and more positive attitudes.

ADDITIONAL PRACTICE | **Maximiser** p.25, Writing 1–4 |
MyEnglishLab: Cambridge Advanced, Writing 12: Knowing the difference between a proposal and a report, Writing 13: Useful language for reports and proposals

Review ▶ CB p.35

Aim
- to revise the structures, vocabulary and exam tasks covered in Unit 3

1 – **3** Ask students to complete the exercises, circulating to provide assistance. Ask students to check answers in pairs before checking as a class on eText. Alternatively, set as a homework activity and then go through the answers as a class, or on eText, to check.

Answers

1 **1** vital that we learn **2** have a deep mistrust of **3** the council that should do **4** astonishing how few people **5** find it embarrassing **6** has an excellent knowledge

2 **1** B **2** C **3** A **4** D **5** C **6** A

3 **1** C **2** B **3** D **4** A **5** C **6** D **7** A **8** B

ADDITIONAL PRACTICE | **Testmaster** online and on **eText**, Unit 3 test, Progress test 1

No gain without pain

Listening and Grammar focus ▶ CB p.36

Sentence completion (Part 2)

Aim
• to complete an exam-style sentence completion task (Listening Part 2)

Warmer: No gain without pain

Ask students to focus on the title of the unit and discuss what it means and how it might apply in the case of the photo. Useful vocabulary for the discussion could include: *Olympic gymnast*, *rings*, *training*, *strength*, *discipline*. Working in pairs, ask students to think of at least three other situations when *no gain without pain* might apply, then elicit some ideas (e.g. getting fit, studying hard to pass an exam, working long hours to launch a business, forgoing small treats to save up for a big purchase, taking a long plane trip to get to an exotic destination).

1 Students work in pairs to add three more statements to the questionnaire. Then ask students to interview at least three other students using their questionnaire.

2 Tell students that Part 2 of the Listening paper involves reading eight sentences with gaps, then listening carefully to a monologue to complete the sentences. The word(s) for the gaps will be exactly the same as in the recording. For more detailed information and strategies for Part 2 Sentence completion, refer students to the **Exam focus** on p.202 and turn to it on eText if you are using it. Give students a minute to read the exam task. Then refer them to the **Exam tip**. Students discuss in pairs what sort of information is missing in each gap (noun, verb, etc.).

3 Play the first part of the talk and elicit the words which could fit grammatically in the gap in question 1. Then elicit the word that makes sense.

4 Play the whole recording while students complete the sentences. Students compare their answers in pairs, then check as a class.

5 Students discuss the question in pairs. Elicit whether they agree with the advice on language learning, playing an instrument or doing a sport.

Answers

2 1 noun   2 noun   3 noun   4 noun   5 noun   6 noun   7 phrase   8 noun

3 could fit grammatically: pot of gold, rainbow, fantasy; makes sense: fantasy

4 2 technique   3 detail   4 accuracy   5 failure   6 time limit   7 less is more   8 potential

Verb patterns: -ing/infinitive

Aim

- to review the -ing form and the infinitive

6 Students work in pairs to think of four qualities you need to be a high achiever. They then swap partners and compare their ideas. Give them a few minutes to read the article, then elicit the qualities mentioned.

7 Elicit a few opinions on whether the advice is helpful or not. In pairs, students discuss which of the advice applies to them.

8 Look at the first gap with the class as an example and elicit the correct form of achieve (to achieve). Students then complete the remaining gaps. Students compare their answers in pairs before you check as a class.

9 Students match the verbs in bold from Activity 6 with patterns 1–5. Check as a class.

10 Read the **Language tip** aloud. Elicit or share a few more examples using the verbs given (e.g. I love to get up/getting up early.). Then tell students that with some verbs, being followed by -ing or infinitive has a significant impact on meaning. In pairs, students discuss the difference in meaning in questions 1–3, then check as a class.

Answers

8 1 to achieve 2 fulfilling 3 having 4 to make 5 to take on 6 failing 7 (to) leave 8 taking 9 to work 10 doing 11 increasing 12 (to) turn

9 1 regret, risk, avoid, keep, consider 2 hope, expect, prepare, dare, help 3 dare, help 4 force 5 prevent

10 1 B 2 A 3 A

Additional activity: More differences in meaning
Write the following three sentences on the board and ask students to discuss the difference in meaning between the alternatives.
1 Jake stopped to smoke/smoking.
2 I regret to let you know/letting you know it was a lie.
3 I remembered to leave/leaving the key under the doormat.

Answers: **1** stopped to smoke = stopped what he was doing in order to smoke; stopped smoking = gave up smoking **2** regret to let you know = I am about to tell you something unfortunate; regret letting you know = I wish I hadn't told you **3** remembered to leave = refers to the thought I had before I left the key; remembered leaving = refers to the memory of leaving the key

To extend in a stronger class, ask each pair to write a sentence with two alternative versions, using the verbs stop, regret or remember with -ing and the infinitive on a piece of paper. Collect these in and check them for accuracy. Read each pair of sentences aloud and allow students time to discuss the difference with their partner, then elicit the answer.

Speaking

Aims

- to practise using -ing/infinitive verb forms
- to provide spoken practice

11 Students discuss the questions in pairs. Invite a few students to share something positive which they learnt about their partner.

ADDITIONAL PRACTICE | **Maximiser** p.26–27, Listening 1–2, Grammar 1–2 | **MyEnglishLab: Cambridge Advanced**, Listening 4: Listening to a longer text

Vocabulary focus ▶ CB p.38

Reading

Aims

- to expand vocabulary related to success
- to provide reading practice

1 Check students understand entrepreneur (someone who starts their own business or arranges business deals to make money, often in a way that involves financial risks). Elicit which syllable is stressed in entrepreneur (entrepre*neur*; the final underlined syllable). Elicit the adjective form entrepreneurial. Get students to discuss the questions in pairs, then elicit a few ideas for each question.

2 Give students a few minutes to read the article about Levi Roots. Tell them that if they come across unknown vocabulary, they should try to guess the meaning from context rather than using dictionaries as it will be dealt with later in the lesson. Elicit what is unusual about Levi Roots' success.

3 Students match the words with their meanings, using the context of the article to help them. Check answers as a class.

Answers

3 1 F 2 C 3 D 4 B 5 A 6 E

Additional activity: Syllable stress

Ask students to work in pairs to underline the stressed syllable for words 1–5 in Activity 3. Check answers as a class. Point out that stress patterns in English are not regular, so students should try to learn the pronunciation and stress patterns of new words.

Answers: exposure, envisage, mantra, granted, venture

Verb/Noun collocations

Aim

● to expand knowledge of collocations related to success

4 Students work through the questions about the verbs with a partner, then check as a class.

Teaching tip

Check students have the correct pronunciation of *seize* by eliciting any rhymes students can think of (e.g. *knees, bees, sneeze, cheese*). Point out that in English, many different letter combinations can represent the same sound.

5 Look at the first phrase with the class (*encounter a setback*). Elicit which of the verbs in the box can also collocate with *a setback* (*suffer*). Students complete the activity, then check as a class.

6 Read the **Language tip** aloud. Students work in pairs to think of as many verbs that collocate with the nouns in the box as possible in five minutes. This could be done competitively, to see which pair can come up with the most collocations. Then they compare their lists with the list on p.162. Ask students to underline any collocations that are new to them.

7 Students write six sentences using some of the collocations in Activity 6. In pairs, they compare their sentences and check them for meaning. Consider collecting in the sentences to check for appropriate use of the collocations.

Answers

4 1 seize 2 grasp, grab, seize 3 A all; B grabbed, took, seized; C take, seize; D grasp; E grabbed, took, seized

5 1 receive, suffer 2 doubt, follow, rely on 3 gain, receive 4 gain, receive 5 exceed, fulfil 6 fulfil, realise

ADDITIONAL PRACTICE | **Maximiser** p.27, Vocabulary 1–2 | **Photocopiable** p.148/175, 4A *Same word, different sentences* | **MyEnglishLab: Cambridge Advanced**, Vocabulary 7: Collocations with *information*, Vocabulary 8: Verbs collocating with *information*

Speaking

Aim

● to provide spoken practice

8 Students discuss the questions in pairs.

Additional activity: More questions

Ask students to look back at the collocations in Activity 5 and use three of them to write a discussion question (e.g. *Where do you get inspiration from? Do you tend to trust your intuition? What advice would you give to a friend who has suffered a setback to starting their own business?*)

Students discuss their questions in small groups.

MyEnglishLab tip

Uploading resources

If you have additional resources you would like to make available for students online, you can add them to the resources folder in MyEnglishLab. Like all MyEnglishLab resources, you have control over whether they are visible or hidden to students at any given time.

Use of English focus

▶ CB p.39

Key word transformations (Part 4)

Aim

- to complete an exam-style key word transformations task (Reading and Use of English Part 4)

Tell students that Part 4, Key word transformations involves completing six sentences using three to six words (including a key word given in capitals) so that each sentence has a similar meaning to another sentence given with it. For more detailed information and strategies, refer students to the **Exam focus** on p.199 and turn to it on eText if you are using it.

1 Students answer the questions, then compare answers in pairs. Check as a class.

2 Students complete the activity, then compare answers in pairs before you check as a class.

3 Focus students' attention on the **Exam tip** and read it aloud. Students complete questions 1–6, then compare answers in pairs, checking they have not used more than six words. Check as a class. Remember that if you are using eText, you can display the included answers.

Answers

1 1 passive   2 negative   3 A
2 1 B   2 C   3 B
3 1 isn't expected to do   2 would have been able
3 may/might not be realised   4 is no point (in) learning   5 is considering taking on   6 prevented me from going

> **Useful resources:** Entrepreneurship in films
> Remind students that watching films in English can be a fun way to get extra listening practice. If students find the dialogues too fast to follow, they can watch with English subtitles turned on to make it easier. Do an internet search for films about entrepreneurship (e.g. *The Social Network, Sunshine Cleaning, The Aviator, Chocolat*) and recommend that students watch some of them.

ADDITIONAL PRACTICE | Maximiser p.28, Use of English 1 |
MyEnglishLab: Cambridge Advanced, Use of English 19:
Using the key word

Reading focus ▶ CB p.40
Speaking

Aims

- to introduce the topic of inventions
- to provide spoken practice

1 Students work in pairs to discuss the questions about inventions. Elicit a few responses to each question.

Answers

1 (Suggested answers)

3 *There is nothing new under the sun.* = It's impossible to invent anything truly different from what has been done in the past. *Necessity is the mother of invention.* = When something is needed or missing, it makes people create something new.

Multiple choice (Part 5)

Aim

- to complete an exam-style multiple-choice reading task (Reading and Use of English Part 5)

Tell students that Part 5 tests their ability to understand a long text in detail and consists of a text with six multiple-choice questions. For more detailed information and strategies, refer students to the **Exam focus** on p.199 .

2 Give students a couple of minutes to read the article quickly and then elicit how the Museum of Failed Products is similar and how it is different from a normal museum.

3 Work through this question with the class, eliciting answers as you go.

4 Tell students that the strategy for this type of task is to a) underline key words in the questions, b) identify the part of the text that the question relates to, c) reread that part of the text carefully and d) choose the option that fits. Either display the **Exam focus** on eText, which has a similar list of strategies, or write these steps up as prompts for students to refer to during the activity. Refer students to the **Exam tip**. Students compare their answers in pairs before checking as a class.

5 Ask students to discuss in pairs why they think most products fail, then elicit a few ideas for the question.

Answers

2 similar: has a very large collection of objects
   different: is not open to the general public

3 1 yes 2 'unlike in a real supermarket, there is only one of each item'; option D

4 2 A ('The museum is home to discontinued brands')

  3 B ('Every failure … embodies its own sad story'; 'It is never far from her mind that real people had their mortgages … riding on the success of products')

  4 C ('merely intended to accumulate a "reference library" of consumer products, not failures per se')

  5 B ('so unwilling to invest time or energy thinking about their industry's past failures')

  6 C ('an aversion to confronting failure'; 'nobody wanted to contemplate the prospect of failure'; 'didn't want to bring it up for discussion'; 'conspired … never to speak of it again'; 'avoid confronting that fact')

Working out meaning from context

Aim

● to practise working out meaning from context

6 Emphasise that students should use the text to help them choose the correct meanings. Check as a class.

Answers

6 1 A 2 B 3 A 4 B 5 B 6 A

Additional activity: Vocabulary check

Ask students to work in pairs. They should find three more words in the text they don't know and try to work out their meaning from the context. They then check their answers in a dictionary .

Useful resources

In pairs, ask students to think of three questions they have about the Museum of Failed Products which are not answered in the article. Then students could spend five minutes online to find the answers (searching in English). They could then look online for another unusual museum that would appeal to them and discuss their findings in small groups.

ADDITIONAL PRACTICE | **Maximiser** p.28–29, Reading 1–4 |
Photocopiable p.149/175, 4B *Get the message?* | **MyEnglishLab:**
Cambridge Advanced, Reading 5: Scanning for specific information A

Grammar focus ▶ CB p.42

Reading

Aim

● to provide examples of modal verbs in context

Warmer: Olympics discussion
Students discuss the following questions in pairs: *Do you follow coverage of the Olympics? What sports does your country tend to have the most success in? Would you prefer to attend the Olympics as an athlete, an official or a spectator? Why?*

1 Focus students' attention on the photo of Roger Black and ask if they know anything about him. Explain that Roger Black is a British Olympic athlete who won two silver medals in Atlanta in 1996 (400 m and 4x400 m relay) and a bronze in Barcelona in 1992 (4x400 m relay). He was also part of the World Championships 4x400 m relay team in 1987, 1991 and 1997. He is now retired from athletics and has a career in television and public speaking. Give students about five minutes to read the article and decide if the statements are true or false. Check as a class.

2 Students discuss the questions in pairs. Elicit a few ideas for each question.

Answers

1 1 T 2 T 3 F 4 F

Modal verbs

Aim

● to review different uses of modal verbs

3 Students read the article again and choose the correct alternatives. Go through the answers as a class.

4 Students find examples in the article of modals used to express uses 1–7, then compare answers in pairs before you check as a class. Read through the **Language tip** with the class. Write another example on the board and elicit the difference in meaning: *He didn't need to bring a present.* (It wasn't necessary and it isn't clear whether he brought one or not.) *He needn't have brought a present.* (He did bring a present but it wasn't necessary.)

5 Go through the modal verbs in the article one by one, eliciting whether they could be replaced by *be able to*, *be allowed to* or *ought to*. Refer students to the **Grammar reference** on p.176. Pick out any points that students struggled with in Activity 3 and deal with any questions students have, then ask them to read the rest for homework. Leave it displayed for students to refer to during Activity 6.

6 Students complete the questions with the correct form of the verbs in brackets. Check the answers as a class, then put students in pairs to ask and answer the questions.

Alternative activity: Move around

If there is room to move around in your classroom, students could ask and answer each of the questions in Activity 6 with a different partner.

Answers

3 1 could   2 needed to   3 couldn't   4 couldn't
5 can   6 had to   7 couldn't   8 could retake
9 could have done   10 should have realised
11 must have done   12 doesn't have to

4 1 couldn't work it out, couldn't complete, can still recall, couldn't go travelling, could have done both   2 should have realised   3 must have done   4 could retake
5 could read medicine   6 needed to do well, had to stay behind   7 doesn't have to be like that

5 be able to: couldn't (work it out), couldn't (complete), can (still recall), couldn't (go travelling), could have (done both)

be allowed to: could (retake)

ought to: should have (realised)

6 1 should have achieved   2 did you have to
3 might come   4 didn't need to do/needn't have done
5 could have done   6 must have seen

ADDITIONAL PRACTICE | MyEnglishLab: Cambridge Advanced,
Use of English 13: Modal auxiliary verbs of obligation

Speaking focus ▶ CB p.43

Collaborative task and discussion (Parts 3 and 4)
justifying an opinion

Aims

- to identify phrases for justifying an opinion
- to complete an exam-style speaking task (Speaking Parts 3 and 4)

Warmer: Hobbies

Working in pairs, ask students to think of at least two hobbies or sports that:

- are very expensive.
- are very cheap.
- take a lot of commitment.
- would appeal to couch potatoes.
- reduce stress.
- need special facilities.
- would appeal to all ages.
- are niche activities. (niche activity = only a select group of people would enjoy it)

Elicit ideas for each category.

1 Students discuss the questions in pairs. Elicit a few examples of hobbies or sports students have given up and why. Then elicit what students remember about Speaking Parts 3 and 4. If necessary, refer students to the **Exam focus** on p.205 to review the task and strategies in more detail.

2 Give students a moment to read the task and then play the recording. Ask students if they agree with Jan and Marisol's opinions.

3 Students complete the phrases. Play the recording again for them to check. Focus students' attention on the word *demotivated* in sentence 3. Point out that both the prefixes *un-* and *de-* can be added to the adjective *motivated*. Ask students to identify the difference between being *demotivated* and *unmotivated* (*demotivated* conveys lost motivation that you had in the past; *unmotivated* only conveys your lack of motivation at the present time).

4 Students match the phrases in Activity 3 with uses A–D. Check as a class. Ask students if they can think of any more phrases that could convey uses A–D. Sample answers could include the following: A *In my view, If you ask me, To my mind*; B *I feel, I am convinced, Personally, I think*; C *In my experience, Speaking from experience*; D *I don't know for sure but, I guess*.

5 Play the recording and elicit which of the candidates answers the question well and why.

6 Tell students that they are now going to do Part 3 and 4 tasks, taking turns to be the 'candidates' and 'examiner'. Read through the **Exam tip** with the class. Working in groups of three, students turn to the task on p.152 and follow the instructions.

7 Refer students to the **Marking guidelines** on p.207. Then give them time to reflect on their performance and make suggestions. If students are keen, give them an opportunity to repeat the task, focusing on the areas which they identified for improvement.

Answers

3 1 the reason   **2** goes a long way   **3** could be wrong
      4 my own experience

4 A 1   B 2   C 4   D 3

5 Jan gives the best answer because he answers the question and gives both sides of the argument. Marisol gives too much personal information and doesn't really answer the question. She also repeats the wording of the question.

ADDITIONAL PRACTICE | Maximiser p.30, Speaking 1–3 |
MyEnglishLab: Cambridge Advanced, Speaking 15: Talking about cause and effect in Part 3 discussions, Speaking 17: Giving examples to support Part 4 answers

Writing focus ▶ CB p.44

Speaking

Aims

- to introduce the topic of positive thinking
- to provide spoken practice

1 Ask students to discuss how useful the tips are for helping people achieve more in their lives. Elicit a few ideas.

Essay (Part 1)

effective introductory and concluding paragraphs

Aims

- to identify the features of effective introductory and concluding paragraphs
- to write an exam-style essay (Writing Part 1)

Elicit whether the essay in the exam is optional or compulsory (compulsory). If necessary, refer students to the **Exam focus** on p.201 to remind them of the parts of the Writing paper. Tell students that in the essay they will always be asked to discuss two or three ideas and then to select one.

2 Students read the exam task and the two introductions. Elicit which of the introductions is better and why. Read the **Exam tip** aloud, then ask students to turn to the **Writing reference** on p.186 for some useful language for outlining issues in the introduction of an essay.

3 Refer students back to Plan A in Unit 1, p.14 for a model of an essay plan. In pairs, students write a plan for the main body of the essay in Activity 2. Circulate, checking students are using a similar model to write their plan.

4 Students decide if the statements are true or false, then compare answers in pairs before you check as a class.

5 Students complete the phrases. Check as a class. Ask students to turn to the **Writing reference** on p.186 for more useful language for conclusions.

6 Ask students to turn to p.162 and allow them five minutes to plan their introduction in pairs.

7 Set the writing task as homework, then collect in to provide individual feedback. Ask students to check their work first, using the checklist on p.185.

Answers

2 A

3 Sample answer:

Benefit 1: reduces stress

+ helps students to put problems into perspective

+ increases general well-being

- positive thinking will not be enough to combat stress for most students

Benefit 2: improves productivity

+ increase achievement

+ more efficient use of time means more time for leisure

- some students might substitute positive thinking for hard work leading to decreased achievement

4 1 T 2 F 3 F 4 T

5 1 sum 2 seems/appears 3 all 4 make/emphasise/stress

6 Sample answer:

We often hear about the many benefits of health and fitness. However, less often do we hear concrete suggestions for how to improve participation rates, particularly among young people. In this essay I will discuss two possible actions that governments could focus on in order to promote health and fitness to youth today.

The first possible action is to improve physical education teaching in schools. Local students have at times complained that the curriculum is rigid and emphasises repetitive activities instead of team sports and enjoyment. Better role models and more adventurous options could lead to improved attitude and participation. Naturally, employing specialist sports teachers would incur considerable cost.

A second option would be to attempt to change the overly competitive attitudes that seem ingrained in many of the sports competitions for youngsters. When adults such as parents and teachers focus on winning above having a good time, it puts undue pressure on the participants. They may feel a sense of failure if they lose and also be less inclined to try a new sport.

To sum up, either approach would be a step in the right direction. In my view, it would be wise to prioritise dealing with reducing competitiveness first because I believe it would help young people feel better about the sports they already do. They could then, in turn, influence their friends to join in.

ADDITIONAL PRACTICE | Maximiser p.30–31, Writing 1–3 |
MyEnglishLab: Cambridge Advanced, Writing 6: Including the correct content in a Part 1 essay

Review ▶ CB p.45

Aim

- to revise the structures, vocabulary and exam tasks covered in Unit 4

1 – **4** Ask students to complete the exercises, circulating to provide assistance. Ask students to check answers in pairs before checking as a class on eText. Alternatively, set as a homework activity and then go through the answers as a class, or on eText, to check.

Answers

1 1 could 2 shouldn't 3 didn't need to 4 must have known 5 would 6 can't

2 1 needn't have booked 2 would have been able to go 3 regretted not applying/(that) she hadn't applied 4 had forgotten to book/make 5 weren't allowed to watch 6 is considering selling

3 1 B 2 B 3 A 4 C 5 C 6 B 7 C 8 A

4 1 helpful 2 characteristics 3 relationships 4 demotivated 5 expectations 6 failure 7 misfortune 8 recognition

ADDITIONAL PRACTICE | Maximiser p.32–33, Use of English 2 |
Testmaster online and on **eText**, Unit 4 test

The feel-good factor

5

Use of English and Speaking focus ▶ CB p.46

Open cloze (Part 2)

> **Aim**
> • to complete an exam-style open cloze task (Reading and Use of English Part 2)

1 Students discuss the questions about happiness in pairs. Elicit a few responses to each question.

2 Tell students that Reading and Use of English Part 2, Open cloze tests their grammar and involves reading a text with eight missing words and putting one word in each gap. For more detailed information and strategies, refer students to the **Exam focus** on p.198 and turn to it on eText if you are using it. Focus students' attention on the title of the article. Working in pairs, students predict what the happiness app might be. Then ask students to read the article for general meaning, without worrying about the gaps yet. Elicit how the writer feels about using technology to help people track their thoughts, activities and moods.

3 Read the **Exam tip** aloud, then ask students to read the article again and fill in the gaps. Students compare their answers in pairs before you check as a class.

Answers

2 He found it annoying but it helped him understand that when he's distracted, he's less happy.

3 1 in 2 part 3 where 4 them 5 than 6 less 7 only 8 else

> **Additional activity:** Mood discussion
>
> Write the following questions on the board. Ask students to complete them with a preposition, then check answers as a class. Give students a few moments to think about their own answers to each question before discussing them in pairs. Elicit a few ideas for each.
>
> 1 Do you have any particular strategies you rely _____ to put you in a good mood?
>
> 2 Would you consider signing up _____ a study like the one in the article?
>
> 3 Do you think you are conscious _____ your feelings most of the time?
>
> 4 Are you able to focus _____ what you're doing or are you easily distracted?
>
> Answers: **1** on **2** for **3** of **4** on

Long turn (Part 2)
speculating (1)

Aims
- to use a range of expressions to speculate
- to complete an exam-style speaking task (Speaking Part 2)

4 Ask students what they remember about Speaking Part 2, Long turn. Refer them to the **Exam focus** on p.204 to check their ideas. Then read the **Exam tip** aloud. Read through the expressions in the box with the class. Then ask students to discuss the questions and pictures using the expressions.

5 Play the recording and elicit which things in the list the examiner does *not* ask the candidate to do.

6 Students complete the activity in pairs. After the activity, Student B should tell Student A which phrases they used. Students then swap roles. To extend with strong students, tell Student A to close their book or not look at the phrases during the task.

7 Play the recording and elicit what the candidate has to do. Students discuss the question with their partner.

8 Tell students that they are going to do another exam task. Students work in pairs and do the tasks on p.153 and p.158.

Answers
5 1, 3, 5

7 The candidate needs to answer the question: *Which group of people do you think looks happiest? Why?*

Additional activity
Ask students to look at the pictures on p.19 and 21. In pairs, they speculate about what the people are talking about using the phrases from Activity 4. Elicit some ideas. Then ask students to select some other pictures of people from Units 1–4 and, in their pairs, speculate what the people were thinking about when the picture was taken.

ADDITIONAL PRACTICE | **Maximiser** p.34–35, Use of English 1–3, Speaking 1–4 | **MyEnglishLab: Cambridge Advanced**, Speaking 5: Using linking words in Part 2

MyEnglishLab tip
Customisable attempt number
The number of attempts students have on each MyEnglishLab exercise is customisable so that you can either set attempts to one or allow unlimited attempts, or anything in between.

Listening focus ▶ CB p.48
Multiple choice (Part 3)

Aim
- to complete an exam-style multiple-choice listening task (Listening Part 3)

1 Students work in pairs and order the professions in the box according to how interesting they think they are. Students then swap partners to compare their ideas.

2 Refer students to the **Exam focus** on p.203 and turn to it on eText if you are using it. Read through it with the students, making sure they understand everything. Ask students to underline the key words in Activity 4, question 1, then elicit possible paraphrases for these.

3 Read the **Exam tip** aloud, then play the recording. Elicit the answers to the questions.

4 Give students a minute to underline key words in questions 2–6. Elicit some possible paraphrases for the key words, then play the recording. Play the recording a second time and then elicit the answers.

5 Elicit the meanings of the underlined words and phrases: *a dead-end job* (a position with no prospects of career advancement), *keep your nose to the grindstone* (stay focused on work), *a real slave driver* (someone who pushes you to work very hard), *up to your ears in work* (have a huge amount of work to do), *a carrot and stick approach* (offering incentives and punishments), *getting a foot in the door* (getting your first opportunity, which could lead to something better). Students read and answer the questions individually, then compare answers in pairs.

6 Pairs turn to the task on p.165. Ask them to take turns to read the sentences aloud, completing them appropriately. They should try and do this without looking back at Activity 5. When they have completed the six sentences, students check their answers on p.48.

Answers

2 What does Diana say the <u>results of the survey</u> <u>show</u> about <u>teaching</u> as a career?
A <u>Teachers</u> find their <u>work</u> makes them <u>happy</u>.
B <u>People</u> working in the <u>media</u> are a <u>lot less happy</u> than <u>teachers</u>.
C <u>Teaching doesn't offer</u> opportunities for <u>creativity</u>.
D <u>Teachers</u> find their <u>work</u> <u>stimulating</u>.

3 1 A and B: 'teaching was rated as the least boring. It came in way ahead of careers in the media or in advertising'; C 'there's some scope for using their creative skills'; D 'all things that keep them engaged'   2 D

4 2 A   3 B   4 D   5 B   6 C

ADDITIONAL PRACTICE | **Maximiser** p.35–36, Listening 1–2 | **MyEnglishLab: Cambridge Advanced**, Vocabulary 17: Career choices, Listening 14: Identifying attitudes and feelings

Grammar focus ▶ CB p.49

Speaking

Aims
- to introduce the topic of job satisfaction
- to provide spoken practice

1 Students discuss the items in pairs. Check they understand *commute* (regularly travel a long distance to get to work) and elicit the word for a person who commutes: *commuter*.

Hypothetical meaning

Aim
- to review a range of ways to express hypothetical meaning

2 Tell students that there are a range of ways to communicate hypothetical meanings in English and in this lesson you are going to review them. Elicit the meaning of *hypothetical* (based on a situation which is not real but might happen or one that didn't happen but potentially could have). Share the collocations *hypothetical situation/example/question*. Students choose the correct alternative in each sentence. Ask them to compare their answers in pairs before you check as a class.

3 Students complete the sentences about hypothetical meaning. Check answers as a class.

4 Read the **Language tip** and elicit a few more ways to complete the sentence *I wish I were … .* Refer students to the **Grammar reference** on p.175–176 for more notes and examples on using the expressions *I wish*, *If only*, *It's time* and *would rather*. Read the instructions for Activity 4 with the class and do the first sentence as an example, eliciting what goes in the gap (*wish I hadn't*). Emphasise the importance of understanding the first sentence before completing the gap. In sentence 1, *wish I had* could fit grammatically but would not have a similar meaning.

5 Students complete the sentences, then compare with a partner. Encourage them to ask at least one question about each of their partner's answers (e.g. *A: I know my friend wishes that she had studied more before she sat her driving test. B: Why, what happened? Did she have to retake the test?*).

Answers

2 1 wouldn't   2 could stop   3 could   4 didn't   5 had chosen   6 would give   7 did   8 Would

3 1 past simple   2 *would* + infinitive   3 *if only*   4 past perfect   5 *could* + infinitive   6 past simple   7 *rather*

4 1 wish I hadn't   2 would stop borrowing   3 you didn't tell   4 only people learnt/would learn   5 wish I didn't have   6 high time I wrote

Additional activity: *The Glad Game*

Ask students if they have ever heard of *Pollyanna* and elicit anything they know about it. Explain that *Pollyanna* is the title of a 1913 novel by Eleanor H. Porter. The novel tells the story of an orphan who cheers up a town by playing *The Glad Game*, which is looking for positives in any situation. The book, considered a children's classic, has been filmed various times, including a version by Disney in 1960.

To play *The Glad Game*, students work in pairs. One student makes a negative statement (which doesn't have to be true) using hypothetical language and their partner has to respond with a positive sentence, e.g.:

A: I wish I wasn't so tired.
B: That's a good excuse for a nap.

A: If only I had a comfortable bed!
B: Have a lie down on this chair instead!

Students continue with four more negative statements and positive responses before swapping roles.

ADDITIONAL PRACTICE | **Maximiser** p.36, Grammar 1–2 | **Photocopiable** p.150/176, 5A *You wish!*

Reading focus ▶ CB p.50

Multiple matching (Part 8)

Aim

● to complete an exam-style multiple matching task (Reading and Use of English Part 8)

1 Students discuss the questions about money in pairs. Elicit a few responses for each. Ask students what they remember about Part 8, Multiple matching. Refer them to the **Exam focus** on p.201 to check their ideas.

2 Give students about three minutes to read the article quickly and match the topics with the sections. Check answers as a class.

3 Focus students' attention on question 1 in the exam task and ask students to find the words/phrases that correspond to the underlined words.

4 Give students about ten minutes to underline key words in questions 2–10 and to choose the sections that correspond to each. Read the **Exam tip** aloud, then ask students to check their answers to questions 6 and 10. Students compare answers in pairs, then check as a class. When checking answers, elicit the sentences in the text that say the same things in different words for questions 6 and 10.

Answers

2 1 E 2 D 3 A 4 B 5 C

3 'they had to spend it by five in the afternoon of the same day'

4 2 C ('Thanks to the care the researchers took')

3 B ('The researchers started out by randomly selecting a group of just over 600 people from the local telephone directory.')

4 D ('Half the people were told to spend the money on themselves and the other half were told they should buy a gift for someone else or donate the money to a charity.')

5 B ('Unfortunately, the researchers couldn't claim that it was the type of spending that made people happy or not')

6 A ('And it is doing just that – using money to help others – that three Canadian researchers, Elizabeth Dunn, Lara Aknin and Michael Norton set out to prove was the key to happiness.')

7 E ('The researchers asked over 100 university students')

8 C ('after receiving a bonus at work')

9 A ('the more they indulge in consumer goods, the more likely they are to obsess about money and the less inclined they will be to use that money to help others')

10 E ('There is clearly a call for teaching people the facts of money and happiness.')

Vocabulary

working out meaning from context

Aim

● to practise working out meaning from context

5 Students find the words and phrases that match meanings 1–8, then compare answers in pairs before you check as a class.

6 Students complete the sentences with the correct forms of words and phrases from Activity 5. They then compare answers in pairs before you check as a class.

7 Students discuss the questions in pairs. Elicit a few ideas as a class.

Answers

5 1 make ends meet 2 intriguing 3 squander
4 randomly 5 come up with 6 clear-cut
7 on two counts 8 call

6 1 call 2 intrigued 3 clear-cut 4 squandered
5 randomly 6 come up with 7 make ends meet
8 on two counts

ADDITIONAL PRACTICE | Maximiser p.36–37, Reading 1–2, Vocabulary 1 | **MyEnglishLab: Cambridge Advanced**, Reading 7: Unfamiliar words, Reading 10: Identifying the writer's attitude A

Grammar focus ▶ CB p.52

Reading

Aim

- to provide examples of substitution and ellipsis in context

Warmer

Students discuss the following question in pairs: *What sorts of suggestions would you expect to read in a book called 'Naturally High'?* Ask students to think of at least four ideas. Elicit some predictions.

1 Ask students to read the extract and then elicit the reviewer's impression.

2 Students discuss the question in pairs. Elicit a few responses as a class.

Substitution and ellipsis

Aim

- to review the use of substitution and ellipsis

3 Focus students' attention on the first underlined word in the review (*it*) and elicit what it refers to (reading the novel). Tell students that this is called *substitution* and is used to avoid repetition of words. Students work out what each of the other underlined words/phrases refer to. Check answers as a class. Check students understand the meaning of *misanthrope* (someone who does not like other people and prefers to be alone).

4 Look at the first instance of ↑ in the article. Read the surrounding sentence aloud and elicit which words have been omitted (*it took me*). Tell students that this is called *ellipsis*. Like *substitution*, it is used to avoid repetition. Read the **Language tip** aloud.

Cultural note

In the UK, a common informal way of saying *How are you?* uses ellipsis:

A: *[Are you] All right?'*

B: *[I'm] All right, thanks. [How are] You?*

5 Students work in pairs to complete the activity.

6 Students complete the sentences, then compare their answers in pairs before you check as a class.

Answers

1 very positive

3 1 reading the book   5 the book   6 suggestions
7 (really hot) chillies   11 hardened misanthropes
13 it won't make them purr with contentment
14 dogs

4 2 it took me   3 ways   4 I'm   8 Are you having/Do you have   9 it will do it   10 of us/you   12 that it

5 My friend Susan wanted me to buy her a book for her birthday but I couldn't find the one that she wanted in our local bookshop, so I got her another one that I found there instead of the one she had asked for.

6 1 do   2 there   3 so   4 one   5 It   6 not
7 either   8 That

Additional activity: Ellipsis: which word?

Write the following sentences on the board or read them aloud one by one. Ask students to discuss in pairs which words or phrases have been left out in these sentences. Then elicit answers as a class.

1 She was tired but (↑) happy.
2 Bring along as many friends as you want (↑).
3 Dan can't make it next weekend. He sent me an email explaining why (↑).
4 They didn't have any yellow sheets. Only pink (↑).
5 That's Bill's bike. This is Kim's (↑).
6 She promised she would write but she hasn't (↑).

Answers: **1** she was   **2** to bring   **3** he can't make it next weekend   **4** sheets   **5** bike   **6** written

Additional activity: Improvise a conversation

Students work in pairs. They choose one of the pairs of sentences in Activity 6 as the first part of a conversation and try to continue the conversation. Encourage them to use more examples of ellipsis. Invite a few pairs to share one of their conversations with the class.

ADDITIONAL PRACTICE | Maximiser p.38, Grammar 1–2

Vocabulary focus ▶ CB p.53

Prefix *mis-* and false opposites

Aims

- to expand knowledge of words beginning with the prefix *mis-*
- to clarify the meanings of some false opposites

Warmer

Focus students' attention on the picture and elicit what is happening. Elicit *mistake*. Write the prefix *mis-* on the board and give students two minutes to work in small groups and think of as many words as they can that start with *mis-*. Invite groups to share their lists and elicit meanings for any that other students are unsure of.

1 Students complete the sentences, then compare answers in pairs before you check as a class.

2 Focus students' attention on the **Language tip** and read it aloud. Elicit the meaning of the false opposites *disease* (serious illness) and *ease* (if you do something *with ease*, it is easy for you, antonym = with difficulty; if you are *at ease*, you feel relaxed, antonym = *unease*). Students discuss the meanings of the underlined words in pairs. Ask them not to use dictionaries as meanings will be clarified in Activity 3.

3 Students match the underlined words from Activity 2 with meanings A–F. Go through the answers with the class and for each underlined word, elicit whether it has a base form and whether it has an opposite, or is a false opposite.

4 Students answer the questions individually, then share their answers in pairs.

Answers

1 1 misunderstanding 2 misguided
3 misconceptions 4 misleading 5 misgivings
6 misinterpretation 7 misprint 8 mistrustful

3 1 F 2 A 3 B 4 E 5 C 6 D

ADDITIONAL PRACTICE | **Maximiser** p.38, Vocabulary 1

Writing focus ▶ CB p.54

Vocabulary

sentence adverbs

Aim

- to review sentence adverbs for use in a review

1 Students work in pairs to discuss the questions. Elicit a few ideas for each question.

Additional activity: What is a sentence adverb?

Check that students understand what a sentence adverb is and how sentence adverbs differ from regular adverbs (A sentence adverb relates to the whole sentence that contains it and is usually used to describe the speaker's attitude, whereas a regular adverb modifies a verb, adjective or other adverb.). Tell students that sentence adverbs are useful for expressing opinions in a review. They are usually placed at the beginning of a sentence. To further illustrate the difference between a regular adverb and a sentence adverb, write the following on the board:

1 Sadly, she left.

2 She left sadly.

Ask students to discuss the difference in meaning between the two sentences, then elicit the answer. The first sentence, where *sadly* is used as a sentence adverb, communicates that the speaker feels sad about the whole sentence, i.e. the fact that she left. In the second sentence, *sadly* modifies the verb *left*, so it communicates that she left in a sad manner.

2 Ask students to cross out the adverb that does not make sense in each extract. If necessary, clarify or elicit the meanings of the adverbs when used as sentence adverbs: *ironically* (used when talking about a situation in which the opposite of what you expected happens or is true), *hopefully* (a way of saying what you hope will happen), *happily*, *thankfully* (used to say that you are glad something has happened, especially because a difficult situation has ended or been avoided), *sadly* (used to say that you are sad or disappointed something has happened, especially when it could have been different), *understandably*, *naturally* (used to say that something is normal and not surprising), *oddly enough*, *curiously*, *surprisingly* (used to say that something seems strange or surprising).

Answers

2 1 Hopefully   2 Understandably   3 Sadly
4 Naturally   5 Ironically   6 Thankfully
7 Understandably   8 Oddly enough

Review (Part 2)
covering key features

Aims

- to identify the key features of a review
- to write an exam-style review (Writing Part 2)

3 Students match extracts 1–8 with features A–D. Check answers as a class.

4 Students work in pairs to read the exam task and discuss which films they would choose.

5 Refer students back to features A–D in Activity 3. Read the **Exam tip** aloud, then ask students to make notes about the two films they chose under those headings.

6 Ask students to read the model review in the **Writing reference** on p.195 and pick out and underline five pieces of useful language. Ask them to share their answers with a partner. Point out the useful language for writing reviews in the **Writing Reference** on p.194. Then set Activity 6 as homework.

7 Give students an opportunity to share their draft with a partner and make changes before you collect the reviews in to provide individual feedback.

Answers

3 1 B   2 C   3 A   4 A   5 C   6 C   7 D   8 A
Sample answer:

In this review I am going to compare two contrasting tales about overcoming adversity. Whereas *The Blind Side* (2009) left me with a huge grin on my face, sadly, *Doctor Zhivago* (1965) left me feeling the weight of the world on my shoulders.

Doctor Zhivago, directed by five-time Oscar winner David Lean, is set in the Bolshevik revolution and follows the title character, who must adapt to the new order while pining for Lara, the beautiful wife of a political campaigner. The director succeeded in creating a film that is thoroughly engaging but full of gritty realism, cruelty and tragic irony. Take the tissues!

The Blind Side, which is based on a true story, is also a bit of a tearjerker, in a completely different way. Starring Sandra Bullock, who won an Academy Award for her portrayal of a rich white mother in Tennessee who takes a homeless black teenager under her roof. Understandably, the gentle giant thinks he isn't good at anything but his new mother sees his potential to become a football star and part of the family. The plot is based on a true story, making it all the more touching.

I would strongly recommend *The Blind Side*. It will appeal to a range of people and is a great choice for a movie night. Although *Doctor Zhivago* is a classic, I think it has more of a niche audience and is best saved for when you want a dose of gloom!

Teaching tip

If a review is one of the Part 2 tasks, it might include items such as a concert, album, film, book or shop. It may help students to brainstorm some examples they might use in each category. However, emphasise that they must only use examples that are relevant to the question asked in the exam. Finally, tell students that they can make up details for the review if they don't know them (e.g. the director of a film or the year a book was published).

ADDITIONAL PRACTICE | **Maximiser** p.38–39 Vocabulary 2, Writing 1–3 | **Photocopiable** p.151/176, 5B *Hit and* mis- | **MyEnglishLab: Cambridge Advanced**, Writing 16: How to write a good review, Writing 17: Useful language: Review writing

Progress test 1 ▶ CB p.55

Aims

- to revise the structures and vocabulary covered in Units 1–5
- to practise Reading and Use of English Parts 1–4 type activities

1 – **8** Ask students to complete the exercises, circulating to provide assistance, or set them as a test. Suggested time limit: 45 minutes for Activities 1–4 and 45 minutes for Activities 5–8. Ask students to check answers in pairs before you check as a class on eText. Alternatively, set as a homework activity and then go through the answers as a class.

Answers

1 1 would stop 2 started 3 had realised
4 wouldn't rain/didn't rain 5 could get 6 didn't go

2 1 C 2 A 3 B 4 A 5 B 6 A

3 1 then 2 as 3 one 4 them 5 this 6 more
7 so 8 It

4 1 C 2 A 3 A 4 C 5 B 6 C

5 1 B 2 B 3 C 4 D 5 B 6 C 7 A 8 C

6 1 More 2 like 3 no 4 to 5 for 6 us 7 have
8 What

7 1 amazement 2 imagination 3 unlikely
4 unexpectedly 5 discovery 6 enthusiastic
7 remarkable 8 agencies

8 1 sooner had I sat down than 2 had a really
good understanding of 3 find it embarrassing
4 prevented me from going 5 had a profound
suspicion 6 wish they didn't have

ADDITIONAL PRACTICE | **Testmaster** online and on **eText**,
Unit 5 test | **MyEnglishLab: Cambridge Advanced**, Progress test 1

Living with the past

Use of English and Listening focus ▶ CB p.58

Word formation (Part 3)

Aim

- to complete an exam-style word formation task (Reading and Use of English Part 3)

1 Focus students' attention on the photo and ask them to discuss in pairs what they think it shows. Elicit a few ideas. Check students understand the meaning of *fossil* (an animal or plant that lived thousands of years ago and that has been preserved in rock). Students work in pairs to discuss the questions. Elicit a few answers for each. Read the **Exam tip** aloud and invite students to share examples of how they record vocabulary. Elicit the word for someone who searches for ancient remains as a job: *archaeologist* (noun). Elicit other word forms of this word, e.g. *archaeology* (noun), *archaeological* (adjective).

2 Elicit what students remember about Reading and Use of English Part 3, Word formation. Refer them to the **Exam focus** on p.198 to check their ideas. Focus students' attention on the title of the article and check that they understand *mammoth* (noun: an animal like a large hairy elephant that lived on the earth thousands of years ago; adjective: extremely large). Give students a minute to read the article for gist, without worrying about the gaps. Then ask them to close their books and see how many facts they can remember in pairs.

3 Focus students on the first word in capitals in Activity 2 (*ASTONISH*) as an example and ask the three questions listed: *Does it form a noun ending in the suffix -tion?* (No, the noun is *astonishment*.) *Does it form a word with the prefix* un-? (no) *Does it have two noun forms with different meanings?* (no) Share the following example of two noun forms with different meanings: *excavator* (a person who excavates) and *excavation* (general noun).

4 With a weaker class, consider eliciting whether the word that fits in each gap is a noun, adjective or adverb before students attempt the activity. If it is a noun, also elicit whether it is singular/uncountable or plural. Students read the article again and form a word that fits each gap. Students compare their answers in pairs before you check as a class.

5 Students discuss in pairs what they think about objects of historical significance in foreign museums and whether they should be returned to their country of origin. Elicit a few opinions from the class.

Additional activity: More word formation

Draw the following table on the board and practise further word formation with words from the article. Students complete the table (answers in brackets).

General noun(s)	Personal noun	Verb	Adjective(s)	Adverb
(preservation, preservative)	—	(preserve)	preserved (preserving)	—
(settlement)	(settler)	(settle)	(settled) settling	—
excitement	—	(excite)	(excited, exciting)	(excitedly)
fight	(fighter)	(fight)	(fighting)	—

Answers

3 1 consideration, confrontation, extinction   2 unfit
3 remains (bones, etc.), remainder (what's left over)

4 1 perfectly   2 remains   3 analysis   4 considerably
5 unfit   6 hunters   7 confrontation   8 extinction

Multiple choice (Part 1)

Aim

- to complete an exam-style multiple-choice listening task (Listening Part 1)

6 Remind students that Listening Part 1 involves listening twice to three short conversations and answering two multiple-choice questions about each. Ask students to work in pairs and discuss what they should do before they listen. Ask students to read Strategy 1 in the **Exam focus** on p.202 to check their answers. Read through the **Exam focus** with students, making sure they understand everything. Ask them to underline key words in the questions and alternatives. Then play the recording. Read the **Exam tip** aloud, then play the recording again. Check answers as a class.

7 Divide the board into two columns headed *in-* and *un-*. Ask students to divide the adjectives in the box into these two groups. Students compare their answers in pairs. To extend with strong students, ask them to think of at least two more words for each column. Finish by checking as a class.

Teaching tip

If students have found any particular questions challenging in a listening task, show the audio script on eText and ask students to find the phrase(s) which support the answer.

Answers

6 1 B   2 A   3 A   4 C   5 A   6 B

7 in-: inaccurate, insignificant

un-: unbelievable, unchanged, unconvincing, uncovered, undiscovered, unfavourable, uninformative, unmodernised

Additional activity: Discussion

Students discuss the following questions in pairs.

1 Would you prefer to learn about dinosaurs by visiting an exhibition or playing a computer game?

2 In what other ways could you learn about dinosaurs?

3 Imagine you have children. What kind of holidays would you like to take them on? Would you want to recreate any vacation experiences from your own childhood with them?

ADDITIONAL PRACTICE | Maximiser p.40–41, Use of English 1–3, Listening 1 **Photocopiable** p.152/177, 6A *Three in a row* | **MyEnglishLab: Cambridge Advanced**, Use of English 5: Word building in context, Listening 2: Agreement and disagreement

Grammar focus ▶ CB p.60
Speaking

Aims

- to introduce the topic of history
- to provide spoken practice

Warmer: History buffs

Write the following events on the board:

A Eiffel Tower completed

B Marie Curie wins her first Nobel Prize

C Michelangelo completes the Sistine Chapel ceiling

D Columbus sails to the Americas

E Nelson Mandela is elected president of South Africa

F Amelia Earhart flies the Atlantic solo

Ask students to work in pairs to decide on the chronological order of the historical events.

Then write the following years on the board: *1492, 1512, 1889, 1903, 1932, 1994.* Ask students to match each year with an event. Share the answers. The pair with the most correct answers are the winners.

Answers: A 1889 B 1903 C 1512 D 1492 E 1994
F 1932

1 Students work in pairs and discuss which of the quotes about history they agree with. Elicit a few opinions.

Comparing

Aim

- to use a range of language for comparing

2 Students look at the sentences and decide if there is any difference in meaning between the phrases in italics. Check answers as a class. Then students tick the statements which are true for them and compare their ideas in pairs.

3 Read the **Language tip** aloud. Elicit what the speaker thinks about watching cricket (it's boring). Share the examples using *as … as*: *He's as tall as his father. Watching cricket is as dull as watching paint dry.* Write the following starters on the board and ask students to complete the sentences verbally with a partner: *Reading historical novels is as … as …; An exhibition about ancient coins? That sounds like …*

Students complete the sentences with one word, then compare answers in pairs before you check as a class.

4 Students read the article quickly for gist, to find out the writer's view of museums as places of entertainment.

5 Students read the article again and choose the correct alternatives. Ask them to compare answers in pairs, then check as a class.

6 Give students about five minutes to discuss the questions, then ask them to present their choice of object to the class. Tell them their presentation should include what the object is and at least three things it would tell future generations about today. If you have a very large class, ask students to present their objects in groups rather than to the whole class.

7 Put students in pairs and ask them to turn to the activity on p.163. Check that they understand the meaning of *posterity* (all the people in the future who will be alive after you are dead). Remind them to use a variety of language to compare the buildings. Students follow the instructions to complete the activity, then swap partners to compare their ideas.

Answers

2 1 no difference in meaning   2 the opposite meaning
3 no difference in meaning   4 *much less fun* is stronger

3 1 much 2 far/much 3 One 4 than 5 as 6 By

4 no

5 1 never 2 far more 3 the briefest 4 More than
ever 5 higher and higher 6 considerably

Additional activity: Guessing meaning from context

Ask students to find and underline the following phrases in the article: *building boom* (a period when a lot of new construction takes place), *old master* (a famous painter from the 15th to the 18th century or a painting by one of these painters), *open round the clock* (open 24 hours). In pairs, students discuss what each phrase means. Check as a class.

ADDITIONAL PRACTICE | Maximiser p.41, Grammar 1

Speaking focus ▶ CB p.61

Long turn (Part 2)

comparing

Aim

- to complete an exam-style speaking task (Speaking Part 2)

Warmer: Which picture?

Write the following words on the board: *ancient past, servants, school trip, guide, memories, legend, cap, apron, granddaughter.* Ask students to discuss in pairs which picture on p.61 they associate each word with.

Suggested answers: Top: servants, school trip, cap, apron; Centre: memories, granddaughter; Bottom: ancient past, guide, legend

1 Play the recording and elicit the three things students need to do for this task.

2 Play the recording and elicit which two pictures Alessandra compares.

3 Play the recording again and ask students to tick the information included.

4 Students discuss Alessandra's answer in pairs.

5 Read through the expressions in the box with the class, then play the recording while students note down the expressions they hear.

Additional activity

Ask students to divide the phrases in the box into those used to introduce a similar idea and those used to present two contrasting ideas (or a contrast to what has been said previously).

Answers: *Similar*: Similarly, What both photos have in common is; *Contrasting*: On the other hand, Having said that, Nevertheless, Whilst, Whereas, Although, However, One significant difference is

6 Students compare the pictures in pairs, using phrases from Activity 5. Circulate, checking the expressions are being used appropriately.

7 Read the **Exam tip** aloud. Ask: *What should you do if you can't think of anything else to say?* (use paraphrases and 'fillers' if necessary; see Strategy 4 of the **Exam focus** on p.204) Students complete the tasks on p.153 and p.159, taking turns to be the examiner.

Answers

1 compare two of the pictures, say why the people might be interested in this kind of information about the past, say how easy it might be for them to remember it

2 The top and bottom photos

3 location, possible reasons for the visit

5 Whilst, Whereas

ADDITIONAL PRACTICE | **Maximiser** p.41, Speaking 1–2 | **MyEnglishLab: Cambridge Advanced**, Speaking 8: Comparing Part 2 pictures

Reading focus ▶ CB p.62

Multiple choice (Part 5)

Aim

- to complete an exam-style multiple-choice reading task (Reading and Use of English Part 5)

1 Students discuss the questions in pairs. Elicit a few ideas. Say: *If someone is your ancestor, you are his or her ... .* Elicit the word *descendant*.

Discuss as a class what the best strategy is for approaching Reading and Use of English Part 5, then refer students to the **Exam focus** on p.199 to check their ideas.

2 Tell students to use the strategies outlined in the **Exam focus** and, if you are using eText, keep these displayed during the activity. Focus students' attention on the **Exam tip**, which corresponds to Strategy 4 in the **Exam focus**. Students compare their answers in pairs, then check as a class.

3 Students discuss the question in pairs. Elicit responses from a few students.

Answers

2 1 B ('I'd accepted the invitation gladly, not because I had any particular interest in my forebears but to understand the bizarre modern craze of ancestor worship.')

2 A ('But the name of the programme is a bit of a sham. Who we actually are is a matter of our own personality, luck, circumstances, education and that of our parents.')

3 D ('People should try to make something of themselves rather than piggy-back on the fact that a distant and long-dead relative was a prince or a prisoner.')

4 C ('every desk was occupied by someone staring at a screen in a sort of rapture. They were poring over microfiches with a focus more intense than any I've ever seen in any other library or anywhere else at all.')

5 D ('Would I have been able to forgive him for abandoning his family?')

6 B ('I was more interested than I'd expected to be in the fate of Amos'; 'I'm not who I thought I was six months ago'; 'Who I am now is a born-again ancestor bore.')

Vocabulary

adjective/noun collocations

Aim

- to expand students' knowledge of adjective/noun collocations

Teaching tip

Point out to students that in English some compound words are hyphenated, others are joined without a hyphen and others remain two separate words. When learning a compound word, students should note and learn whether it is hyphenated or not.

4 Check students understand that a *compound word* is one that is made up of two (or more) other words to form a new unit of meaning. Students work out the meanings of the underlined compound adjectives in the article. They compare in pairs, then as a class.

5 Students underline the nouns that collocate with the adjectives. Check as a class.

6 Students make collocations, then compare answers in pairs before you check as a class.

7 Give students a moment to make a few notes, then put them in small groups to discuss their family trees.

Answers

4 tailor-made: designed especially for an individual; consumer-driven: focused on material things (in this context); high-minded: having high moral standards

5 1 trip, course, suit, service   2 fashion, technology, design   3 person, ambition, reason, principle

6 1 close, distant, immediate   2 common, direct, distant, early   3 close, distant, extended, immediate, nuclear

Additional activity: Compound word treasure hunt

Challenge students in pairs to see how many more compound words they can find and underline in the article. They may be hyphenated, joined or two separate words.

Suggested answers: travel company, ancestor worship, fastest-growing, runaway, social history, family tree, piggy-back, long-dead, upstairs room, microfiche, great-grandfather, psychobabble, great-great-grandfather, clergyman, snakebite, humble pie, born-again.

ADDITIONAL PRACTICE | Maximiser p.42–44, Reading 1–5, Vocabulary 1 | **MyEnglishLab: Cambridge Advanced**, Reading 9: Focusing on detail, Vocabulary 1: Adjective/Noun collocations

Vocabulary focus ▶ CB p.64

Speaking

Aims

- to present prefixes and suffixes in context
- to provide spoken practice

Warmer

Write the following questions on the board and discuss as a class: *What is DNA? What reasons might someone get a DNA test?*

Suggested answers: DNA (or deoxyribonucleic acid) is a substance that carries genetic information in the cells of the body. Reasons people might get a DNA test could include testing for susceptibility to a genetic condition or disease, evidence in a crime or to see if you are related to someone.

1 Give students a few minutes to read the article without worrying about the gaps at this stage. Elicit an answer to the question.

2 Students discuss the questions in pairs. Elicit a few different opinions.

Answer

1 no

Useful resources

For more information on DNA testing, do an internet search for companies that offer the service or for the International Genome project.

Prefixes and suffixes

3 Look at the first gap with the class and elicit the correct adjective form (*respectable*). Students complete the article with the correct adjective forms, then compare in pairs before you check as a class.

4 Students discuss the questions in pairs. Check answers as a class.

5 Students work in pairs to answer the questions. Check as a class. Focus students' attention on the **Language tip** and read it aloud.

6 Elicit any adjectives ending in *-ive/-ing* from Activity 4 and also any others that students can think of.

7 Students choose the correct alternatives, then compare answers in pairs before you check as a class.

8 In pairs, students play the word association game on p.162 and p.169. Encourage them to think of at least five ideas for each word.

Answers

3 1 respectable 2 reliable 3 affordable 4 predictable
5 unremarkable 6 revealing/revelatory 7 exciting
8 unthinkable

4 -able: believable, changeable, comfortable, comparable, excitable, identifiable, imaginable, movable, noticeable, profitable, variable

-ible: accessible, comprehensible, resistible, reversible, visible

5 un-: unbelievable, unchangeable, uncomfortable, unexcitable, unidentifiable, unimaginable, unmovable, unnoticeable, unprofitable

in-: inaccessible, incomparable, incomprehensible, invariable, invisible

ir-: irresistible, irreversible

6 -ive: comparative, comprehensive, imaginative

-ing: changing, comforting, exciting, varying

7 1 imaginable 2 imaginative 3 changeable
4 variable 5 excitable 6 comforting 7 changing
8 comprehensive

ADDITIONAL PRACTICE | Maximiser p.44, Vocabulary 2–3

Grammar focus ▶ CB p.65

Modifying adverbs

Warmer: I'm into …
Draw the following continuum on the board.

not at all————————————*totally*

Then write: *I'm _____ into history.*

Ask students to draw the continuum and discuss in pairs where the following adverbs would go on it:

quite, seriously, really, not really.

Answers:

not at all, not really, quite, really, seriously, totally.

Now ask students to complete the sentence with one of the adverbs so it is true for them and share it with their partner. Quickly elicit ten other topics/interests and write them on the board, e.g. sports, dancing, shopping, travel, reading biographies, vintage clothing, trivia, classical music, organic food, anime (Japanese cartoons). Ask students to discuss in pairs how 'into' each of these things they are using the adverbs. Encourage them to ask their partner a follow-up question about each topic or interest.

1 Check students understand the meaning of *ungradable* (If an adjective is ungradable, it means that there are no degrees of it. For example, something is either *impossible* or it isn't – it can't be *slightly impossible* or *very impossible*.). Focus students' attention on the examples, then go through the questions with the class, eliciting the answer to each one.

2 Students discuss in pairs which of the adjectives are ungradable. Elicit the answers.

3 Use *disappointed* as an example with the class and go through each modifier in the box, eliciting whether it can be used with this word. Ask students to turn to the **Grammar reference** on p.170. Highlight the collocations (2) and the **Watch out** box at the end. Ask students to read through the rest of the notes and examples.

Read the **Language tip** aloud. Write on the board: *quite nice, quite perfect, quite angry.* Elicit which of these is ungradable (*perfect*) and elicit the meaning (completely perfect). Then elicit the meaning of *quite nice* (fairly nice) and *quite angry* (fairly angry).

Teaching tip

Point out that in addition to modifiers, the strength of an adjective can also be conveyed in speaking by vocal expression, e.g. *She is pretty disappointed.* could sound very strong or moderately strong, depending on the expression of the speaker.

4 Focus students' attention on the heading and picture and elicit some ideas about what the article might be about. Then ask students to read the article. Elicit what *infantile amnesia* is.

5 Students choose the correct alternatives, then compare answers in pairs before you check as a class.

Answers

1 1 A modifier is used for emphasis. In sentence A, *fairly* makes *predictable* weaker; *quite* makes *unremarkable* slightly less unremarkable. In sentence B, *absolutely* makes *enormous* stronger.

   2 enormous

2 all except *disappointed*

3 *Completely*, *pretty*, *quite*, *really* and *totally* can be used with *exceptional*, *furious*, *impossible*, *perfect* and *terrified*. *Bitterly*, *pretty*, *quite*, *really*, *seriously* and *somewhat* can be used with *disappointed*.

4 Infantile amnesia is how people's early childhood memories completely disappear. Researchers discovered that by ages 4–7, infantile amnesia is already evident.

5 1 somewhat 2 scarcely 3 rather 4 highly
   5 virtually 6 completely 7 deeply 8 seriously

Speaking

Aim

• to provide spoken practice

6 Students read the questions and may make a few notes if they wish. They then compare their answers in pairs.

7 Ask for a show of hands for each topic. Elicit what the other first memories were about that weren't mentioned in the list.

Additional activity

This activity works best in classes where students know each other, as they need to know each other's names. Give students a few minutes to briefly describe an early memory on a piece of paper. Tell them that it will be shared with the class, so it shouldn't be anything too personal.

Collect the memories, number them and stick them up around the classroom. Students walk around the class with pen and paper, reading the memories and noting down who they think wrote each one. Finish by revealing who wrote each memory. The person who guessed the most correctly is the winner.

ADDITIONAL PRACTICE | Maximiser p.44, Grammar 1–2 |
Photocopiable p.153/178, 6B *Absolutely right*

Writing focus ▶ CB p.66

Essay (Part 1)

structuring an argument

Aim

• to provide well-structured arguments in an exam-style essay (Writing Part 1)

1 Students discuss the task in pairs. Ask a few pairs to share their ideas.

2 Underline the key words with the class, on eText if you are using it.

3 Read the **Exam tip** aloud. Students read the statements and then discuss their opinions on each one in pairs.

4 Students should write *P* next to the main points and *E* next to supporting evidence. They compare answers in pairs before you check as a class.

5 Ask students to underline useful phrases in Activity 3. Then ask them to turn to the useful language in the **Writing reference** on p.186 to review more useful phrases for other parts of the essay.

6 Students plan their essays and then share their plans with a partner.

7 Set the writing task as homework and then collect in to provide individual feedback.

Answers

2 Your class has attended a lecture on the <u>action</u> <u>governments</u> can take to make sure <u>cultural heritage</u> is <u>preserved</u> for <u>future generations</u>. You have made the notes below.

<u>Priorities</u> for governments aiming to preserve cultural heritage

- increase <u>funding</u> for <u>museums</u>

- <u>protect old buildings</u>

- <u>teach</u> the importance of <u>cultural heritage</u> in schools

Some <u>opinions</u> expressed in the discussion

- 'Cultural heritage <u>isn't just about buildings</u> – it's about a <u>way of life</u>.'

- 'It's the <u>responsibility</u> of the <u>older generation</u> to <u>pass on</u> a <u>cultural heritage</u> to the next generation.'

- '<u>Museums</u> are the <u>best places</u> to keep <u>shared memories</u> of a <u>community</u>.'

Write an <u>essay</u> for your tutor discussing <u>two</u> of the <u>priorities</u> in your notes. You should <u>explain which priority you think is more important</u>, <u>giving reasons</u> to support your opinion. You may, if you wish, make use of the opinions expressed in the discussion but you should <u>use your own words</u> as far as possible.

Write your essay in <u>220–260 words</u> in an <u>appropriate style</u>.

4 1 P 2 P 3 E 4 E 5 P 6 E

5 Giving main points: I would argue that, It's become clear in recent years, An urgent priority is

Giving supporting evidence: Perhaps, I'm sure, For example

Sample answer:

Cultural heritage is an invaluable asset for all generations to enjoy. It is about knowing where we have come from and having pride in the place we live. In this essay I will discuss two priorities for the government's support of the cultural heritage in our community.

The first idea is to increase funding to museums. People say that museums are the heart of cultural heritage preservation. Not only do they display objects, they also teach and provide information about them. Increased funding could attract better care of objects, more specialised staff and more fun displays, in turn attracting more people to visit and learn. On the other hand, I would argue that it's unreasonable to expect governments to give more money to museums when they have got more important things to spend people's taxes on.

The second idea is to protect old buildings. It has become clear in recent years that governments can no longer afford to provide generous grants to help people maintain their historically significant houses. I am sure there are many voluntary organisations which would be

prepared to work on conservation projects. Nevertheless, the government could provide protection to ensure that old buildings are not demolished or transformed out of character.

In my view, the most pressing priority is to provide protective legislation for old homes and buildings. I'm not alone in my concern about the loss of historical features which take such pride of place in and give character to our communities.

ADDITIONAL PRACTICE | Maximiser p.45, Writing 1–4 |
MyEnglishLab: Cambridge Advanced, Writing 7: Essay writing

Review ▶ CB p.67

Aim

- to revise the structures, vocabulary and exam tasks covered in Unit 6

1 – **4** Ask students to complete the exercises, circulating to provide assistance. Ask students to check answers in pairs before checking as a class on eText. Alternatively, set as a homework activity and then go through the answers as a class, or on eText, to check.

Answers

1 1 so 2 much 3 nothing like 4 great 5 far
6 like 7 ever 8 worse and worse 9 just as
10 simplest

2 1 B 2 A 3 B 4 C 5 A 6 C 7 B 8 A 9 C
10 A

3 1 favourable 2 unconvincing 3 misinformed
4 imaginative 5 irreversible 6 inaccessible
7 disbelief 8 inaccurately 9 incomprehensible
10 invisible

4 1 trip 2 principles 3 design 4 ambition
5 course 6 person 7 service 8 reason

ADDITIONAL PRACTICE | Maximiser p.46–47, Use of English 3 |
Testmaster online and on **eText**, Unit 6 test, Progress test 2 |
MyEnglishLab: Cambridge Advanced, Practice Reading test

MyEnglishLab tip

Practice tests

The MyEnglishLab Practice tests are an opportunity for students to practise a full exam paper for each of the four papers: Reading and Use of English, Writing, Listening and Speaking. They are able to re-attempt the questions multiple times for extra practice.

The hard sell

Vocabulary and Grammar focus ▶ CB p.68

Collocations: sales and marketing

Aim

- to introduce collocations related to sales and marketing

Warmer

Focus students' attention on the picture on p.68 and ask students to discuss what it is about and why it is printed sideways. (The advertisement is for Vegemite, a yeast spread commonly eaten on toast for breakfast in Australia and New Zealand. The text is printed sideways as a humorous appeal to pretend the audience for the billboard is looking at it from a lying position.)

1 Working in pairs, students discuss whether they have ever been persuaded to buy something by a clever salesperson. Ask each pair to briefly report their discussion back to the class.

2 Students read the article quickly. Elicit why Joe Girard's approach was so successful.

3 Students complete the article with the words in the box, then compare answers in pairs before you check as a class.

4 Elicit a few answers to the question, encouraging students to give reasons for their answers.

5 First ask students to find any collocations with the words *sales*, *product*, *mail*, *business* and *customer* in the text. Students then work in pairs to make more collocations and share their ideas with the class. To support a weaker class, write the words from the Answers below on the board (out of order) for them to pair with the words to form collocations.

Answers

2 He made sure his customers liked him.

3 1 retail   2 marketing   3 campaign   4 product   5 rapport   6 sales
7 mail   8 loyal

5 (Suggested answers)
sales figures, sales conference; product placement, product launch; mail order; business acumen, business partner; customer service, customer complaints, customer relations

Review of conditionals

Aim

- to review conditionals

6 Students read the article, then discuss whether anyone has ever used the sales techniques mentioned on them. Elicit a few responses. Ask the class: *Which of the techniques do you think is the most effective? Why?*

7 Give students time to read the numbered sentences again and decide what type of conditional they are. If necessary, briefly review the conditionals as follows:

- zero conditional: used to describe a general truth, e.g. *If I dent a car, it costs a fortune to fix.*

- first conditional: used to describe what is possible or likely in the present/future, e.g. *If I work extra hours, I'll make more sales.*

- second conditional: used to describe something unlikely/contrary to present facts or to give advice, e.g. *If I were rich, I'd buy a new car.*

- third conditional: used to describe something in the past that could (or should) have happened but didn't, e.g. *If I had got that promotion, I'd have become rich.*

For more information on conditionals, refer students to the **Grammar reference** on p.172.

8 Ask: *What are the advantages of online shopping over regular shopping?* Elicit a few ideas, then ask students to read the article and see if the writer's explanation was the same as theirs.

9 Go through the questions with the class, eliciting the answers. Read through the **Language tip** with the class. For more information on mixed conditionals, refer students to section 5.6 in the **Grammar reference** on p.173.

10 Complete the first sentence with the class as an example. Students complete the remaining sentences, then compare their answers in pairs before you check as a class.

11 Students complete the sentences so that they are true for them. Ask a few students to read out some of their sentences and correct errors as a class if necessary. Then ask students to check and correct their own sentences before moving into small groups to compare their ideas.

Answers

7 1 first conditional 2 second conditional 3 third conditional 4 zero conditional

8 It is attractive to shoppers because it is more fun, less stressful and less tiring.

9 A 1 B 2

10 1 had done, would understand 2 would be, had had 3 were/was, would have made 4 hadn't opened, wouldn't be 5 would have got, were/was 6 were/was, would have stopped

Sentences 1, 3, 5 and 6 could be written as third conditional sentences. Only 6 has no change in meaning.

ADDITIONAL PRACTICE | Maximiser p.48, Vocabulary 1–2, Grammar 1–2

Listening focus ▶ CB p.70

Multiple choice (Part 3)

Aim

- to complete an exam-style multiple-choice listening task (Listening Part 3)

1 Students discuss the questions in pairs. If necessary, pre-teach *evoke* (to produce a strong feeling or memory in someone). Share the related collocations *evoke sympathy* and *evoke a response*.

2 Elicit what students remember about Listening Part 3 and the strategies to use. If necessary, refer students to the **Exam focus** on p.203 to review the strategies. Ask students to underline key words in the questions and alternatives in Activity 3.

3 Read the **Exam tip** aloud, then play the recording twice, pausing in between. Go through the answers with the class.

4 Play the recording again while students write expressions that match meanings 1–6. Check answers as a class.

Answers

2 (Suggested answers)

1 attitude, sophisticated scent marketing; A a little concerned, some instances; B not think people, anxious; C brilliant innovation; D not terribly impressed

2 people, feel, tricked; A food smells, encourage, spend; B products on display, different smell; C find out, no connection, products on display; D so inviting, making unplanned purchases

3 choice, toy shop; A should, more subtle; B known, good mood; C not possible, be certain, why, chosen; D only worked, London

4 attitude, milk board campaign; A not surprised, complaints; B shares, dislike, smell; C original concept; D skilful use

5 reaction, complaint, allergy sufferers; A unsure, why, complained; B sympathises, poses, health risk; C should be warned; D more research

6 opinion, people, design; A all companies need, services; B rewarding profession; C great admiration, knowledge, professionalism; D unfairly held responsible, loss

3 1 A 2 C 3 C 4 D 5 B 6 C

4 1 get wind of 2 manipulated 3 can't be sure 4 raise objections 5 is potentially dangerous 6 take my hat off to

Additional activity: Write sentences

In pairs, students choose three of the expressions from Activity 4 and write a sentence using them. They then swap partners and share their sentences.

Speaking

Aim

- to provide spoken practice

5 Students discuss the questions in pairs. Elicit a few responses from the class.

Teaching tip

Before the discussion, elicit a few different ways for students to introduce their opinions (e.g. *in my view, actually, well*). To extend with strong students, encourage them to try starting some sentences with *although, while* or *whereas* (e.g. *While I think it's a bit sneaky to use smells, it can actually be quite pleasant for the consumer!*).

ADDITIONAL PRACTICE | Maximiser p.49, Listening 1 | **MyEnglishLab: Cambridge Advanced**, Listening 11: Identifying the main point, Listening 17: Listening for gist

Use of English focus

▶ CB p.71

Multiple-choice cloze (Part 1)

Aim

- to complete an exam-style multiple-choice cloze task (Reading and Use of English Part 1)

1 Students work in pairs to discuss the four tastes. Elicit them and write them on the board. Elicit three example foods or drinks for each taste (e.g. *sweet*: ice cream, *fudge, lollipop*; *salty*: salt, crisps, crackers; *sour*: lemon, lime, sherbet; *bitter*: coffee, dark chocolate, olives).

2 Elicit what students remember about Part 1. If necessary, refer students to the **Exam focus** on p.197 to review what is required. Students read the article quickly and answer the question without worrying about the gaps yet.

3 Students discuss the example (0) in pairs. Elicit why the other alternatives are not possible. Read the **Exam tip** with the class.

4 Students fill in the gaps 1–8, then discuss their answers in pairs before you check as a class. For each gap, elicit reasons why the other alternatives are not possible.

5 Students discuss their answers in pairs. Elicit a few different ideas.

Answers

1 sweet, sour, salty, bitter

2 Umami. For many years it was thought that people couldn't taste umami.

4 1 B 2 A 3 B 4 C 5 B 6 D 7 B 8 A

Vocabulary

collocations with *go*

Aim

- to expand students' knowledge of collocations with *go*

6 Start by eliciting the meanings of *bald* (having no hair on your head), *bankrupt* (not having enough money to pay what you owe), *deaf* (unable to hear), *hysterical* (unable to control behaviour or emotion because you are very upset, afraid, excited, etc.; extremely funny) and *mouldy* (covered in mould, a substance that grows on food which has been kept too long or on objects that are in warm, moist places). Students then answer the questions in pairs before you check as a class.

7 Do the first sentence with the class as an example, eliciting the collocation *go downhill*, and the correct form (*gone downhill*). Students complete 2–8, then compare answers in pairs before you check as a class.

Answers

6 1 bad, bald, bankrupt, deaf, downhill, grey, mad, mouldy, off, sour **2** become

7 1 gone downhill **2** go deaf **3** gone mouldy
4 went bankrupt **5** going grey **6** gone off
7 gone bald **8** goes mad

Additional activity: Make up a story

Put students in pairs and ask them to write three collocations from the lesson on a piece of paper (e.g. *go bald*, *go hysterical*, *go mouldy*). Pairs exchange their lists. Each pair makes up a story using the collocations they were given. Invite each pair to share their story with the class.

ADDITIONAL PRACTICE | Maximiser p.49, Use of English 1, Vocabulary 1 **| MyEnglishLab: Cambridge Advanced**, Use of English 1: Nouns followed by prepositions

MyEnglishLab tip

Messaging
In MyEnglishLab you can send online messages to individuals or groups of students. Use the 'Message' feature for reminders or encouragement. It can also be a forum for students to ask you a question which you can reply to at a time that suits you.

Reading focus ▶ CB p.72

Gapped text (Part 7)

Aim

● to complete an exam-style gapped text task (Reading and Use of English Part 7)

Warmer

Write the advertising terms *brand*, *logo*, *slogan*, *jingle* and *product* on the board and ask students to discuss in pairs what each word means in relation to advertising. Elicit the meanings as a class, then ask each pair to think of three examples for each term.

Definitions:

brand: a type of product made by a particular company that has a particular name or design

logo: a small design that is the official sign of a company or organisation

slogan: a short phrase that is used to advertise a product

jingle: a short song used in advertisements

product: something that is grown or made in a factory in large quantities, usually in order to be sold

1 Students discuss the question in pairs. Elicit some ideas as a class.

Alternative activity

Bring in a few common products (e.g. a breakfast cereal box, a soft drink bottle) and ask students to think of why these brand names were chosen. Alternatively, find some pictures of common products (with brand names visible) to display on the projector or IWB and discuss why the brand names are successful.

2 Give students a few minutes to read the article on p.73 and then elicit any reasons students discussed in Activity 1 that were mentioned in the article. (The article discusses the relationship between sounds, especially vowels, in the brand name, and people's perception of the product.)

3 Elicit what students remember about the task and strategies for Part 7. If necessary, refer students to the **Exam focus** on p.200 to check their ideas. Give students a few minutes to read the first two paragraphs of the article and the paragraphs A–G which were removed. Then focus students on the reason a student gave for correctly choosing one of the missing paragraphs, and read through it with the class. Elicit which paragraph the student is referring to.

4 Read the **Exam tip** with the class. Then ask students to underline any clues in the paragraphs (nouns, pronouns, linking words, etc.), which help them identify where the missing paragraphs fit (Strategy 4 from the **Exam focus**). Students then complete the task.

5 Students compare their answers and reasons in pairs before checking as a class. As you go through the answers with the class, elicit justifications for why each answer is correct.

6 Elicit some ideas from the class.

Answers

3 1 G

4 2 B (*The study* in paragraph B refers to the study in the second paragraph. *In fact* at the beginning of the third paragraph introduces supporting evidence to the hypothesis in paragraph B that it would be better to give ice cream brand names with back vowels.)

3 D (*This* in paragraph D refers to the assertion that people prefer back vowels for ice cream flavours (third paragraph). *They* in the fourth paragraph refers to *researchers* in paragraph D.)

4 A (*So* in paragraph A links the result in the fourth paragraph with the question in paragraph A. *The most widely accepted theory* (fifth paragraph) is in answer to the questions posed in paragraph A.)

5 E (*This link of high pitch with deference or friendliness* at the beginning of the sixth paragraph is a paraphrase of *smaller animals naturally make high-pitched sounds … [so animals] … try to appear smaller and less threatening when they are not [aggressive]* in E.)

6 F (*Smiling* is mentioned in the sixth and seventh paragraphs and in paragraph F. *Smiling evolved …* in paragraph F relates to *the origin of the smile* in the sixth paragraph.)

Additional activity: Pronunciation
Ask students to try saying some of the front and back vowels from the article. If you are using eText, open up the phonetic chart. Identify where the front and back vowels are on the chart, and have students listen and repeat.

Vocabulary
working out meaning from context

Aim
* to practise working out meaning from context

7 Students choose the correct meaning, then compare answers in pairs before you check as a class. Elicit any clues that students used to help them work out the correct answer.

Answers

7 (Possible clues in brackets)
1 B (the speech marks around her observation)
2 A (*hypothetical*)
3 A (*it … that* wouldn't make sense with the meaning *evict*)
4 B (*deference*)
5 A (*this shrinks the size of the front cavity in the mouth*)
6 B (*expressing; of enjoyment and other emotional meanings; complex meanings*)

Additional activity: Discussion
Write the following questions on the board and ask students to complete them with the correct form of one of the words from Activity 7. Students then discuss their own answers to the questions in pairs.

1 What are some good ways to _____ someone you have offended?
2 Do you prefer films where everything _____ well in the end?
3 At a social gathering, do you prefer to be the life and soul of the party or a quiet _____?

Answers: **1** appease **2** turns out **3** observer

ADDITIONAL PRACTICE | **Maximiser** p.50–51, Reading 1–5 | **Photocopiable** p.154/178, 7A *Make your pitch* | **MyEnglishLab: Cambridge Advanced**, Reading 2: Predicting the text B

Speaking focus ▶ CB p.74

Collaborative task and discussion (Parts 3 and 4)
agreeing and disagreeing

Aims
* to review phrases for agreeing and disagreeing
* to complete an exam-style speaking task (Speaking Parts 3 and 4)

1 Students discuss the questions in pairs. Elicit a few opinions in open class.

2 Play the recording and elicit the answer.

3 Play the recording again for students to listen and tick the phrases they hear.

4 Students match the uses 1–5 with expressions from Activity 3.

5 Encourage students to add at least one expression in each category. After checking answers as a class, elicit a few more expressions for each category and write them on the board.

Teaching tip

Display
Display these phrases for agreeing and disagreeing in your classroom for students to use during discussions.

Additional activity

Write on the board (or read out) the following statements about Speaking Parts 3 and 4. Ask students to discuss in pairs whether each one is true or false. (They are all true.)

1 For Part 3, you will first be given a task sheet with ideas to discuss with your partner for two or three minutes.

2 Then the examiner will ask you to make a joint decision about a related topic for one minute.

3 In Part 4, the examiner will ask you both questions for about four minutes.

4 In Part 4, you can add to or disagree with what your partner says.

5 In Part 4, you can ask related questions of your own.

If students find this challenging, refer them to the **Exam focus** on p.205 to quickly read the task description and strategies.

6 Students look at the exam task and listen to the recording. They then discuss in pairs. Encourage them to use a range of language from Activities 3–5 in their discussions.

7 Read the **Exam tip** aloud, then give students a minute to discuss which would work best.

8 Students change partners and discuss their answers.

9 Tell students that they are going to do another exam task, taking turns to be the examiner and the candidates. In groups of three, they follow the instructions on p.154.

Teaching tip

If your class does not divide easily into groups of three, either make a group of four with two examiners or join a group yourself.

Answers

2 the girl

3 2, 4, 5, 6, 8

4 1 I couldn't agree more. Absolutely! Indeed it is.
  2 I'm afraid I just don't see it like that at all. Surely not!
  3 We'll just have to agree to differ.
  4 I can't argue with that, but …
  5 That's not quite the way I see it.

5 (Suggested answers)
  1 You're absolutely right about that! I couldn't have said that better myself. Great minds think alike!
  2 I'm afraid we don't see eye to eye on this one. I beg to differ. Actually, I'm going to have to disagree with you there.
  3 I'm afraid we'll have to agree to disagree. It seems we both have strong views on this subject.
  4 I suppose you do have a point. I'm not completely convinced, but …
  5 I see it slightly differently. You have a point, but … There's some truth in what you're saying, but …

ADDITIONAL PRACTICE | **Maximiser** p.52, Speaking 1–2 | **MyEnglishLab: Cambridge Advanced**, Speaking 12: Agreeing and disagreeing in Parts 3 and 4, Speaking 16: Producing balanced Part 4 answers, Speaking 20: Structuring Part 4 responses

Grammar focus ▶ CB p.75

Conditionals: advanced features

Aim
• to review how conditionals are used to sound more formal/polite/hypothetical

Warmer: Discussion
Students discuss the following questions in pairs: *How important is personal recommendation to you when making purchasing decisions? Do you often recommend products to others in person or on social networks?*

1 Play the recording and elicit what *stealth advertising* is (advertising by getting people to promote products to their friends without them knowing). Elicit the techniques described (paying people to promote products to their friends, giving free samples, then suggesting people recommend them to their friends, using people's blog photos in advertisements without permission). Elicit some opinions about the techniques.

2 Check students understand the explanations. If necessary, clarify *hypothetical* (based on a situation that is not real but that might happen) and *imposition* (something that someone expects or asks you to do for them, which is not convenient for you). Students find the words and phrases. Check answers as a class.

3 Students cross out the alternative which is *not* possible. They then compare answers in pairs before you check as a class.

4 Look at the first sentence with the class as an example. Elicit how it would be changed (adding a conditional to make it more hypothetical *If you were to inherit a lot of money, would you give up working?*).

5 Students write their dilemmas, then exchange with another pair and discuss. Students can swap two or three more times for extra practice.

Alternative activity

In place of Activity 5, put students into small groups. Write the following scenarios on the board. Give students a few minutes to discuss each one.

What would you do if

- you found an MP3 player in the street?
- a friend forgot to log out of a social networking site on your laptop?
- a friend invited you to watch a film that you knew had been illegally downloaded?
- a friend posted a status which you found offensive on a social networking site?

Answers

2 1 A If I were to   2 C Should you   3 B If you happen to
  4 D Had (inversion)

3 1 If the weather improves   2 if we won   3 unless
  4 Provided   5 supposing   6 If

4 1 If you were to inherit a lot of money, would you give up working?

  2 Should you require assistance, contact a member of staff.

  3 Had we interviewed a larger number of people, we would have obtained more reliable results.

  4 If you happen to see Joe, can you remind him to give me a call?

  5 If your brother were to phone me in the next couple of days, I might be able to arrange an interview.

  6 Had I known working as a journalist was so demanding, I would have done something else.

ADDITIONAL PRACTICE | Maximiser p.52, Grammar 1 |
Photocopiable p.155/179, 7B *Just supposing*

Writing focus ▶ CB p.76

Speaking

Aims

- to introduce the topic of attitudes to advertising
- to provide spoken practice

1 Students respond to the questions, then compare their answers in small groups.

Report (Part 2)

formal language

Aims

- to review features of formal language
- to use these features to write an exam-style report (Writing Part 2)

2 Students look at the results on p.169, then read the report on p.76. Elicit the answer.

3 Students underline examples of features 1–4 in the report. Check as a class.

4 Ask students to read the task. Read the **Exam tip** aloud and elicit possible headings for the exam task.

5 Refer students to the model report on p.192 and the useful language on p.193 of the **Writing reference**. Set the writing task as homework. Make sure students understand that they can invent research in their reports. Collect the reports to provide individual feedback.

Answers

2 yes

3 1 While …; Strange as it may seem, …; On the one hand, … On the other hand, …; Notwithstanding …

  2 respondents, participants, those surveyed, those whose opinions we sought

  3 regard, consider

5 Sample answer:

Introduction

In this report I will provide a description of common types of advertising in Australia and present results of consumer responses to these. The final section makes recommendations for possible changes to increase the effectiveness of campaigns.

Common approaches

Television and radio continue to play an important part in advertising campaigns and celebrity endorsements often feature prominently. Print media, including billboards, posters and flyers, are also ubiquitous, especially in large cities. Some companies target consumers by giving away samples in public places and supermarkets, aggressive telemarketing or door-to-door sales. Many companies use social media strategies such as online competitions or special offers for 'likers'.

Consumer responses

I conducted an online survey with 200 Australian contacts. An overwhelming majority cited that they found telemarketing and door-to-door sales people intrusive, annoying and rude. Nevertheless, over half admitted to buying something from someone through one of these channels. People generally said that they liked advertising when it was suited to their interests or used humour. A number of respondents mentioned that they 'loved free stuff' and would tell others about something they had been given.

Recommendations

In light of the results above, I recommend the following:

- Make sure telemarketers and door-to-door salespeople have adequate customer service training.
- Target young people such as university students for giveaways as this will likely result in positive word-of-mouth advertising and online reviews.

Additional activity: Word hunt

Write the following on the board:

1 mentioned	6 second group
2 discourage	7 unreasonably high
3 unpleasant	8 take advantage of
4 eating out	9 big
5 split	10 ride a bike

Tell students that there are formal words or phrases with meanings 1–10 in the model report on p.192. Working in pairs, give students five minutes to see how many of the formal words and phrases they can find, awarding a point for each correct one. The pair with the most points wins.

Answers: **1** cited **2** deter **3** disagreeable **4** dining **5** division **6** latter **7** inflated **8** capitalise **9** major **10** cycle

---

ADDITIONAL PRACTICE | **Maximiser** p.53, Writing 1–3 |
MyEnglishLab: Cambridge Advanced, Writing 5: Using nouns in formal English, Vocabulary 20: From informal to formal language

Review ▶ CB p.77

Aim

- to revise the structures, vocabulary and exam tasks covered in Unit 7

1 – **3** Ask students to complete the exercises, circulating to provide assistance. Ask students to check answers in pairs before checking as a class on eText. Alternatively, set as a homework activity and then go through the answers as a class, or on eText, to check.

Answers

1 **1** I had more money **2** she had got better **3** unless we save **4** I studied the piano for longer **5** you buy one, you can **6** wouldn't be necessary **7** you were to see **8** should you require

2 **1** D **2** C **3** B **4** A **5** B **6** A

3 **1** C **2** A **3** C **4** D **5** B **6** D **7** D **8** C

ADDITIONAL PRACTICE | **Testmaster** online and on **eText**, Unit 7 test |
MyEnglishLab: Cambridge Advanced, Practice Writing test

MyEnglishLab tip

Practice Writing test
For the Practice Writing test, students access the tasks online then write their tasks on separate sheets of paper. Collect these in to provide individual feedback using the **Marking guidelines** for writing on Coursebook p.206.

Passing through

Listening and Grammar focus ► CB p.78

Sentence completion (Part 2)

Aim
- to complete an exam-style sentence completion task (Listening Part 2)

Warmer
Write the following questions on the board and put students into pairs to discuss them: *What sorts of trips appeal to you: action-packed or relaxed? Guided or independent? City or nature? What else?* Students discuss the questions in pairs. Ask a few pairs to share whether they have similar or different tastes in holidays.

1 Students work in pairs and think of three reasons for and against using a guidebook during a trip.

2 Ask students to look at the exam task in Activity 3 and elicit some possible answers for questions 2 and 4. Then ask the class: *In the sentence completion task, in Listening Part 2, will you hear the exact word or phrase for each gap in the recording?* (yes). Tell students that there are six useful strategies listed in the **Exam focus**. Ask students to discuss with a partner what they might be, then refer them to the **Exam focus** on p.202 to check their ideas. Read the **Exam tip** on p.78 aloud and give students a few minutes to work in pairs to predict the kind of information that would go in the other gaps. Elicit some ideas.

3 Play the recording for students to complete the sentences. Play the recording a second time, then give students a couple of minutes to check that their spelling and grammar are correct and that each sentence makes sense. Go through the answers or show them on eText. Ask: *How accurately did you predict the answers to questions 2 and 4?*

4 Give students no more than five minutes to discuss their preparations. Consider putting a few ideas on the board as prompts for students to choose from, or some pictures of famous places on the IWB (e.g. Disneyland, the Sydney Harbour Bridge, the Forbidden City, Ipanema Beach, Stonehenge). Ask each pair to share one of their preparations with the class.

Answers

3 1 comedy club **2** publication date **3** restaurant suggestions
4 photos/photographs **5** navigation **6** tailor-made **7** recent
8 (huge) cave

Reported speech

Aim

- to review reported speech

5 Students choose the correct alternatives, then compare answers in pairs before you check as a class.

6 Tell students that they are going to listen to a conversation between two friends, Mia and Matt, about travel. Play the recording, then ask students to work in pairs and summarise what each speaker said. Elicit a summary.

7 Students work in pairs to choose the correct alternatives. Check as a class.

8 Students match comments A–E with sentences 1–5 from Activity 7. For more detailed notes, refer students to the **Grammar reference** on p.178 and read through the table in 16.1 with the class. Ask students to read through the rest, answering any questions that arise.

9 Read the **Language tip** aloud. Refer students back to the statements in Activity 7 and elicit where *that* has been omitted: *3 Mia says* (that) …, *4 Mia said* (that) … . Students complete the reported statements.

Answers

5 1 not to believe 2 don't check 3 wouldn't buy
4 wouldn't 5 should visit 6 might have missed

7 1 had been/was 2 could 3 she'll 4 is travelling
5 this/that

8 1 B 2 C 3 E 4 A 5 D

9 1 wishes/wished she had been advised

2 not to visit/(that) they shouldn't visit

3 goes/went again, he will make sure he sees/would make sure he saw

4 had been planning/were planning to be; shouldn't miss

5 if/whether anyone had stayed

6 is/was the most beautiful place in the world; must/ had to go there at least once

Speaking

Aim

- to practise reporting speech using correct verb tenses

10 Check students understand *tourist trap* (scams that target tourists or overpriced places for tourists that locals never go to) and *get off the beaten track* (visit remote places or places that tourists wouldn't normally see). Give students a few minutes to plan their itinerary in pairs. Suggest that they include four places to visit and at least one recommendation on each of the other listed categories. Students swap partners to give their recommendations. They should make a few notes about what the recommendations were but shouldn't write down full sentences. Then students work again with their original partner to report what was said. Circulate and make sure students are using correct verb forms for reporting their speech.

ADDITIONAL PRACTICE | Maximiser p.54–55, Listening 1–2, Grammar 1–2 | **MyEnglishLab: Cambridge Advanced**, Listening 3: Listening for detail and inferring meaning

Use of English focus

▶ CB p.80

Speaking

Aims

- to practise selecting correct word forms
- to provide spoken practice

Warmer: Word association game
Students work in small groups. Call out a word from the lesson and give the groups 30 seconds to brainstorm as many associated collocations as they can (e.g. *travel: pack a suitcase, catch a plane, dream holiday*). Ask each group to share their list. For each acceptable collocation, they get one point. They get two points for every collocation that no other group got. If you have a weaker class, ask them to brainstorm individual words instead of collocations. Suggested words: *travel, luxury holiday, postcard, remote location, camping, souvenir.*

1 Students choose the correct alternatives. Check as a class. In sentence 1, check students understand the difference in meaning between the two adjectives *respectful* (someone who respects others) and *respected* (someone who others respect). Students tick the ideas they agree with and compare their answers in pairs.

2 Draw the following table on the board and ask students to complete it with the rest of the words in italics from Activity 1. Check as a class.

General nouns	Verb	Adjectives	Negative prefix(es)
respect	respected	respected/ respectful	dis-

Answers

1 1 respectful 2 awareness 3 appealing 4 familiar 5 knowledge 6 discoveries 7 reminder 8 expectations

2 1 respect (n), disrespectful (adj) 2 unaware (adj) 3 appeal (v) 4 familiarise (v), unfamiliar (adj), unfamiliarity (n) 5 know (v), (un)knowledgeable (adj) 6 discover (v), undiscovered (adj) 7 – 8 expect (v), expectant (adj), (un)expected (adj)

Word formation (Part 3)

Aim

● to complete an exam-style word formation task (Reading and Use of English Part 3)

3 Read the **Exam tip** aloud, then ask students to read the article quickly. Ask a student to summarise the article, then ask for a show of hands to find out who agrees and who disagrees with the writer's attitude towards souvenirs. If necessary, clarify the meaning of *snob* (someone who thinks they are better than other people), *kitsch* (an adjective to describe objects that are cheap and unfashionable) and *driftwood* (wood floating in the sea or left on the beach).

4 Students form a word to fit in each gap, then compare answers in pairs before you check as a class. If students get stuck on one of the gaps, ask them the questions from Strategy 2 in the **Exam focus**: *Does the word in the gap need to be positive or negative? Plural or singular? A noun, verb, adjective or adverb?*

5 Students discuss the questions in pairs. Elicit a few responses for each question.

Answers

4 1 awareness 2 earthly 3 existence 4 massive 5 reminders 6 appealing 7 unexpected 8 strangest

ADDITIONAL PRACTICE | **Maximiser** p.55, Use of English 1–2 | **MyEnglishLab: Cambridge Advanced**, Use of English 17: Agreement

MyEnglishLab tip

Exam links
Each exercise in MyEnglishLab has a tip text included. This usually links the exercise with the skills and part of the Cambridge English Advanced exam that it provides practice for. Encourage students to click on the 'tip' before they try the activity.

Speaking focus ▶ CB p.81

Long turn (Part 2)

speculating (2)

Aims

● to use a range of language to speculate
● to complete an exam-style speaking task (Speaking Part 2)

Warmer: 5 *W*s and an *H*

Elicit the question words in English: *what, when, where, who, why* and *how*. Point out that they begin with five *W*s and an *H*. Then write the following questions on the board:

What's happening?

When is it?

Where is it?

Who are the people?

Why are they doing what they are doing?

How are they feeling?

Students take turns to ask each other these questions about the three pictures.

1 Students discuss the pictures in pairs.

2 Ask students the following questions about Speaking Part 2: *How many pictures will you be given?* (three) *How many questions will you be asked?* (two, then the partner will be asked a shorter one) *How long will you be given to speak?* (one minute to answer both questions). If necessary, refer students to the **Exam focus** on p.204 to read the information about the task type. Then elicit some possible instructions for the task on p.81.

3 Play the recording and elicit what the instructions were. Ask students if they guessed right in Activity 2.

4 Play the recording for students to tick the things the candidate speculates about. Elicit the answers.

5 Students complete the phrases for speculating, then compare answers in pairs. Play the recording again for students to check. Check answers by writing the phrases on the board or showing them on eText if you are using it.

Teaching tip

If you are using eText, remember that you can display the answers for every exercise.

6 Tell students that they are going to work in pairs and take turns to practise a Speaking Part 2 task. Read the **Exam tip** aloud. To support a weaker class, keep the phrases displayed on the board/eText as a prompt while they do the task. To extend with a strong class, encourage them to use a range of phrases without referring back to the book.

7 Consider asking students to swap partners to work with someone new. Students complete the Communication activity on p.166. Before they begin the activity, focus on the pictures and elicit what kinds of souvenirs they show (T-shirts, mugs, caps, ties, scarves, an elephant statue).

Answers

4 3 and 5

5 **1** would **2** doubt **3** pretty **4** couldn't
5 likelihood **6** be surprised

ADDITIONAL PRACTICE | **Maximiser** p.56, Speaking 1–3 |
MyEnglishLab: Cambridge Advanced, Speaking 6: Giving reasons for speculation in Part 2

Reading focus ▶ CB p.82

Cross-text multiple matching (Part 6)
identifying attitude and opinion

Aims

- to practise identifying attitude and opinion
- to complete an exam-style cross-text multiple matching task (Reading and Use of English Part 6)

1 Elicit the difference between the terms *expat* and *immigrant* (*expat* is usually used by people to describe themselves when they live abroad temporarily; *immigrant* is usually used to refer to other people who move permanently to a new country). Put students in pairs to discuss the second question. Elicit some of the things they would find most difficult to cope with.

2 Students read the extracts quickly, to decide which issues in Activity 1 are mentioned by each writer. Check as a class.

3 Remind students that in the cross-text multiple matching task they will read four texts by different writers and answer four questions that test their ability to identify and compare attitude and opinion. Ask students to match the underlined words and phrases in Text A with uses A–D. Check as a class.

4 Ask students to find three examples of adverbs of attitude and two impersonal phrases for making recommendations in Texts B–D. Students could work in pairs for this, then check as a class. Point out to students that there is only about ten minutes in the exam to complete the cross-text multiple matching activity, so being able to recognise words and phrases that express attitude and opinion will help students identify these quickly in the texts.

5 Before students do the task, refer them to the list of strategies for Part 6 in the **Exam focus** on p.200. Keep these displayed as a reference on eText if you are using it. Students work through the strategies to answer the questions, then compare answers in pairs before you check as a class.

6 Students work in pairs to find the words and phrases in italics in the texts. Elicit the meaning of each one in context, then ask students to discuss their answers to questions 1–4 with their partner. Suggested meanings: *nurture* (make an effort to look after), *live up to* (achieve/ meet), *daunting prospect* (frightening possibility), *blend in* (fit in).

Answers

2 all of them except 'being cut off from your roots'

3 **1** B **2** C **3** A **4** D

4 adverbs: thankfully, mistakenly, understandably; phrases: It's best to …, The only way to overcome this is …

5 1 A (D: 'compounding a sense of loneliness and isolation'; A: 'The polite detachment of New Yorkers is of no consequence')

  2 B (C: 'The only way to overcome this is to try and blend in by picking up an American accent, vocabulary and expressions.' B: 'it's best to embrace and even celebrate your "charming" or "cute" manner of speaking')

  3 C (D: 'It takes people a little while before it eventually dawns on them that true acceptance by New Yorkers will have to be earned over a minimum of five years'; C: 'This over-confidence can prompt something of an identity crisis at first, once it becomes clear that many New Yorkers regard them in the same light as any other expat.')

  4 C ('A: Adjusting to life in New York can seem overwhelming for newly arrived expats.'; C: 'Many expats from English-speaking countries arriving to work in New York mistakenly assume that fitting in will be easy.')

Speaking

Aim
- to provide spoken practice

7 Students work in pairs and discuss how far they agree with the statements. Elicit some ideas.

ADDITIONAL PRACTICE | Maximiser p.56–57, Reading 1 | **Photocopiable** p.156/180, 8A *Four texts* | **MyEnglishLab: Cambridge Advanced**, Reading 4: Skimming for gist B, Reading 14: Following the theme A

Vocabulary focus ▶ CB p.84

Describing trends

Aim
- to review vocabulary for describing trends

Warmer: Discussion
Ask the following questions for students to discuss in pairs: *Do you like the sound of New York City as a holiday destination? How about as a place to live? Give reasons for your answers.*

1 Start by focusing on the picture and asking the class: *Where do you think this is? When was the photo taken? Who are the people?* In pairs, students check they understand the meaning of the underlined words/phrases. To check, write the following meanings on the board and ask students to match each one with one of the underlined words/phrases: *A to go down very quickly, B to go down, C to stay the same, D to reach a high point, E was higher than, F a short drop before rising again* (Answers: **1** D **2** C **3** E **4** F **5** B **6** A).

2 Play the recording. Students decide if the statements in Activity 1 are true or false. Elicit the answers.

3 Play the recording again for students to note words which match meanings 1–4. Check as a class.

4 Students discuss the questions in pairs. Check they understand the difference between *emigrate* (to move permanently *from* a country), *settle* (to make a place your permanent home) and *immigrate* (to move permanently *to* a country).

5 Students complete the text with the words in the box. They then compare answers in pairs before you check as a class.

Answers
2 1 T 2 F 3 T 4 F 5 T 6 F
3 1 substantially, sharp **2** moderate **3** grow, surge, boost **4** drop, decline
5 1 risen **2** decline **3** overtaken **4** sudden **5** dropping **6** peak

Speaking

Aims
- to practise using vocabulary to describe trends
- to provide spoken practice

6 Encourage students to make at least five predictions about future trends where they live.

7 Students discuss the question with their partner.

Useful resources

Search for an article, blog post or a few facts about future worldwide trends on population growth, immigration and emigration for students to use in conjunction with their discussion in Activity 7.

ADDITIONAL PRACTICE | Maximiser p.58, Vocabulary 1–2 |
MyEnglishLab: Cambridge Advanced, Vocabulary 6: *Evidence, data, issue,*
Vocabulary 19: Collocations for talking about academic topics

Grammar focus ▶ CB p.85

Verb patterns with reporting verbs

Aim

● to review verb patterns with reporting verbs

Warmer: Reporting verbs brainstorm

Write the following reporting verbs on the board: *blame, persuade, object, urge*. Ask students to discuss in pairs the difference between each, then elicit the meanings: *blame* (think that someone is responsible for something bad), *persuade* (try and get someone to do or believe something), *object* (vocally disagree with an idea), *urge* (tell someone forcefully they should do something). Put students in small groups and give them two minutes to brainstorm other verbs for reporting speech. Elicit these and write them on the board.

1 Work through this activity with the class, eliciting possible answers for each statement. Read the **Language tip** aloud.

2 Students complete the statements. Point out that more than one verb is possible for each, and tell students that they should note all possibilities in each case.

3 Students complete the activity. Go through the answers with the class. Ask students to turn to the **Grammar reference** on p.179 and read through 16.3 with the class, on eText if you are using it. Check that students understand everything. If students find reported speech difficult, refer them back to 16.1 on p.178 of the **Grammar reference**, for an overview of reported speech.

4 Tell students that they are going to read about some statements that young Irish people made about emigrating. Change the first sentence into direct speech with the class as an example. Read the reported sentence aloud, then elicit what the direct speech might have been (e.g. One possible answer is: *There is no alternative to me emigrating*. But a more likely way of saying this directly might be: *I don't have any other choice but to emigrate*. or *I have to emigrate – I don't have a choice*.). Ask students to change the statements in Activity 4 into direct speech. Remind them that when they report speech, they move the tenses one step back into the past, but here they will have to do the opposite. Play the recording for students to compare their answers.

Answers

1 1 advised, urged   2 recommended, suggested
   3 recommended, suggested   4 recommended, suggested

2 1 admitted, claimed, doubted   2 persuaded, warned
   3 admitted, regretted   4 admitted, announced, claimed   5 invited, permitted, persuaded   6 accused
   7 blamed   8 objected

3 1 admit, announce, claim, doubt, regret   2 admit, regret   3 invite, permit, persuade, warn   4 accuse, blame   5 admit, object

4 1 I hate to admit it but I've got no choice. I have to leave here to find work.

   2 Don't worry, Mum, I'm not lonely. I've made loads of friends here already.

   3 I wish I hadn't left. I think I would have had a better chance of starting my own business at home.

   4 The government hasn't done enough to create jobs – that's why so many people are leaving.

   5 Listen, son, I really think you should stay in Australia. You've got lots more opportunities there.

   6 I don't regret emigrating for one minute. It's the best decision I've ever made.

Impersonal reporting verbs

Aim

● to practise using impersonal reporting verbs to sound more formal

5 Invite a student to read the two sentences aloud. Then ask students the questions. Tell them that *It is believed (that)* is a common impersonal reporting phrase. Elicit other similar phrases that students can think of (e.g. *It is thought, It is said, It is claimed*).

6 Ask students to tick the statements they agree with and discuss with a partner. Then rewrite the first sentence with students as an example. Read the sentence aloud, then focus on the verb in brackets (*accepted*). Elicit how this could be changed to an impersonal reporting form (*It is accepted*). Students rewrite the other sentences. Check answers as a class.

7 Share an example with the class (e.g. *It is said that the more languages you know, the easier it is to pick up another one.*). Put students in pairs and ask them to think of at least three other facts to present to the class.

Alternative activity

Write on the board a selection of topics that you think will be of interest to your class for students to choose from for Activity 7 (e.g. football, texting, indie music, fashion).

Answers

5 2 (found in formal written texts)

6 1 It is accepted   2 It is suggested/It's been suggested
   3 It is claimed   4 It is expected   5 It was assumed
   6 It has been argued

ADDITIONAL PRACTICE | Maximiser p.58, Grammar 1–2 |
Photocopiable p.157/180, 8B *The whole sentence*

Writing focus ▶ CB p.86

Proposal (Part 2)

using an appropriate style

Aim

• to write an exam-style proposal using an appropriate style (Writing Part 2)

Warmer: Discussion

Ask these questions for students to discuss in pairs: *Have you ever been on a student exchange to study abroad in another country? Think of five benefits of participating in an exchange programme.* Elicit some responses.

1 Students read the task and discuss the questions in pairs. Ask students to underline the information they need to include in the task question to make sure they don't miss anything.

2 Students make a plan using the headings given. Suggest they include three benefits, three ways to promote the exchange programme and three recommendations.

3 Elicit what style a proposal should be written in (relatively formal and impersonal). Invite six students to read each of the recommendations aloud. After each one, elicit whether it is in an appropriate style for a proposal.

4 Students discuss in pairs. Check as a class. Refer students to the **Writing reference** on p.193 for more useful language for proposals.

5 Refer students to the **Marking guidelines** on p.206 and ask them to choose which task to complete. Set the writing task for homework.

6 Students swap their proposal with a partner and make suggestions on ways it could be improved. They should make the suggested changes before handing in their proposals for individual feedback.

Teaching tip

Activity 6 could also be set as a homework task. If students do not see each other between classes, they could send the draft and suggestions to their partner electronically.

Answers

3 2, 3, 4, 6

4 2, 3, 4

5 Sample answer:

Introduction

This proposal is intended to outline common issues students have when studying abroad, and suggest ways that a course could help them to deal with these. The final section makes recommendations about what should be included in the course curriculum.

Problems when studying abroad

Interviews were conducted with 20 students who have recently completed a student exchange programme. The majority of students were of the opinion that overcoming the language barrier in their new country was the biggest challenge and nearly half also said that they experienced culture shock. Other problems cited included unrealistic expectations, loneliness and packing the wrong things – particularly being unprepared for a different climate.

Ways a course could address these

A course could prepare students for culture shock by raising awareness of the phenomenon and describing cultural differences that students may encounter in their host country. To aid participants with language, a course could include some useful phrases for the first days after arrival, in addition to some resources for language learning. The course could also include a discussion about combating isolation and adjusting expectations.

Recommendations

I would like to make the following recommendations:

- Invite students who have previously studied abroad to share aspects of the culture they found surprising and give advice on what to take.

- Provide a list of useful phrases, together with suggestions of useful resources for language learning such as websites, blogs or e-books.

- Facilitate a discussion about engaging with people to avoid loneliness and isolation.

If these recommendations are implemented, young people are bound to feel more prepared for their experience.

ADDITIONAL PRACTICE | Maximiser p.59, Writing 1–3 | **MyEnglishLab: Cambridge Advanced**, Writing 15: Report and proposal checklist

Review ▶ CB p.87

Aim

- to revise the structures, vocabulary and exam tasks covered in Unit 8

1 – **4** Ask students to complete the exercises, circulating to provide assistance. Ask students to check answers in pairs before checking as a class on eText. Alternatively, set as a homework activity and then go through the answers as a class, or on eText, to check.

Answers

1 1 B   2 C   3 B   4 A   5 A   6 C   7 B   8 C

2 1 recommended Sam travel/that Sam should travel
2 will remain stable   3 reached a peak in   4 was a drop in demand   5 is/was/has been accused of not building   6 have to be so knowledgeable about

3 1 increasing   2 steadily   3 rise   4 growth   5 lower   6 overtaken   7 expected   8 drop

4 1 off   2 maintain   3 shock   4 belonging   5 barrier   6 assimilate

ADDITIONAL PRACTICE | Maximiser p.60–61, Use of English 4 | **Testmaster** online and on **eText**, Unit 8 test | **MyEnglishLab: Cambridge Advanced**, Practice Listening test

Reading the mind

Use of English and Vocabulary focus ▶ CB p.88

Open cloze (Part 2)

Aim

- to complete an exam-style open cloze task (Reading and Use of English Part 2)

Warmer: Discussion

Focus students' attention on the picture on p.88. Write the following questions on the board for students to discuss in pairs: *Have you ever learnt a musical instrument? What do you think is the ideal age to start learning? Do you believe that musical ability depends more on genetics, exposure to music or something else?* Elicit some responses to each question.

1 Elicit what is meant by *nature or nurture* in the first question (the genes you are born with or your environment growing up). Allow students time to answer the questions, then put them in pairs to discuss their answers. Elicit a few answers to each question.

2 Students read the article quickly, without worrying about the gaps. Elicit why researchers in the 1980s thought babies understood physics. Elicit what students know about Reading and Use of English Part 2 and how to approach the task. If necessary, refer them to the **Exam focus** on p.198 to review the task and strategies.

3 Read the **Exam tip** aloud. Focus students' attention on gap 1, where they might expect *stared* to be followed by the preposition *at*. However, the word in the gap (*in*) combines with the words *apparent disbelief* to form an adverbial phrase. Ask students to complete the remaining gaps and then compare answers in pairs before you check as a class.

Answers

2 Because the babies seemed surprised when they were shown images that defied the laws of physics.

3 **1** in **2** out **3** something **4** same **5** would **6** for **7** no **8** nothing

Additional activity

Write the sentence beginnings and pairs of endings below on the board. Ask students to discuss in pairs what the gapped word would be for each sentence ending. Elicit the answers. Ask students to think about their own response to sentence 3B (something interesting that happened in their childhood) and share it with their partner.

1 She listened
A _____ the radio until she fell asleep.
B _____ a while and then turned the radio off.

2 I want you to promise you'll have
A _____ to do with these people anymore.
B _____ more contact with these people.

3 Tell me
A _____ interesting story about your childhood.
B _____ interesting that happened in your childhood.

Answers: **1** A to, B for **2** A nothing, B no **3** A an, B something

Speaking

Aims

- to expand students' vocabulary related to developmental milestones
- to provide spoken practice

4 Students work in pairs to put the developmental milestones in order. Play the recording for them to check their answers.

5 Play the recording again for students to note down the phrases the speaker uses for each milestone. Students compare answers in pairs before you check as a class.

Answers

4 **1** return a smile **2** recognise familiar faces **3** know her own name and respond to it **4** enjoy hiding games **5** try to be a help **6** learn to put on her own clothes

5 recognise familiar faces – know who's who

know her own name and respond to it – recognise her own name and react to it

enjoy hiding games – get a real kick out of the game of *peekaboo*

try to be a help – display helpful behaviour

learn to put on her own clothes – get the hang of dressing herself

Additional activity

Ask students what other milestones they consider significant in childhood (e.g. saying your first word, starting school). Ask if anyone in the class has young family members (nephews, nieces, cousins) or friends. Elicit what stage they are at and what they can/can't do. If most students have young contacts, they could share information about their stage with a partner.

Expressions with *brain* and *mind*

Aim

- to use a range of expressions with *brain* and *mind*

6 Students look at the words in the box and answer the questions. Check as a class, then read the **Language tip** aloud.

7 Elicit whether each expression in Activity 1 is two separate words, a hyphenated two-word compound or one word (see Answers to Activity 6).

Students complete the sentences with compound nouns or verbs from Activity 6. Remind them to check that their compound words are correctly written and hyphenated. Students compare answers in pairs before you check as a class.

8 Invite a student to read the first question aloud. Elicit from the class some things that might have happened beforehand (e.g. *You might have broken or lost something of theirs. You might have had to cancel plans.*). Students discuss the questions in pairs. Finish by eliciting a few ideas for each question.

Answers

6 1 brainchild, brain damage, brain drain, brain scan, brainstorm, brain teaser, brainwash, brainwave

2 A mind-boggling, B mind reader

7 1 brain drain 2 brainchild 3 brain damage
4 brainstorm 5 brainwave 6 brain teasers
7 brainwashing 8 brain scan

8 (Suggested answers)

1 something disappointing or upsetting

2 No, she'll just think about it.

3 They want one.

4 Because another person has used a taboo word in front of a child or someone who might find it offensive.

5 Because you are about to say something that partially contradicts something you or another speaker have previously said.

6 a question that might cause embarrassment or be understood as an invasion of privacy

Additional activity: Dialogues

In pairs, students make up a short conversation for one of the scenarios they thought of in Activity 8. It should include the relevant phrase using *mind*. Invite pairs to share their conversations with the class.

ADDITIONAL PRACTICE | **Maximiser** p.62–63, Use of English 1–2, Vocabulary 1–2 | **Photocopiable** p.158/181, 9A *As quick as you can* | **MyEnglishLab: Cambridge Advanced**, Use of English 20: Spelling practice

Grammar focus ▶ CB p.90

Reading

Aim

- to present narrative tenses in context

1 Start by asking: *What groups of people need to work together as a team to be successful?* (a sports team, a work team, a board, a political party, etc.). In pairs, students think of at least three activities that might help develop team spirit in a group or organisation. Elicit some ideas.

2 Give students a couple of minutes to read the blog extract to find out whether any of the activities mentioned are similar to the ideas they discussed in Activity 1. Elicit the activities that the author took part in to develop team spirit (a series of problem-solving games, including building a shelter out of cardboard and duct tape).

Additional activity: Find …

Ask students to find the following in the text: a phrasal verb that means *withdraw* (*pull out*), an adverb that means *working together* (*collaboratively*), a phrase that means *have doubts about my decision* (*have second thoughts*).

Review of narrative tenses

Aim

- to review the use of narrative tenses

3 Students find examples of uses 1–5 in the extract. Check as a class. For more examples of the past perfect, refer students to **Grammar reference** 18.7 on p.182. There are also examples of the other narrative tenses in the rest of Grammar reference 18, which students can read for homework.

4 Read the **Language tip** aloud. Tell students that *After I had spoken to Victoria* is also possible but not necessary because of the time adverbial *after* making the order of events clear. Explain to students that sometimes both the past simple and the past perfect are possible but have a difference in meaning, e.g. *I had cooked dinner when they arrived.* (I finished cooking before they arrived.) *I cooked dinner when they arrived.* (I started cooking dinner when they arrived.). Students complete the gaps in the second part of the blog entry, then compare answers in pairs before you check as a class.

5 Students discuss the questions in pairs. Tell them that they can describe a bad experience that has some sort of benefit using the idiom *a cloud with a silver lining*, which is often reduced to simply saying that a situation had *a silver lining*. Invite a few students to share their experiences with the class.

Answers

3 1 was actually thinking, was talking   2 had started
3 went, started   4 had been looking   5 heard, knew,
didn't, consisted, involved, were, had, weren't, weren't,
started

4 1 took   2 had hardly said/hardly said (no difference
in meaning)   3 asked   4 had been/was (*had been*
implies that he was silent during the game but isn't
now; *was* could mean that he is still silent)   5 had felt/
had been feeling/was feeling (no difference in meaning)
6 were playing   7 made   8 had realised/realised (*had
realised* implies that this happened while the game was
being played; *realised* could mean that this happened
when the instructor asked him the question)   9 felt
10 had wanted/wanted (no difference in meaning)
11 didn't think   12 was pulling

ADDITIONAL PRACTICE | **Maximiser** p.63, Grammar 1 |
MyEnglishLab: Cambridge Advanced, Use of English 15: Review of
tenses

Speaking focus ▶ CB p.91

Long turn (Part 2)

paraphrasing

Aim

- to practise paraphrasing in an exam-style speaking
task (Speaking Part 2)

1 Focus students' attention on the pictures and elicit
what is happening in each picture. Then ask students
to discuss with a partner how often, if ever, they do any
of these activities alone.

2 Elicit what students remember about Speaking Part 2.
If necessary, refer students to the **Exam focus** on p.204
to review the task and strategies. Play the recording,
then elicit the instructions. Write these on the board for
students to refer to in Activity 3.

3 Students work in pairs, following the examiner's
instructions from Activity 2.

4 Play the recording. Elicit which pictures the candidate
compared. Ask students if she followed the
instructions.

5 Allow students time to read the gapped sentences,
then play the recording again for students to fill in the
gaps. Check as a class.

6 Play the recording once for students to listen to the
question and answer. Discuss as a class whether the
candidate responds effectively.

7 Tell students that they are going to try a long turn
activity and take turns to be the candidate and the
examiner. Read the **Exam tip** aloud. Tell students that
both tasks relate to the topic of learning. On the board,
write *learning* and brainstorm some related words and
phrases that could be useful for the task (e.g. *study,
teach, pick up something new, try something, gain a new
skill, knowledge*). Students work in pairs and follow the
instructions for the activities on p.155 and p.156.

Answers

2 The examiner asks the candidates to compare two of
the pictures and say why people might be doing these
things on their own and what reactions they might get
from other people.

4 Yes. She compares two of the pictures, says why people
might be doing these things and suggests possible
reactions people might have.

5 1 by herself   2 without anyone else   3 all to herself
4 solitary   5 lone   6 unaccompanied

6 The examiner asks who is happiest doing these things on
their own and why. The candidate responds effectively.

ADDITIONAL PRACTICE | **Maximiser** p.63, Speaking 1–3 |
MyEnglishLab: Cambridge Advanced, Vocabulary 12: Paraphrasing

Reading focus ▶ CB p.92

Gapped text (Part 7)

Aim

- to complete an exam-style reading task (Reading and
Use of English Part 7)

1 Start by asking students to think about what they
remember about their first day at primary school and
their first teacher, then to compare answers in pairs.
Elicit a few experiences.

2 Allow students time to read the list of comments then
discuss them in pairs.

3 Elicit what students remember about Reading and Use of English Part 7. If necessary, refer them to the **Exam focus** on p.200 to review the task and strategies. Give students about five minutes to read the article quickly and find out which of the difficulties in Activity 2 are mentioned. This corresponds to the **Exam tip** and Strategy 2 in the **Exam focus**.

4 Remind students that Strategies 3–5 in the **Exam focus** are very helpful when deciding how to fill the gaps, especially the strategy of looking for and underlining textual clues in the article and the missing paragraphs. Ask students to follow Strategy 7 with a partner as they compare answers. Then check answers as a class.

Answers

3 It took me ages to be able to tell the time.
I don't know why but I sometimes couldn't understand what I read or what the teacher explained to us.

4 1 B (Paragraph B provides further evidence and examples of the last statement in the first paragraph: *She didn't know what was wrong.*)

2 F (*somebody*, *His* and *he* in the third paragraph refer to Aleksandr Luria in paragraph F.)

3 G (*an area of my brain wasn't working* in the third paragraph is a paraphrase of *The bullet had lodged in a part of the brain where information from sight, sound, language and touch is synthesised, analysed and made sense of.*)

4 A (*this* in the fifth paragraph refers to the clock face exercise described in paragraph A.)

5 D (*It* in the sixth paragraph refers to the *exercises* she developed (paragraph D).)

6 E (*so many children get written off* in the final paragraph is a paraphrase of *Thousands of children dismissed as impossible to teach* (paragraph E).)

Vocabulary

working out meaning from context

Aim
• to practise working out meaning from context

5 Focus students' attention on the underlined words in the text and ask them to discuss in pairs the meaning of each one. Students complete the sentences using the correct form of the underlined words. Check the answers as a class.

6 Students tell their partner about something they had difficulty learning and answer the questions. Elicit a few experiences.

Answers

5 1 dismal   2 breakthrough   3 devised   4 got
5 premise   6 written off

ADDITIONAL PRACTICE | Maximiser p.64–65, Reading 1–4 |
MyEnglishLab: Cambridge Advanced, Reading 8: Unfamiliar words B

Listening focus ▶ CB p.94

Speaking

Aims
• to introduce the topic of forgetfulness
• to provide spoken practice

1 Read through the comments with the class. Check students know the literal meaning of *sieve* (a round wire kitchen tool with a lot of small holes, used for separating small pieces of food from large pieces). Elicit the meaning of the expression *have a memory like a sieve* (forget things easily) and elicit whether there are any similar expressions in the students' own languages. Ask students what *absent-minded* means (likely to forget things, especially because you are thinking about something else). In pairs, students discuss which of the comments apply to them.

Multiple matching (Part 4)

Aim
• to complete an exam-style listening task (Listening Part 4)

2 Elicit what students know about Listening Part 4 and how to approach the task. If necessary, refer students to the **Exam focus** on p.203 to review the task and strategies. Then students look at Task 1 and discuss the question. Elicit some ideas.

3 Focus students' attention on Task 2. Elicit some answers to the questions.

4 Read the rubric and **Exam tip** aloud. Ask students to highlight key words in lists A–H, then play the recording. Play the recording again, then go through the answers with the class.

5 Students turn to p.164 and p.169 and complete the matching activity. Go through the answers as a class, eliciting the meaning for each sentence.

6 Encourage students to use phrases from Activity 5 and remind them to use a range of narrative tenses when they tell their story. Give students a moment to think about what they are going to share, then put them in pairs to talk about their experiences.

Answers

4 Task 1 1 C 2 G 3 A 4 F 5 H

 Task 2 6 D 7 C 8 G 9 H 10 E

5 1 F (didn't actually write it down but told myself to remember it) 2 D (fix the problem) 3 E (I forgot about it completely) 4 B (confused) 5 C (trying really hard to remember) 6 A (create)

ADDITIONAL PRACTICE | **Maximiser** p.66, Listening 1 | **MyEnglishLab: Cambridge Advanced**, Listening 12: Interpreting context, Listening 19: Listening for examples

Grammar focus ▶ CB p.95

Emphasis

cleft sentences with *what*

Aim
● to review cleft sentences with *what*

Warmer: How good is your memory?
Tell students there are 16 pictures in Units 7 and 8. Give them two minutes to look at them and then ask them to close their books. Put them in pairs and give them two minutes to remember as many as they can. Elicit ideas and make notes on the board. Students can look in their books to see which ones they missed.

1 Elicit the meaning of *neuroscience* (the study of the brain) and the related personal noun *neuroscientist*. Check students understand *witness* (someone who sees a crime or an accident and can describe what happened). Ask students to read the extract and explain why we are 'unreliable witnesses' to a partner. Elicit the answer.

2 Focus students' attention on the underlined sentences and ask a student to read each one before you elicit answers to the questions.

3 Give students a moment to reread the sentences and discuss in pairs, then elicit the answers. Read the **Language tip** aloud. Share or elicit a few examples of cleft sentences, emphasising an emotional response with the verbs given (e.g. *What I loathe is hearing about other people's exotic island vacations when I am stuck in the office.*). Ask students to turn to the **Grammar reference** on p.175 and read through the examples with the class, on eText if you are using it.

4 Do the first sentence as an example with the class. Read the sentence aloud, then the word in capitals, then the sentence with the gap. Elicit the answer. Students complete the remaining sentences, then compare answers in pairs before you check as a class.

5 Elicit possible ways to complete the first sentence (e.g. *What the world needs now is to take united action on climate change.*). Students complete the sentences with their own ideas, then tell a partner about them. Ask each student to share one of their sentences.

Additional activity: Mingle
After completing the sentences in Activity 5, students mingle to find out if anyone has finished any of the sentences in a similar way. Finish by eliciting some things that students had in common with their classmates (e.g. *We both think that our generation is much more impatient than previous ones. We can't stand waiting for more than three seconds.*).

Answers

1 Because our memories of events are inevitably distorted. The distortion occurs because we blend elements from different events together.

2 The second part of the sentence is emphasised in all three sentences.
   1 What this means is 2 What is more worrying is
   3 What we're actually doing is

3 1 sentence 1 2 sentence 3 3 sentence 2

4 1 to do is to go 2 surprised me was (the fact) that
   3 is what I 4 we had was chicken 5 motivated was the fact that 6 I dislike about her is

ADDITIONAL PRACTICE | **Maximiser** p.66, Grammar 1–3 | **Photocopiable** p.159/182, 9B *Beginnings and endings*

Writing focus ▶ CB p.96

Reading

Aim

- to provide an example of informal tone

Warmer: Discussion

Discuss the following question in pairs: *If you arrived in a new country not speaking any of the language, how would you go about learning it?*

1 Students read the blog entry and discuss the question in pairs. Elicit a few ideas.

Email (Part 2)

adopting the right tone

Aim

- to write an email using an informal tone

2 Give students time to read the blog again. Elicit answers to the question, asking students to justify them with examples from the blog.

3 Working in pairs, students decide if each piece of advice is formal or informal. Check as a class.

4 Ask students to work with their partner to rewrite the formal items in a less formal tone. Check as a class. In pairs, students decide whether they agree with each piece of advice.

5 Students read the exam task and points for inclusion. They put them in order to make a coherent plan. Elicit the correct order.

6 Refer students to the **Writing reference** on p.190 for useful language for emails. Set the writing task for homework.

7 Students share their writing in groups of three and make any improvements suggested. Collect in the emails to provide individual feedback.

Teaching tip

If students normally type their writing tasks, suggest that they complete writing tasks by hand from now on to practise for the exam.

Answers

2 The text is informal. The following features tell us this: contractions (e.g. *I'd read*); *and* is used frequently as a linker; simple vocabulary (e.g. *got it wrong*) and phrasal verbs (e.g. *work out, end up*).

3 1 F 2 I 3 F 4 F 5 I 6 I 7 F 8 I

4 (Suggested answers)

1 It wouldn't be a bad idea to get yourself a dictionary.

3 If I was thinking of learning a language, I'd most probably do a course.

4 Reading as widely as you can could help.

7 I wouldn't try learning a language by yourself.

5 1 Acknowledge receipt of the message and apologise for not writing before.

2 Express pleasure about friend's plans to relocate and reiterate the question in the email.

3 Comment briefly on my experience of learning English.

4 Make a series of suggestions about learning my language drawing on my own and others' experience.

5 Express the hope of having been of some assistance.

6 Conclude with the wish to receive a reply and the usual salutation.

6 Sample answer:

Dear Emma,

Thanks so much for your email. It was so good to hear from you. I'm really sorry not to have been in touch earlier but I've been up to my eyes preparing for my exams.

What great news that you're finally coming to France – I can't wait to catch up in person! And you're going to learn French too – fantastic!

I've been learning English since I was a kid as you know, and by far the most useful experience was going to that language school in Brighton for three months last summer. If I were you, I'd definitely enrol in a course like that to keep you focused. I'd also suggest reading as widely as possible, online newspapers, blogs, books, the back of a cereal packet – anything, really! Don't be tempted to buy one of those 'Learn French in a weekend' courses though – a waste of time if you ask me. Learning a language takes time and effort.

What seems to work for a lot of people is learning songs. My brother reckons that he has learnt more English from the Top 40 than he has at school. And you know my friend Lucie? She raved about her fortnight with a host family, so that's worth a try too. Of course, you could also get a French boyfriend to speed up your progress!

Anyway, I hope that's helped give you a few ideas. Do write back as soon as you can – I'd love to hear all the details of your plans.

Lots of love,

Sandrine

ADDITIONAL PRACTICE | Maximiser p.67, Writing 1–3 | **MyEnglishLab: Cambridge Advanced**, Writing 8: Planning a letter or email

Review ▶ CB p.97

Aim

- to revise the structures, vocabulary and exam tasks covered in Unit 9

1 – **3** Ask students to complete the exercises, circulating to provide assistance. Ask students to check answers in pairs before checking as a class on eText. Alternatively, set as a homework activity and then go through the answers as a class, or on eText, to check.

Answers

1 1 were saying   2 all forms are possible   3 was impressing, had impressed, had been impressing   4 had been reading   5 were always thinking, had always been thinking   6 had been learning   7 had been trying   8 was giving, had been giving

2 1 brainstorming   2 wave   3 brain   4 Brainteaser   5 brain   6 damage

3 1 need to do is spend   2 is what would   3 is the fact that   4 doing in five years' time is   5 are what make   6 is what people in this class   7 makes travelling to Australia difficult is   8 I love most about the house

ADDITIONAL PRACTICE | Testmaster online and on **eText**, Unit 9 test, Progress test 3 | **MyEnglishLab: Cambridge Advanced**, Practice Speaking test

MyEnglishLab tip

Practice Speaking test activities

Students will need a partner for the MyEnglishLab Practice Speaking test activities and someone to act as 'examiner'. You can print the tasks for use in class if necessary. Before students do the task, ask them to reread the **Marking guidelines** for speaking on p.207. Students could do the practice test in groups of four, with one pair completing Parts 1–4 as candidates while the other pair act as examiners, time-keeping and noting down any good vocabulary/phrases the candidates use. After pairs swap roles, give them time to discuss the feedback and what they need to improve on.

Things to come

10

Vocabulary and Use of English focus ▶ CB p.98

Speaking

Aims
• to introduce the topic of attitudes towards the future • to provide spoken practice

1 In pairs, students think of definitions for *idealist, realist, optimist* and *pessimist*. Discuss the meaning of each word as a class. Students discuss with their partner what kind of person it is best to be. Elicit some ideas from the class.

Past participles + dependent prepositions

Aim
• to review common past participle + dependent preposition combinations

2 Remind students that knowledge of dependent prepositions (prepositions that follow a verb, adjective, etc.) is often tested in Reading and Use of English Parts 1 and 2. Students choose the correct alternatives and decide what sort of person made each statement. They compare their answers in pairs before you check as a class.

3 Students decide which statements in Activity 2 are true about them and which they would like to be true, then compare their ideas with their partner. Read the **Language tip** aloud.

4 Ask students to complete the sentences with the correct prepositions, then discuss the question in pairs. Go through the answers as a class.

Answers

1 idealist: someone who tries to live according to high standards or principles, especially in a way that is not practical or possible; realist: someone who accepts that things are not always perfect and deals with problems or difficult situations in a practical way; optimist: someone who believes that good things will happen; pessimist: someone who believes that bad things will happen

2 1 about 2 by 3 to 4 of 5 by 6 on 7 by
8 with 9 by 10 to

4 1 by/with 2 by/with/about 3 for 4 with/in (*by*
also possible in other contexts) 5 to 6 about (*by* also
possible, with different meaning)

Additional activity: Feelings

Students use the feelings adjectives in Activities 2 and
4 and discuss their own ideas in small groups (e.g. *I am
absolutely terrified of spiders. How about you?*).

Alternatively, each student (or group) selects one of the
feelings and uses it to write a question (e.g. *What are you
motivated by?*). They walk around surveying the other
students and select three or four responses to share with
the class.

Multiple-choice cloze (Part 1)

Aim

- to complete an exam-style multiple-choice cloze task
  (Reading and Use of English Part 1)

5 Students discuss the questions in pairs.

6 Elicit what students remember about Reading and
Use of English Part 1. If necessary, refer students to the
Exam focus on p.197 to review the task and strategies.
Students then read the article quickly, ignoring the
gaps, and describe the writer's attitude to his future
self with their partner. Elicit the answer.

7 Students complete each gap, then compare answers
in pairs before you check as a class. Read the **Exam tip**
aloud and point out that in this activity gap 5 tested
verb/noun collocations and gaps 1, 2, 3 and 8 tested
dependent prepositions.

8 Students discuss the questions in pairs.

Answers

6 He expects his future self to be disappointed despite his
hard work.

7 1 A 2 B 3 D 4 B 5 C 6 C 7 D 8 B

Additional activity: Dependent preposition chart

To help students remember and record dependent
prepositions, ask them to draw up a word map to visually
divide the verb/preposition combinations on p.98–99
into groups, e.g.

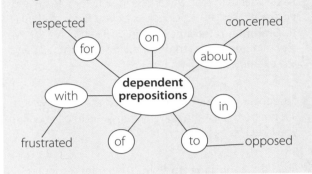

ADDITIONAL PRACTICE | **Maximiser** p.68–69, Vocabulary 1, Use of
English 1–3

Grammar focus ▶ CB p.100

Listening

Aim

- to introduce future forms in context

Warmer: Mapping out the future
Write the following on the board: *Do you <u>have your future
mapped out</u> or tend to <u>take each day as it comes</u>?* Check
that students understand the underlined expressions
(have long term plans; make decisions according to what
happens each day), then put them in pairs to discuss the
question. Elicit a few responses. Then write the following
on the board: *find a …, get a …, start a …, buy a … .*

Working in pairs, ask students to think of ways these
phrases could be completed with possible medium-
and long-term goals (e.g. *find a job, get a degree, start a
business, buy a car*). Elicit some ideas and write them on
the board in a word map.

1 Give students a few minutes to read the article and
elicit what goals Chris has (start a family and get
promoted or find another job). Students then discuss
in pairs what he should do to achieve his goals. Play
the recording for students to compare their answers
with the advice a life coach gives.

2 In pairs, students discuss how useful it would be to
have a life coach. Elicit a few responses.

Future forms

Aim

- to review future forms

3 Ask students to read the article in Activity 1 again and find examples of 1–6. Check as a class. Refer students to **Grammar reference** 18.8 on p.182 and give them a few minutes to read through the future form uses and the examples.

4 Students cross out the verb forms in the article which are *not* possible, then compare answers in pairs before you check as a class.

5 Read the **Language tip** aloud, then refer students to **Grammar reference** 18.9 on p.182 for further examples of time expressions used with future forms. Students complete the sentences with the correct future forms of the verbs in brackets, then compare answers in pairs before you check as a class.

6 Using the time expressions in Activity 5, students talk in pairs about their own plans and predictions. They could also use some of the ideas they brainstormed in the warmer.

Answers

3 1 They're moving to a bigger house soon   2 We're going to start a family   3 they think they'll have enough money   4 Perhaps I'll start   5 I'll have been promoted   6 I'll be doing exactly the same job

4 1 I'm starting   2 I'm doing   3 I'm achieving   4 I do   5 I'll have spent   6 I see   7 I'll have stayed   8 I'm finding

5 1 will be doing   2 will have left   3 will have found   4 am going to/will pass   5 meet   6 find   7 am living/will live   8 will learn   9 got   10 will be

ADDITIONAL PRACTICE | Maximiser p.69, Grammar 1–3

Speaking focus ▶ CB p.101

Speaking

Warmer: Discussion
Write the following on the board and ask students to work in pairs to discuss: *Think of at least three things that might help someone achieve a goal and three things that might be a hindrance.* Elicit some ideas.

1 Students read the advice about goal setting. Make sure that they notice that the headings spell the acronym *SMART* down the page. Elicit some opinions on how useful the advice is.

2 Do an example with the class of making a goal *SMART* (e.g. *I'm planning to read more English books.* becomes *I'm going to read two English library books by the end of this month.*). Students follow the advice in the article to make the goals *SMART*. Elicit some ideas.

3 Suggest that students think about some goals around learning English or another area of their own choice. Students work in pairs to make their goals *SMART*.

Collaborative task (Part 3)
reaching a decision

Aim

- to practise reaching a decision in the collaborative task (Speaking Part 3)

4 Elicit what students remember about Speaking Part 3. If necessary, refer students to the **Exam focus** on p.205 to review the task and strategies. Read the **Exam tip** with the class. Focus students' attention on the word map, then play the recording. In pairs, students do the first part of the task.

Teaching tip

Practise *timed* exam speaking tasks to help students get a feel for how long they need to speak for. In Part 3, Collaborative task, candidates will be given around two minutes for the first part of the task and one minute for the second part.

5 Play the recording of the second part of the task and elicit which of the items 1–5 candidates need to do to complete this part successfully.

6 In pairs, students add a second useful phrase for each strategy. Elicit some ideas, writing them on the board for reference in Activity 7.

7 Play the recording again, then give students about one minute to do the second part of the task. For additional practice, students could swap partners and do the task again. This time, play recording 39 and give students two minutes to complete the first part of the task, then immediately play recording 40 and give students one minute to complete the second part.

Answers

5 Candidates should do 1, 3 and 4. It is fine to disagree politely with each other and there is no 'right' answer.

6 (Suggested answers)

1 X or Y seem like the most obvious choices to me./ I would probably say either X or Y sound best.

2 I'd say we can discount X straightaway. What do you think?

3 So you think that …

4 You do have a point about X, I'll go along with that./ Although X was actually my first choice, I'm willing to go with Y.

ADDITIONAL PRACTICE | **Maximiser** p.70, Speaking 1 |
MyEnglishLab: Cambridge Advanced, Speaking 14: Making a decision in the second part of Part 3

Reading focus ▶ CB p.102

Multiple matching (Part 8)

Aim

- to complete an exam-style multiple matching task (Reading and Use of English Part 8)

1 Students discuss the questions in pairs. Elicit a few responses. If you have internet access and a projector, do a search for 'unusual foods' or 'food production' and display a few pictures on the board as an additional prompt. You could also ask students if they have ever eaten anything they consider unusual.

2 Focus students on the picture on p.103 and elicit ideas of what it is (a seaweed farm). Ask the class if anyone has visited a farm or a factory where food is produced, and what it was like. Give students a few minutes to quickly read the article and put the four developments in order of importance. Explain that there is no 'right' answer but students should order the developments according to their own view. They then compare answers in pairs.

3 Elicit what strategies students would use for this task (Reading and Use of English Part 8, Multiple matching). If necessary, refer students to the **Exam focus** on p.201 to check their ideas. Read the **Exam tip** aloud. Remind students of the following advice from **Exam focus**, Strategies 4 and 5: *Don't just choose a paragraph because it contains the same words as in a question or statement.; Highlight possible answers in pencil. You may find similar – but not exactly the same – information in other sections.* Students reread the article and complete questions 1–10. They then compare answers in pairs before you check as a class.

4 Students discuss the questions in pairs. Elicit a few responses to each.

Answers

3 1 A ('its texture, smell and colour and are put off by this')

2 C ('the production method is perhaps even more important than the rice itself. That is because it can be applied to other crops, such as wheat, that feed millions of people.')

3 B ('There are other people who say you will never be able to make it taste exactly the same as meat. So there are lots of sceptics.')

4 A ('it's more than likely that salt could be replaced by seaweed granules in many supermarket ready-meals, for example, and people wouldn't even notice the difference')

5 D ('One possible location might be the desert, which, although not usually associated with either fish or water, is actually ideal')

6 B ('We are working under the assumption, which might be naive'; '"Whether that's true, we'll find out," Mark confesses.')

7 C ('Rice production must double in this region in order to support a rapidly rising population and we believe GSR technology is the answer.')

8 D ('cobia is preferable to salmon for fish farmers because it … reaches maturity in half the time')

9 C ('One example is a weed-tolerant GSR variety, which establishes itself much faster than weeds. This means the chemicals aren't needed to control the weeds, which makes it both cheaper to produce and less harmful for the environment.')

10 A ('While we're not anticipating it becoming a staple part of the local diet')

Vocabulary
working out meaning from context

Aim
- to practise working out meaning from context

5 Students look at the underlined words in the article and use the context to choose the correct meaning. They then compare answers in pairs before you check as a class.

Answers

5 1 B   2 A   3 B   4 A   5 B   6 B   7 A   8 B

Additional Activity: Think of five …
In pairs, students think of five words:

- to describe texture (e.g. *smooth, rough, silky, bumpy, rigid, coarse, lumpy*).
- for food cupboard staples (e.g. *flour, sugar, jam, rice, salt*).
- that collocate with *viable* (e.g. *viable outcome/ alternative/solution/option, financially/economically viable, be/seem/sound/become/remain viable*).

Elicit some ideas from the class.

ADDITIONAL PRACTICE | Maximiser p.70–71, Reading 1–3 |
MyEnglishLab: Cambridge Advanced, Reading 20: Recognising paraphrase B

Listening focus ▶ CB p.104

Speaking

Aims
- to introduce the topic of behaviour change
- to provide spoken practice

1 Read through the questions with the class and check students understand *peer pressure* (a strong feeling that you must do the same things as other people of your age if you want them to like you). Put students in pairs to discuss their thoughts on each question. Elicit a few ideas for each.

Sentence completion (Part 2)

Aim
- to complete an exam-style listening task (Listening Part 2)

2 If necessary, refer students to the **Exam focus** on p.202 to review the task and strategies for Listening Part 2. Then ask them to look at the exam task and predict the kind of information missing in each gap. Elicit the kind of information that is missing, then remind students that they must use between one and three words in each gap. Elicit some possible answers.

3 Read the **Exam tip** with the class. Play the recording twice for students to complete the task, then go through the answers as a class.

4 Check students understand the meaning of *nudge* (push someone gently, usually with your elbow, in order to get their attention). Elicit why it is in inverted commas (it is being used figuratively). Students discuss the questions in pairs.

5 Students complete the phrases with the verbs in the box, then compare answers in pairs before you check as a class.

6 Ask students to turn to the activity on p.165 and discuss in pairs which of the 'nudges' in A–D would be most effective for the people in 1–3. Ask pairs to think of three more pieces of advice they would give to each group and then choose their best tip to share with the rest of the class.

Answers

3 1 habit   2 (the) lights off/off (the) lights   3 long-term   4 gap   5 (green) footsteps   6 fines   7 regulation   8 recycling

5 1 cut   2 cause   3 move   4 lead   5 act   6 follow

ADDITIONAL PRACTICE | Maximiser p.72, Listening 1–2 |
Photocopiable p.160–161/183, 10A *That's what you need* |
MyEnglishLab: Cambridge Advanced, Listening 6: Listening for detail, Vocabulary 16: The environment

Grammar focus ▶ CB p.105

Conjunctions

Aim

- to review the form and function of a range of conjunctions

Warmer: Collaborate

Write *collaborate* on the board and elicit the meaning (work together) and word class (verb). Elicit other related word forms: *collaborative* (adjective), *collaboration/collaborators* (nouns), *collaboratively* (adverb). Ask students to discuss the following question in pairs, then elicit a few responses: *How has modern technology made collaboration easier?*

1 Students read the article and answer the first question. Elicit a definition of *collaborative consumption* and a few opinions about it. Ask if anyone has taken part in it before.

Elicit the meaning of *hand-me-down* in the last line of the article (something, usually clothing, that has been used by someone and then given to another person). Students discuss the meanings of the statements. Elicit the meanings and ask students if there are any similar expressions in their own language.

2 Ask students to match the underlined conjunctions in the article with their functions. Check as a class. Read the **Language tip** aloud. Refer students to the **Grammar reference** on p.174 for more notes and examples of conjunctions.

3 Students choose the correct alternatives, then compare answers in pairs before you check as a class.

4 Read the instructions with the class, ensuring that students understand that the words in the box match the meanings of the underlined words but cannot necessarily be used to replace them in the sentences. Students complete the activity, then check answers as a class.

Answers

1 (Suggested answers)
1 sharing the cost of buying new items such as cars or lawn mowers with other people
2 people get on better with each other if they have privacy; attempting to make sure everything you have is as good as or better than your neighbours, friends or colleagues; sharing and hand-me-down are completely different

2 1 whereas, whether   2 as long as, provided   3 nor

3 1 as   2 nor   3 As yet   4 whereas   5 Provided   6 as long as

4 1 While   2 Regarding   3 until now   4 current   5 Since   6 Starting on

Additional activity: Quote dictation

Dictate the following three gapped quotes. Ask students to discuss in pairs which conjunction they think fits in each gap. Check as a class, then ask students to discuss with a partner whether they agree with each quote.

1 _____ you think you can, or you think you can't, you're right. (Henry Ford)

2 It doesn't matter how slow you go, _____ you don't stop. (Confucius)

3 No printed word _____ spoken plea can teach young minds what they should be. Not all the books on all the shelves, but what the teachers are themselves. (Rudyard Kipling)

Answers: **1** Whether   **2** as long as   **3** nor

ADDITIONAL PRACTICE | Maximiser p.72, Grammar 1–2 **|
Photocopiable** p.162/184, 10B *Transport links* | **MyEnglishLab: Cambridge Advanced**, Use of English 9: Connectors

Writing focus ▶ CB p.106

Formal letter (Part 2)

using an appropriate range of language

Aim

- to write a formal letter using an appropriate range of language for the exam (Writing Part 2)

Write *rubbish* on the board and elicit what students associate with it. If the following items are not mentioned, elicit them: *landfill, pollution, hazard, discard, waste, dispose, litter.* Ask: *What sort of rubbish is the most problematic in your area? What do you think should be done to tackle the problem?* Put students in pairs to discuss the questions.

1 Tell students that they are going to read a letter to the editor of a newspaper about a rubbish issue. Students read the text and discuss in pairs whether they agree with the writer. Elicit a few opinions.

2 Students find more 'advanced' words in the letter for meanings 1–6. Check as a class.

3 Ask students to find one or more examples of 1–6, then check as a class. Remind them that in the exam they should try and show off the more advanced words and features they know but they must ensure that any vocabulary or structures they use are relevant to the task.

4 Ask the class what is being done to reduce the use of plastic bags where they live. Ask: *What other measures could be taken to reduce plastic bag usage?*

5 Focus students' attention on the exam task and ask them to plan their answer. If students find this challenging, they could work in pairs to generate some ideas. Read the **Exam tip** box aloud. Refer students to the **Writing reference** on p.188 for useful language for formal letters. (Note that if a letter is included in Part 2, it could be in response to a given letter or to some other prompt. However, the letter in the exam will *not* be a letter of application or character reference.) Set the writing task for homework.

6 This task can also be set for homework.

7 Students work in pairs and check their partner's letter. Ideally, they should have the chance to add additional features if necessary before submitting their writing for individual feedback.

Answers

2 1 discourage   2 manufactured   3 discarded   4 hazard   5 consumption   6 yet

3 1 It is hoped   2 being sent, was introduced, to be gained   3 If we accept   4 drastically reducing the amount of waste being sent   5 Countries which have already introduced   6 yet

Sample answer:

Dear Mr Hudson,

In response to your request of 30 September, I am writing to suggest possible actions to reduce the wasteful disposal of plastic water bottles at our school in order to comply with the latest government targets.

There are several ways in which this might be drastically reduced. Firstly, water fountains could be installed at the cafeteria so that students can access quality water for free. Secondly, free reusable drink bottles could be distributed. Thirdly, an education programme could be put in place, focusing on the environmental impact of consumer choices.

In addition to increasing compliance with the regulations, other advantages of providing free water and bottles could include students consuming fewer sugary drinks. If we have the bottles printed with the school logo, this would provide an advertising opportunity. It is also anticipated that implementing education programmes could spark further ideas for future sustainability initiatives.

With regard to ensuring student co-operation, I would recommend starting a student club to oversee the project. The fact that the bottles and water fountains are free would be very attractive for young people as a money-saving measure. It is also hoped that with the education programme in place, students would understand the reasons behind the changes and take an active role in self-monitoring and behaviour change.

I very much hope you will consider the above points. I look forward to working with you to ensure a more sustainable future for Dartfield Community College.

Yours sincerely,

Mahesh Kumar

ADDITIONAL PRACTICE | Maximiser p.73, Writing 1–3 |
MyEnglishLab: Cambridge Advanced, Writing 9: Useful language for formal letters, Writing 10: Error correction: formal letters and emails

Progress test 2 ▶ CB p.107

Aims

- to revise the structures and vocabulary covered in Units 6–10
- to practise Reading and Use of English Parts 1–4 type activities

1 – **8** Ask students to complete the exercises, circulating to provide assistance, or set them as a test. Suggested time limit: 45 minutes for Activities 1–4 and 45 minutes for Activities 5–8. Ask students to check answers in pairs before you check as a class on eText. Alternatively, set as a homework activity and then go through the answers as a class.

Answers

1 1 about 2 will/may/might 3 is/becomes 4 have 5 will 6 While/Although/Though 7 Nor/Neither 8 whether/if

2 1 F 2 A 3 E 4 C 5 D 6 B

3 1 B 2 C 3 C 4 B 5 B 6 B 7 A 8 C

4 1 whether 2 as 3 As yet 4 as long as 5 Since 6 nor 7 As from 8 While

5 1 C 2 A 3 B 4 A 5 B 6 D 7 D 8 B

6 1 own 2 was 3 up 4 along 5 well 6 less 7 to 8 by

7 1 unemployment 2 shortage 3 perceptions 4 prospective 5 assumptions 6 recruitment 7 openings 8 exceptional

8 1 if I had waited 2 you happen to pass/be passing 3 quite impossible for me to attend 4 if any of us/ them/you had 5 regretted having told/telling Angela 6 for as long as (is)

ADDITIONAL PRACTICE | **Maximiser** p.74–75, Use of English 5 | **Testmaster** online and on **eText**, Unit 10 test | **MyEnglishLab: Cambridge Advanced**, Progress test 2

A perfect match

11

Vocabulary and Grammar focus ▶ CB p.110

Expressions for describing compatibility

Aim
• to introduce a range of expressions for describing compatibility

Warmer: Chameleon

Focus on the unit title and introduce the idea of *compatibility* (the ability to have a good relationship with someone because you are similar). Elicit the adjectives *compatible* and *incompatible*. Focus students' attention on the photo. Ask the class the following questions: *What kind of animal is it?* (a chameleon, a type of lizard) *Why does it represent the idea of compatibility?* (It can change colour to make itself more compatible with its environment at a given time.) *Why might you describe a person as a chameleon?* (They change their ideas and/or behaviour depending on who they are with.)

1 In pairs, students discuss whether compatibility is the most important thing for them in a friendship and why or why not. Elicit a few answers and if students answer *no*, then elicit what elements they consider more important (e.g. loyalty, honesty).

2 Students complete the questions, then check as a class. Elicit the meaning of the expressions *be on the same wavelength* (think in a similar way and understand each other well), *be as different as chalk and cheese* (be very different) and *get on like a house on fire* (get on very well). Students ask and answer the questions with a partner.

3 Elicit/Introduce a few other expressions to talk about compatibility, e.g. *kindred spirits* (two people who think or feel exactly the same way), *hit it off straightaway* (get on extremely well from the first time you meet), *get along famously* (get along extremely well) and *(not) have a lot in common*. Pairs write a short conversation using some of the expressions. Invite pairs to act out their conversations for the class. If you have a very large class, each pair could perform their conversation for a group instead.

4 Students complete the sentences, then check as a class. Focus students' attention on the **Language tip** and read it aloud. Elicit a few more possible examples using *suit* in this way (e.g. *I'm afraid that time doesn't suit me.; Which day would suit you better: Monday or Thursday?*).

5 Students discuss clothes and fashion with a partner, using words from Activity 4. If you have a projector and internet access, display some pictures of current fashions as an additional prompt.

Answers

2 **1** with **2** from **3** on **4** as, as, on **5** to/with, with

4 **1** match **2** suit **3** fit **4** match **5** match
  6 match

Additional activity: It doesn't suit, doesn't match and doesn't fit.

In pairs, students take the roles of shopkeeper and customer, and role-play the exchange of a piece of clothing. The customer needs to give reasons for returning the item (e.g. it doesn't suit them, it doesn't match something else they own, it doesn't fit). The customer needs to convince the reluctant shopkeeper to exchange the item.

Reading

Aim

- to present *whenever*, *whichever* and *whatever* in context

6 Give students a moment to read the questions and think about their answers, then ask them to compare answers with a partner.

7 Students read the article. Elicit how the writer feels about her profile.

Suggested answer

7 She is slightly amused by it.

whoever, whatever, etc.

Aim

- to review the use of *whoever*, *whatever*, etc.

8 Students rewrite the underlined sentences in Activity 7 without using *-ever* words. Elicit the rewritten sentences, then discuss the answers to the questions as a class.

9 Students complete the sentences, then compare answers in pairs before you check as a class.

10 Rewrite the first piece of advice with the class. Students then rewrite the rest, comparing answers in pairs before you check as a class.

11 Students discuss the advice in pairs, then write two more pieces of advice. Elicit some of the students' additional advice.

12 Read the **Language tip** aloud, pointing out that it can sound impatient or rude to use *whatever* by itself. Share or elicit how to use *like/prefer* to make the response more polite: *Whatever you like./Whatever you prefer.* Tell students that you can make it sound even more polite by using the conditional: *Whatever you'd like./Whatever you'd prefer.* Then students work in pairs to make suggestions and respond politely.

Answers

8 (Suggested answers)

1 Every (single) time I did an internet search … (adverb)
2 Google was matching who they thought I was … (pronoun) **3** … but regardless of which computer I happened to use, … (pronoun) **4** It doesn't matter what they happen to search … (object)

9 **1** Whatever **2** However **3** whenever
  4 whichever **5** wherever **6** whoever

10 **1** However well you know and trust the person, never share your log-in details.

 2 Set your notifications to tell you whenever someone tags you in a photo.

 3 However much you like an image, think carefully before you post it on your wall.

 4 Wherever you're going on holiday, don't put the details up on your wall. You might not want everyone to know you're away.

ADDITIONAL PRACTICE | **Maximiser** p.78, Vocabulary 1, Grammar 1–2 |
MyEnglishLab: Cambridge Advanced, Vocabulary 13: UK universities

Reading focus ▶ CB p.112

Speaking

Aims
- to introduce the topic of online dating
- to provide spoken practice

1 Elicit the meaning of *match-make* (try and find a suitable partner for someone else) and elicit the noun forms *match-maker* and *match-making*. Students discuss the statement in pairs.

2 Students read the article and choose the best title.

Answer
2 1

Multiple choice (Part 5)

Aim
- to complete an exam-style multiple-choice reading task (Reading and Use of English Part 5)

3 Focus students' attention on the underlined word *dozen*. Even if students know what it means (twelve), ask them to find the information later in the paragraph that would help (*the eleventh*). Read the **Exam tip** aloud and elicit what students remember about the strategies for tackling Reading and Use of English Part 5. If necessary, review the strategies in the **Exam focus** on p.199.

4 Give students ten minutes to complete the activity.

5 Students replace the underlined verbs with phrasal verbs from the article. Elicit the answers.

Teaching tip

Time limits
At this stage of the course, start giving students limited time to complete Reading and Use of English activities, to get them used to working quickly in the exam. Students are given 90 minutes to complete the eight parts in this paper, which works out to around 11 minutes per part.

Answers
3 twelve

4 1 D ('Although he had met lots of girls during his first semester at college, he just hadn't clicked with any of them.')

2 C ('In my opinion, the claimed success of matching sites may have more to do with narrowing the pool of eligible daters than psychological tests or computer science.')

3 B ('noting that none have ever subjected their algorithms … to peer scrutiny')

4 D ('In fact, a "selection bias" – a statistical bias that occurs when your sample population is different from the norm – may be at work.'; ' claimed success of matching sites may have more to do with narrowing the pool of eligible daters')

5 B ('online matching services may work because the couple believe their coupling has been validated by relationship experts using complex computer science')

6 D ('Matching software, it seems, is no match for a good chat up line.')

5 1 signing up   2 turned him down   3 cut back
4 back up   5 chatting up   6 weed out

Additional activity: Seeking my perfect match

Ask students to discuss the following question in pairs: *What do you think is the best way for people to meet a partner?* Elicit some ideas.

For a bit of fun, ask students to write their profile for an online dating site in under 50 words. They should include what they are looking for, either a friendship or relationship, and information about themselves. Put students in small groups and ask them to swap profiles with someone else in the group. Each profile is read aloud and the other students in the group need to guess whose profile it is.

ADDITIONAL PRACTICE | **Maximiser** p.76–77, Reading 1–5 |
MyEnglishLab: Cambridge Advanced, Reading 11: Identifying the writer's attitude B, Reading 18: Understanding text development

Use of English focus

▶ CB p.114

Open cloze (Part 2)

Aim

- to complete an exam-style open cloze task (Reading and Use of English Part 2)

1 Students discuss the questions in pairs.

2 Elicit what students remember about the strategies for tackling Reading and Use of English Part 2 and if necessary, review them in the **Exam focus** on p.198. Ask students to read the title and the article quickly, then elicit the answer to the question.

3 Students work in pairs to choose the correct alternatives, discussing in each case why the other alternative is not possible.

4 Read the **Exam tip** aloud, then give students about seven minutes to fill the gaps. Check as a class, eliciting reasons for the choice for each gap.

Answers

2 It is about professional contexts.

3 1 few (a matter of)   2 does (make something = create)   3 out (set up = establish)   4 next (*against* not followed by *to*)   5 up (*out* not followed by *on* and different meaning)   6 all (some of)

4 1 one   2 further   3 of   4 way   5 as   6 few   7 next   8 about

Speaking

Aim

- to provide spoken practice

5 Students answer the questions. They may make a few notes but should not write full sentences. Then they compare their responses in pairs.

Additional activity: Speed networking

If possible, set up your classroom like the photo on p.114 so that there is a long table with chairs for pairs of students facing each other on either side. Alternatively, ask students to stand up and find a partner. Using a timer, tell students that they have two minutes to talk to their partner to find out as much as possible about them in that time. Depending on your class demographic, you could ask them to focus on learning about their partner's career, education or family. After two minutes, students swap partners, either by one side of the table moving down one place or by students walking around to find a new partner. Repeat this until students have spoken to at least four different people. Ask each student to share something they found out about one of their classmates.

ADDITIONAL PRACTICE | Maximiser p.78, Use of English 1–2

Listening focus ▶ CB p.115

Multiple matching (Part 4)

Aim

- to complete an exam-style listening task (Listening Part 4)

Warmer: Personality test
Write the following short personality test on the board:

I am a person who

1 never gives _____ , even if things get really tough.

2 is always coming _____ with great ideas.

3 works well _____ pressure.

4 works best _____ collaboration with others.

5 gets anxious _____ disruptions to my routine.

Ask students to work in pairs to complete the gaps, then check as a class. Students then grade each statement so that it is true for them on a scale of 1–5, where 1 represents 'strongly disagree' and 5 represents 'agree completely'. Students compare their answers with their partner. Invite each person to share something they learnt about their partner's personality.

Answers: **1** up   **2** up   **3** under   **4** in   **5** about

Pronunciation

Ask students to look at the phrases on the board and find three different spellings for the sound /ʃ/ as in _sheep_. If you are using eText, select the phonetic chart tab and play the phoneme /ʃ/.

Answers: ss- (pre<u>ss</u>ure), t- (collabora<u>t</u>ion, disrup<u>t</u>ions), x- (an<u>x</u>ious)

Check students can pronounce _tough_ correctly (it rhymes with _stuff_). Students practise reading the phrases aloud.

1 Elicit what students can remember about the strategies for tackling Listening Part 4 and if necessary, review them in the **Exam focus** on p.203. Then ask students to look at the exam tasks in Activity 3 and discuss the questions in Activity 1 in pairs.

2 Read the **Exam tip** aloud, then give students time to underline key words in the tasks. Play the recording and elicit whether the information comes in the same order as the two tasks.

3 Play the recording for students to complete the tasks. Play the recording a second time for students to complete and check their answers, then go through the answers as a class.

Answers

2 no
3 **Task 1** 1 B 2 C 3 F 4 A 5 D
   Task 2 6 F 7 D 8 C 9 E 10 A

Speaking

Aims

- to practise using vocabulary related to personality tests
- to provide spoken practice

4 Put students in small groups to discuss the questions about personality tests. Elicit some ideas from each of the groups.

ADDITIONAL PRACTICE | **Maximiser** p.79, Listening 1–2 | **Photocopiable** p.163/184, 11A _Compatibility_ | **MyEnglishLab: Cambridge Advanced**, Listening 9: Listening for attitudes and opinions, Listening 20: The speaker's opinion

Grammar focus

▶ CB p.116

Reading

Aim

- to present participle clauses in context

1 Students discuss in pairs what the positive and negative aspects of working as a stylist would be. Encourage them to think of at least two positive and two negative things. Elicit some ideas.

2 Give students a couple of minutes to read the article. Elicit whether the stylist mentioned any of the aspects students discussed in Activity 1. Ask: _What other aspects does she mention?_ (positive aspects: travel, learning new skills, working in close collaboration with others; negative aspects: long hours, demanding work, can be challenging to help celebrities).

Participle clauses

Aim

- to review the structure and use of participle clauses

3 Focus students' attention on the underlined sentences in the article in Activity 2. Elicit what the main clause in each sentence is. If necessary, explain that a main clause is a clause that could stand alone as a complete sentence (main clauses: 1 – _I knew there were only two real career paths open to me_; 2 – _Celebrities often hire stylists to help them out._). Then ask students to identify the _participle clause_ in each case. Explain that a participle clause is one that begins with a present or past participle (participle clauses: 1 – _Having studied fashion at college_; 2 – _hoping to improve a tarnished image or simply trying to make the most of their assets_). Go through the two questions with the class, eliciting answers to each one.

4 Ask students to underline four more participle clauses in the article. If you are using eText, underline these on the board using the pen tool. Elicit the answers with the class. Tell students that participle clauses are used as an alternative to relative pronouns, to make writing more concise. For more notes and examples of participle clauses, refer students to the **Grammar reference** on p.177.

5 Focus students' attention on the example. Students match 1–6 with A–F, then rewrite the sentences using participle clauses. Students may work in pairs for this activity. Check as a class, then read the **Language tip** aloud. Elicit how the example could be changed so that the subject of both clauses is the same (e.g. *Picking up the phone, I heard an unfamiliar voice greet me.*).

6 Students work in pairs. They should decide who is A and B before turning to p.164 and p.166 because they are going to do an activity individually and then check each other's work. When students are ready to do the checking, make sure they do it verbally rather than looking at their partner's work.

Answers

3 1 hoping to improve a tarnished image (sentence 2)

2 Having studied fashion at college (sentence 1)

4 The wardrobe stylist, <u>holding responsibility for pulling all the elements of the show together</u>, often ends up …

The fashion houses <u>chosen by the magazine</u> provide …

<u>Having worked in these areas for several years</u>, I decided …

… has given me a range of new skills, <u>including learning to do research</u>.

5 1 D Realising I was going to be late, I tried to find a taxi.

2 E Having not/Not having slept a wink the night before, I was really tired.

3 B I was worried about finding myself in another tense situation with Andrea having not/not having actually spoken to her since our last disastrous encounter.

4 F Not wanting to have to be responsible for running the meeting, I asked Victoria if she would chair it for me.

5 C Convinced everyone knew about the situation with Andrea, I decided it was pointless to behave as if nothing had happened.

6 A Feeling very nervous as I walked into the room, I tried not to look anybody in the eye.

ADDITIONAL PRACTICE | Maximiser p.80, Grammar 1–3 |
Photocopiable p.164/185, 11B *Participle clause bingo*

Speaking focus ▶ CB p.117

Collaborative task and discussion (Parts 3 and 4)

negotiating and co-operating

Aim

- to practise negotiating and co-operating in an exam-style speaking task (Speaking Parts 3 and 4)

Warmer: Discussion

Write the following questions on the board and ask students to discuss them in pairs: *Have you ever been to a job interview? What advice would you give to someone preparing for one? What sorts of job applications might require a portfolio?* Elicit some responses to each.

1 Elicit what is involved in Speaking Parts 3 and 4 of the exam. If necessary, refer students to the **Exam focus** on p.205. Ask them to look at the Part 3 task and the Part 4 questions in Activity 1. Play the recording and elicit whether Nadia and Anton talk about all the methods listed.

2 Read the **Exam tip** aloud. Tell students that using phrases to negotiate and co-operate can help them sound confident without being too direct. Play the recording again for students to complete the phrases. Elicit the answers or show them on eText if you are using it.

3 In pairs, students read the task on p.154. Ask all students to start at the same time and give them two minutes to discuss how useful the methods would be when trying to make new friends and business contacts. Stop everyone after two minutes and say: *Now you have one minute to decide which would be the best method to recommend to someone who is very shy.* Give students one minute to negotiate, then ask who managed to come to an agreement in that time.

4 Play the recording and elicit which of the questions from the task in Activity 1 the examiner asks.

5 Give students a moment to read the phrases, then play the recording again for students to tick the phrases they hear.

6 Write the three headings from Activity 6 on the board and ask students to decide which headings the phrases should go under. Check answers and write the phrases on the board, under the correct headings. Leave this displayed for reference during Activity 7.

7 Students take turns to ask and answer the Part 4 questions on p.158, giving each other about one minute to answer each.

Answers

1 yes

2 1 Would you go along with that   2 up to a point   3 would you be happier with   4 we may well   5 just wonder how   6 I think we can agree that

4 What is the most important quality for a stylist to have?

Some people prefer to have someone choose their clothes and accessories for them. Why do you think this is?

Some people say that we can change our style and appearance but not our basic character. What do you think?

5 1, 2, 3, 5, 7, 8

6 A: 5, 8, 9   B: 1, 4, 10   C: 2, 3, 6, 7

ADDITIONAL PRACTICE | **Maximiser** p.80–81, Speaking 1–3 |
MyEnglishLab: Cambridge Advanced, Speaking 13: Managing a Part 3 and 4 discussion, Speaking 18: Analysing Part 4 answers

Writing focus ▶ CB p.118

Formal letter (Part 2)
including relevant information

Aim
● to practise including all relevant information in a formal letter

Warmer: Discussion
Students discuss the following question in pairs: *What did you look for when choosing an English course?* Elicit a few ideas.

1 Students read the task and discuss the question in pairs. Elicit the answers.

2 Students read the letter and underline the irrelevant information. They discuss their answers in pairs before you check as a class. Read the **Exam tip** aloud.

3 Students turn to p.165. In pairs, they follow the instructions to make a plan for the task. Set the writing for homework. There is 90 minutes to complete two writing tasks in the exam. Suggest that students set a timer for 45 minutes while they write their letter, to practise working within the time limit. Remind them about the useful language for formal letters in the **Writing reference** on p.188.

Answers

1 points not to be included: your opinion about these students, what is not taught at the school, other subjects you would like to see introduced, why you can't offer some courses at the moment, what you've heard people say about your school

2 paragraph 2: Apparently, there is some discussion about offering Chinese at some time in the future but it is not currently available. (too vague and negative)

paragraph 3: It can be very difficult to find accommodation here, so it is a good thing that the school provides such a service. (too negative)

paragraph 4: The oldest student we've ever had was seventy-eight years old. (too specific)

3 Sample answer:

Dear Ms Florandez,

I am writing to apply for the exchange programme at San Marino High School and to describe my current studies, suitability and what I hope to learn from the experience.

Currently in my final year at Fredrikson College, my studies have included mathematics and three foreign languages, including Portuguese and science. I expect to complete my final exams next month, after which I would like to come to your institution in Brazil for three months.

I believe I have the qualities needed to have a successful exchange. I have been described as open, friendly and responsible. I hold a part-time position at the local tourist office, so am accustomed to conversing with people from other cultures. My prior experience with Portuguese will ensure that I am able to hold basic conversations from the outset.

In addition to improving my conversational Portuguese, I hope to learn more about Brazilian culture, especially music and celebration. If I am fortunate enough to visit some of the sights of your country, which I have read so much about, I would also find that exhilarating and enjoyable. This would be my first time outside of Europe and I would like to challenge myself by travelling further away from home without my family, to step outside my comfort zone.

I very much hope you will look favourably on my application and I look forward to receiving your response.

Yours sincerely,

Jana Novic

ADDITIONAL PRACTICE | Maximiser p.81, Writing 1–2 | **MyEnglishLab: Cambridge Advanced**, Writing 11: Letter of complaint

Review ▶ CB p.119

Aim

● to revise the structures, vocabulary and exam tasks covered in Unit 11

1 – **3** Ask students to complete the exercises, circulating to provide assistance. Ask students to check answers in pairs before checking as a class on eText. Alternatively, set as a homework activity and then go through the answers as a class, or on eText, to check.

Answers

1 1 doesn't matter what 2 makes no difference how 3 having heard it was going 4 how much you like them 5 regardless of what 6 wherever I happen 7 don't mind what we 8 you would like to come around

2 1 with 2 from 3 on fire 4 on 5 to 6 do with

3 1 C 2 D 3 A 4 C 5 B 6 B 7 C 8 A

ADDITIONAL PRACTICE | Testmaster online and on **eText**, Unit 11 test | **MyEnglishLab: Cambridge Advanced**, Mock Reading and Use of English paper

MyEnglishLab tip

Mock Reading and Use of English paper
The mock tests are complete papers for exam practice. Suggest to students that they allow 90 minutes to complete the mock Reading and Use of English paper Parts 1–8 as a block, to get a feel for the progression in the exam.

Soundtracks

Use of English and Grammar focus ▶ CB p.120

Word formation (Part 3)

Aim

● to complete an exam-style word formation task (Reading and Use of English Part 3)

Warmer: Sounds

Ask students to look at the picture on p.120, then close their eyes and imagine all the sounds they could hear if they were in the picture (e.g. waves, seagulls, people on the beach). Elicit some ideas. Then ask students to think of five sounds they heard on the way to the class and compare them with a partner.

1 Students discuss the question in pairs.

2 Elicit what students remember about the strategies for tackling Reading and Use of English Part 3 and if necessary, review them in the **Exam focus** on p.198. After students have read the article, elicit what was the most popular sound.

3 Look at the first word in capitals with the class as an example and elicit as many forms of it as possible. If necessary, remind students to consider whether any prefixes or suffixes can be added. Working in pairs, students brainstorm word forms for each of the words in capitals, then decide what sort of word form fits in each gap. Check as a class.

4 Give students around five minutes to complete the gaps. Then read the **Exam tip** aloud and ask students to compare their answers and check spelling in pairs. Check answers and point out that the words for gaps 0, 2, 3, 5 and 7 involve losing the final -e.

5 In pairs, students try to predict five more unpopular sounds that might have been listed on the survey. Elicit some ideas, then ask students to turn to p.167 to check.

Answers

2 the sound of waves crashing against rocks

3 (Suggested answers)

1 resistance, (ir)resistible, (ir)resistibly   2 (un)surprising, (un)surprised   3 soothing, soothed   4 ranking, rank   5 anticipation, anticipated   6 powerful, powerfully, empower, empowering, empowered   7 central, centred, centre   8 (un)predictable, (un)predictably, prediction

Missing words: **1** adjective   **2** adverb   **3** adjective   **4** noun   **5** noun   **6** adverb   **7** adjective   **8** adverb

4 1 irresistible   2 unsurprisingly   3 soothing   4 ranking(s)   5 anticipation   6 powerfully   7 central   8 Predictably

---

Additional activity: Pronunciation spot

Write the following pairs on the board (without underlining) and ask students to work in pairs to underline the stressed syllable in each word.

pre*dict*, pre*dict*ion

an*tic*ipate, antici*pa*tion

re*ass*ure, re*ass*urance

re*sist*, re*sist*ance

Ask the following questions: *In which pair does the stressed syllable change?* (an*tic*ipate/antici*pa*tion) *In which pairs is there a change in consonant sound when the suffix is added?* Point out that in *predic**t*** and *anticipa**t**e*, the final consonant sound /t/ becomes /ʃ/ (as in *sheep*) in *predic**ti**on* and *anticipa**ti**on*. Check students know that the *-ss* in *re**ss**ure/rea**ss**urance* is also pronounced /ʃ/, and the first *-s* in *re**s**ist/re**s**istance* is pronounced /z/. If you are using eText, click on the phonetic chart tab and ask students to locate the phonemes /ʃ/, /z/ and /s/ on the chart, then play the sounds.

Future in the past

Aim

- to present examples of future in the past in context

6 Focus students' attention on the picture and elicit some predictions about what might be making the teenager cover his ears. Ask students to read the article, then elicit two uses of the Mosquito.

7 Students discuss the questions in pairs. Elicit a few ideas from different students.

8 Focus students' attention on the first underlined verb in the article (*was aiming*). Ask students to read the whole sentence aloud, then ask: *Does the verb 'aiming' refer to a future plan or a prediction about the future that was made in the past?* (a prediction about the future that was made in the past). In pairs, students discuss the other underlined verbs in the article. Elicit the answers as a class.

9 Refer students to **Grammar reference** 18.10 on p.183 and read through the notes and examples on *Future in the past* 1–3. Tell students that points 4–7 in the **Grammar reference** will be dealt with in more detail later in this unit (see p.127). Ask students to complete the activity, then check as a class. Read the **Language tip** aloud and share an additional example using future in the past (e.g. *I was hoping to buy/would have bought/was going to buy you a wonderful present but I simply couldn't find anything classy enough.*).

10 Students choose the correct alternative in each sentence, then compare answers in pairs before you check as a class.

Answers

6 to discourage teenagers from lingering around certain places; a ringtone that only young people can hear

8 1 is a future plan. All the others are predictions made in the past about the future.

9 … is aiming to repel teenagers from loitering around shops near his home in Wales. The idea behind it is that teenagers will be put off by the noise and leave before they can cause any trouble. And older shoppers will be able to get on with their shopping undisturbed by either groups of teenagers or the sound that, in theory, will drive them away.

Changes from future to future in the past: present continuous – past continuous, *will – would, can – could, would be – would have been*

10 1 was considering   2 was going to be   3 would win   4 were hoping   5 would have been   6 was going to take

Speaking

Aim

- to practise using future in the past to make excuses

11 Working in pairs, students read the scenarios on p.163 and p.164, then take turns to apologise to each other using future in the past.

Additional activity: More excuses

Use the additional scenarios below for extra practice in Activity 11.

1 Student B was going to meet Student A for a coffee yesterday but didn't show up.

2 Student A promised to lend Student B an English novel but no longer can.

ADDITIONAL PRACTICE | Maximiser p.84, Use of English 1, Grammar 1–2

Reading focus ▶ CB p.122

Speaking

Aims

- to introduce the topic of silence
- to provide spoken practice

1 Check students understand the meaning of *bland* (boring) and *canned music* (generic, easy listening music which often is set on a loop and doesn't have lyrics; often played in shopping malls and lifts, and when holding on the phone). Students tick the statements they agree with, then compare their answers in pairs.

Multiple matching (Part 8)

Aim

- to complete an exam-style multiple matching task (Reading and Use of English Part 8)

2 Elicit what students remember about the strategies for tackling Reading and Use of English Part 8 and if necessary, review them in the **Exam focus** on p.201. Read the **Exam tip** aloud. Check students are clear on what they need to do, then give them 11 minutes to complete the activity. Students compare answers in pairs before you check as a class.

Answers

2 1 B ('absence of man-made noise')

2 A ('Silence unsettles us. Silence both widens our attention and focuses it'; 'It's not that we hear nothing – we hear everything.')

3 D ('People began whispering to one another and some people began to walk out'; 'For those who actually widened their awareness and listened carefully, they would have heard a world of unintended sound.')

4 B ('And in the American West? Maybe twelve.')

5 A ('At 2 a.m. a silent house can be an unsettling house. It creaks. It clicks. It shuffles.')

6 B ('Instead of nothing, he heard')

7 A ('[the sounds] were gone and with it, my sense of tranquillity')

8 C ('Gordon Hempton, an acoustic ecologist … noted that in a dense moss-covered forest it is possible to be aware of something as delicate as the sound of a falling rain drop – undetectable in any city.')

9 D ('the audience burst into an uproar – "infuriated and dismayed"')

10 C ('Man-made noise dulls us. Thought narrows. Sitting by a river or waterfall, or on a secluded stretch of beach, our thoughts become expansive. Our nervous system slows and soothes.')

Speaking

Aims

- to encourage students to engage further with the text
- to provide spoken practice

3 Students discuss the questions in pairs. Elicit a few ideas for each.

Answers

3 3 (Suggested answers) birdsong in the city, the hum of bees, acoustic instruments, some minority languages

Vocabulary
working out meaning from context

> **Aim**
> - to practise working out meaning from context

4 Students answer the questions, then compare answers in pairs before you check as a class.

5 Working in pairs, students discuss and choose the correct meaning for each underlined word or phrase. Check as a class.

Answers

4 1 incessant, immensity   2 randomness, amplification
   3 irritated, annoyed, uproar, infuriated

5 1 A   2 A   3 B   4 A   5 A   6 B

ADDITIONAL PRACTICE | Maximiser p.82–83, Reading 1–3 |
MyEnglishLab: Cambridge Advanced, Reading 6: Scanning for specific information B

Vocabulary focus

▶ CB p.124

Onomatopoeic words

> **Aim**
> - to practise onomatopoeic words

Warmer
Check students know the meaning of *onomatopoeia* (a word that sounds similar to the sound it describes). Focus students' attention on the picture and ask them what sort of sounds they could use to describe rain (e.g. *splish, splosh, splash, drip, plop*). Ask: *Are these words similar to the onomatopoeic words for rain in your language?* Tell students that onomatopoeic words are another aspect of lexical range which can add more interest to speech and (informal) writing.

1 Students match verbs 1–8 with things they could describe A–H, then compare answers in pairs before you check as a class.

2 Students discuss the uses of the verbs in pairs. Check as a class.

3 Students choose the correct alternative in each sentence, then compare answers in pairs before you check as a class. Read the **Language tip** aloud.

4 Ask students to be silent for 20 seconds and listen carefully to see how many sounds they can hear. Students then take turns to describe the sounds using the example as a model.

5 Read through the words in the box with the class and check they understand them all. Students complete the sentences, then compare answers in pairs before you check as a class.

Answers

1 1 D   2 A   3 B   4 E   5 F   6 C   7 H   8 G

2 1 hum, buzz   2 roar   3 snap   4 gurgle, whoosh
   5 patter   6 creak   7 rustle   8 whisper, sigh

3 1 buzzing   2 clicks   3 snapped   4 popping
   5 gurgling   6 pattered   7 creaking   8 chattering

5 1 ducks   2 birds   3 owls   4 frogs   5 penguins
   6 snakes

> **Additional activity:** Animal sounds
> For a bit of light-hearted fun, get enough small pieces of paper for everyone in the class and write down pairs of animals from this lesson (e.g. write *frog* on two pieces of paper). Distribute the pieces of paper and tell students not to show anybody. Students have to move around making the onomatopoeic sound of the animal to find their partner. Alternatively, other items/events from the lesson which make sounds can be used instead of animals (e.g. thunder, rain). After students have found their partner, they can work with them for the speaking section below.

Speaking

> **Aims**
> - to reflect on onomatopoeia
> - to provide spoken practice

6 Students discuss the questions with their partner. Elicit some ideas for each.

7 Play the recording, pausing after each sound for students to discuss the sound with their partner. Elicit a few ideas then give the answer.

Answers

7 1 waterfall 2 frog croaking 3 cat hissing 4 tap dripping 5 creaking floorboard 6 music heard through someone else's headphones

ADDITIONAL PRACTICE | Maximiser p.85, Vocabulary 1–2 |
Photocopiable p.165/186, 12A *It sounds right to me* | **MyEnglishLab: Cambridge Advanced**, Vocabulary 5: Review of Activities 1–4

Listening focus ▶ CB p.125

Multiple choice (Part 1)

Aim

- to complete an exam-style multiple-choice listening task (Listening Part 1)

Warmer: Musical genres

On the board, brainstorm with the class as many genres of music as you can (e.g. *hip hop, indie, rock, heavy metal, pop, classical, country, jazz, electronica, reggae, Latin*). For any genres that students (or you) are unsure of, ask the person who suggested it to describe it, e.g. typical speed, instruments, themes, etc. Then put students in pairs to discuss what the best sort of music is for: a) studying, b) exercising, c) a party with friends, d) a ringtone.

1 Students read the statements and discuss in pairs whether they agree or disagree. Elicit a few ideas.

2 Elicit what students remember about Listening Part 1 and if necessary refer them to the **Exam focus** on p.202 to review the task and strategies. Read the **Exam tip** aloud, then give students two minutes to complete Strategy 1: read the questions and options and highlight the key words before they listen. Play the recording twice, leaving a minute in between. Then go through the answers as a class.

Answers

2 1 B 2 B 3 A 4 B 5 C 6 B

Speaking

Aims

- to expand vocabulary related to music and personality
- to provide spoken practice

3 Check students understand the adjectives in the box. Working in pairs, students discuss the questions. Elicit a few answers from the class.

4 Students discuss the questions in pairs.

Answers

3 1 imaginative, gentle, introverted

ADDITIONAL PRACTICE | Maximiser p.85, Listening 1–2 |
MyEnglishLab: Cambridge Advanced, Listening 5: Understanding specific information

Speaking focus ▶ CB p.126

Speaking

Aim

- to provide spoken practice

1 Working in pairs, students discuss the questions. Elicit a few ideas with the class. Share two more collocations with *sense*: *sense of direction, common sense*.

Collaborative task (Part 3)

using a good lexical range

Aim

- to practise using a good lexical range in an exam-style speaking task (Speaking Part 3)

2 Check students understand the meaning of *lexical* (vocabulary). Elicit what strategies students remember for tackling Speaking Part 3. If necessary, refer them to the **Exam focus** on p.205 to review the task and strategies. Read the **Exam tip** aloud. Allow students time to read the task, then play the recording. Elicit whether the students agreed with the candidates.

3 Students complete the activity in pairs. Elicit answers and write them on the board. Keep these displayed for reference during Activity 4.

4 Give students two or three minutes to complete the task. Ask them to reflect on the lexis (vocabulary) they used, then swap partners and try the task again, aiming to use a greater range of lexis.

5 Play the recording, then give students one minute to continue their discussion.

6 Ask students to swap partners. Focus their attention on the word map, then give them three minutes to do the exam task.

Alternative activity: Feedback groups

As students are now quite familiar with the exam tasks, they could work in groups of four for Activities 6 and 7, with one pair doing the task at a time while the other pair listens and notes down good vocabulary or repetitions, to feed back on the lexical range.

7 Point out that these questions are examples of Part 4 questions and students should try to use as great a range of lexis as possible when answering. Students should talk for about one minute when they answer the questions. Students take turns to ask and answer the questions in pairs.

Answers

3 (Suggested answers)

   1 advantageous, helpful, valuable, useful   **2** unhelpful, detrimental, harmful   **3** stimulating, calming, comforting, motivating   **4** I believe, I'd say that, I would argue that   **5** since, for this reason, as   **6** right, fine, well

ADDITIONAL PRACTICE | Maximiser p.86, Speaking 1–3 |
MyEnglishLab: Cambridge Advanced, Speaking 10: Using a wide range of vocabulary in Part 3

Grammar focus

▶ CB p.127

Future in the past: advanced features

Aim

- to use future in the past to describe unfulfilled intentions

Warmer: Discussion

Write the following questions on the board: *Are you good at keeping surprises hidden or do you tend to let the cat out of the bag? Would you enjoy having a surprise party thrown for you or would you prefer to know in advance?* Elicit the meaning of *let the cat out of the bag* (share something that was supposed to be a secret). Students discuss the questions in pairs. Elicit a few responses. Tell students that in this lesson they will look at ways to describe something that was going to happen but didn't or something that wasn't supposed to happen but did.

1 Focus students' attention on the first sentence (1) as an example. Look at each phrase in the box in turn, eliciting whether it could replace the underlined phrase, and any changes that would need to be made. Students work through the remaining sentences, then compare answers in pairs before you check as a class.

2 Go through the examples with the class, eliciting the answers as you go.

3 Ask students to turn to **Grammar reference** 18.10 on p.183 and read 4–7. Leave these displayed for students to refer to during the activity. Students complete the sentences and then discuss their answers as a class.

4 Point out that this is an example of a Reading and Use of English Part 4 task. Students complete the activity, then compare answers in pairs before you check as a class. Read the **Language tip** aloud to the class.

Answers

1 1 was about to   2 weren't meant to, was meant to
3 was meant to/due to leave (verb form changes here)
4 were thinking of inviting (verb form changes here)
5 was about to   6 was about to

2 1 no   2 yes   3 yes   4 yes

3 1 were to have left   2 was to have become   3 were
to perform   4 were to be informed   5 were to sign
6 was to have been fired

4 1 was supposed to be/have been finished   2 were
due to release   3 were to have been told   4 was
thinking of asking (for)   5 was about to close
6 would have invited Sarah

Speaking

Aim

- to practise using future forms to describe past
  situations
- to provide spoken practice

5 Students work in pairs to think of some examples
of each situation and explain what went wrong.
Alternatively, brainstorm examples as a class, then put
students in pairs to discuss what went wrong.

Additional activity

Ask students to think of a time when their plans changed
because something unexpected happened. Students
share their experience with a partner using future in the
past. As a prompt, you could share a brief anecdote of
your own or share the following for times when plans
may change: *unseasonable weather, a delayed connection,
an unexpected phone call/visit, winning something, losing
something.*

ADDITIONAL PRACTICE | **Maximiser** p.86, Grammar 1–3 |
MyEnglishLab: Cambridge Advanced, Use of English 11: Past tenses with
future meaning

Writing focus ▶ CB p.128
Review (Part 2)
making recommendations

Aim

- to use a range of language to make
  recommendations in a review (Writing Part 2)

Warmer: Song

In pairs, students think of:

- a song with a catchy melody that makes you want to
  hum along.
- a song with great vocals.
- a powerful song.
- a song that makes you want to dance like crazy.

Ask pairs to join with another pair to see if any of the
same songs were mentioned.

1 Students read the review, then discuss the questions in
pairs. Elicit the answers.

2 Check students know what a simile is (an expression
which uses *like* or *as* to compare one thing to another).
Ask students to underline colourful, lively language,
put a star next to a simile and circle examples of
specialised topic vocabulary. Elicit some examples
for each. Ask students if the review uses a formal or
informal style (informal).

3 Students match the sentence halves. Check as a class,
then ask students to discuss in pairs whether each
sentence is formal or informal. Go through the answers
as a class.

4 Students can complete this as a homework activity.
Focus their attention on the **Exam tip** and remind
them to set a timer for 45 minutes to simulate the
exam time limit. The Review section on p.194 of the
Writing reference has more useful language for this
task, including music vocabulary under the heading
concert.

5 This could also be set as a homework task. Collect in
the work to provide individual feedback, focusing on
lexical range.

Answers

2 1 awesomeness, bubbly, so fantastic, amazing
   2 dance along like a local crazy, feeling like you just won the *X Factor*   3 melody, track, vocals, riffs

3 1 D (I)   2 A (I)   3 B (F)   4 E (I)   5 C (I)

Sample answer:

I'm certainly not alone in my choice of favourite album. In fact, Michael Jackson's 'Thriller' has sold over 50 million copies worldwide since being released in 1982, and still currently holds the much coveted title of 'best-selling album of all time'. A toe-tapping blend of pop, funk and R&B, it's sure to get everyone grooving at a party, yet also contains unexpected emotional power in the lyrics.

Jam-packed full of catchy melodies such as the opening 'Wanna be startin' something' and the famous 'Beat it', almost every song makes you want to hum along. It's like a feast for the ears, with a range of styles from the soft duet ballad with Paul McCartney 'The Girl is Mine' to the rock/pop of the title track. The album will leave you with no doubt of the unique and extraordinary talent of the King of Pop. What disco would be complete without a few of his renowned numbers?

Unlike much of today's modern pop, this album actually deals with a huge number of deep themes such as jealousy, loneliness and obsession. The song 'Billie Jean', for example, chronicles a story of a crazed fan who insists that she has his baby. Not hard to imagine that the artist was channelling some real experiences in his writing.

It doesn't surprise me at all that this remains the best-selling album of all time and I challenge even the most cynical listener to play 'Thriller' without tapping along.

ADDITIONAL PRACTICE | **Maximiser** p.87, Writing 1–6 |
Photocopiable p.166/186, 12B *A great album* | **MyEnglishLab:**
Cambridge Advanced, Writing 18: Useful expressions for review writing,
Writing 19: Review writing

Review ▶ CB p.129

Aim

- to revise the structures, vocabulary and exam tasks covered in Unit 12

1 – **3** Ask students to complete the exercises, circulating to provide assistance. Ask students to check answers in pairs before checking as a class on eText. Alternatively, set as a homework activity and then go through the answers as a class, or on eText, to check.

Answers

1 1 was planning   2 was meant to be coming   3 was going to ask   4 would be   5 were working   6 was supposed to   7 were due to play   8 would have been

2 1 roar   2 croaked   3 hooted   4 shuffled   5 whooshing   6 buzzing   7 humming   8 snapped

3 1 forgettable   2 attachment   3 comfort   4 dedicated   5 founders   6 clicking   7 audible   8 nostalgic

ADDITIONAL PRACTICE | **Maximiser** p. 88–89, Use of English 6 |
Testmaster online and on **eText**, Unit 12 test, Progress test 4 |
MyEnglishLab: Cambridge Advanced, Mock Writing paper

MyEnglishLab tip

Mock Writing paper
For the Mock Writing paper, students write their tasks on separate sheets of paper. Collect these in to provide individual feedback using the **Marking guidelines** on p.206.

Face value

Vocabulary and Use of English focus ▶ CB p.130

Speaking

Aims
- to introduce the topic of emotions
- to provide spoken practice

1 Students work in pairs to decide if the statements are true or false. If necessary, pre-teach *frown* (a facial expression used to indicate displeasure). Ask for a show of hands for who thinks each statement is true or false, then ask students to turn to p.167 to check their answers.

Alternative activity: *True/False* game

Give each pair two pieces of paper and ask them to write *TRUE* on one and *FALSE* on the other. Read each statement aloud and allow students about 20 seconds to discuss their answer and hold up their piece of paper. Reveal the answer. Each correct answer scores one point and the pair with the most points at the end wins.

Words to describe emotions

Aim
- to expand students' knowledge of vocabulary for describing emotions

2 Ask students to discuss how to form adjectives from the words in the box. Then read the **Language tip** aloud.

Additional activity: Forming adjectives

Write the following nouns on the board: *plenty, congratulations, pain, custom, acid, poison, success, tribe*. Ask students to change the nouns into adjectives using the suffixes in the **Language tip** box.

Check answers and elicit any spelling changes that students noticed between the nouns and the adjective forms (*-y* to *-i* in *plentiful*, drop *-e* in *tribal*).

Answers: plentiful, congratulatory, painful, customary, acidic, poisonous, successful, tribal

3 Students discuss the questions in pairs. Elicit some ideas for each one.

Answers

2 amusement – amused/amusing; astonishment – astonished/astonishing; bitterness – bitter; confusion – confused/confusing; contentment – content/contented; delight – delightful/delighted; embarrassment – embarrassed/embarrassing; exhilaration – exhilarated/exhilarating; frustration – frustrated/frustrating; hysteria – hysterical; indifference – indifferent; nervousness – nervous; relief – relieved; shame – shameful/ashamed

Open cloze (Part 2)

Aim

- to complete an exam-style open cloze task (Reading and Use of English Part 2)

4 Elicit what it means to have something *written all over your face* (it is obvious how you feel about it). Students discuss the questions in pairs. Elicit a few responses to each question.

5 Give students two minutes to read the article for gist and see if they can tell which smile is of frustration and which expresses delight.

6 Elicit what strategies students would use for a Part 2 task. If necessary, refer students to the **Exam focus** on p.198 to review the task and strategies. Give students eight minutes to complete the task.

7 Read the **Exam tip** aloud, then ask students to compare their answers to Activity 6 and answer the questions in Activity 7 as they discuss questions 6 and 8. Check answers as a class.

Answers

6 1 more   2 do   3 As   4 when/being/if   5 by
   6 little   7 On   8 while/whereas

7 1 hardly any   2 in contrast to

Speaking

Aim

- to provide spoken practice

8 Elicit the meaning of the phrase *when you're smiling, the whole world smiles with you* (when you're happy, other people want to be around you). Students discuss the questions in pairs. Elicit some responses to each. Write the next part of the saying on the board: *cry and you cry alone*. Ask what students think it means (when you're upset, other people don't want to be around you) and whether they agree.

ADDITIONAL PRACTICE | **Maximiser** p.90, Vocabulary 1, Use of English 1 | **Photocopiable** p.167/187, 13A *The right word, the right form* | **MyEnglishLab: Cambridge Advanced**, Vocabulary 11: Collocations with *highly*, Use of English 6: Reflexive and personal pronouns

Listening focus ▶ CB p.132

Speaking

Aims

- to introduce the topic of laughter
- to provide spoken practice

Warmer

Check students remember the meaning of *onomatopoeia* from Unit 12. Focus their attention on the picture and ask what sort of onomatopoeic words could be used to describe laughter in English (e.g. *ha ha, hehehe, teehee*). Then ask: *What words are used to describe laughter in your language?*

Write on the board *lol* and *rotfl/rofl*. Ask students if they have seen these and what they mean. (They are acronyms used in online chat: *lol* = laughing out loud; *rotfl/rofl* = rolling on (the) floor laughing.)

1 Students discuss in pairs what sort of situations they laugh in. Elicit some ideas.

Multiple choice (Part 3)

Aim

- to complete an exam-style multiple-choice listening task (Listening Part 3)

2 Elicit what strategies students would use for Listening Part 3 and if necessary, refer them to the **Exam focus** on p.203 to review them. Give students a couple of minutes to underline key words in the questions and alternatives. Read the **Exam tip** aloud, then play the recording twice, pausing for a minute in between. Then check answers as a class.

3 Students discuss the questions in pairs.

4 Students choose the correct alternatives to complete the sentences. Play the recording for students to check.

Answers

2 1 A   2 D   3 A   4 B   5 B   6 C
4 1 advocating   2 longevity   3 impulses
   4 anecdotes   5 contagious

Additional activity: Pronunciation

Ask students to find and write down three adjectives ending in -ous in Activity 4 (*spontaneous, contagious, dangerous*). Ask students to discuss in pairs the number of syllables in each word and to underline the stress.

Answers: spont<u>a</u>neous (4), cont<u>a</u>gious (3), <u>dan</u>gerous (3)

Check students are pronouncing the final vowel sounds in this as a *schwa* /ə/. If you are using eText, click the phonetic chart tab and play the schwa /ə/ phoneme.

ADDITIONAL PRACTICE | Maximiser p.91, Listening 1 | **MyEnglishLab: Cambridge Advanced**, Listening 15: Identifying main ideas and understanding definitions, Listening 16: Identifying stressed words

Grammar focus

▶ CB p.133

Speaking

Aims

- to introduce the topic of the value of art
- to provide spoken practice

1 Students discuss the questions in pairs. Elicit a few responses for each.

Passive forms

Aim

- to review the forms and uses of the passive

2 Check students understand the basic difference between the active and passive. Explain, if necessary, that in an active sentence, the agent (or person doing the action) is also the subject of the sentence, whereas in a passive sentence, the agent is not the subject.

Ask students to match the examples of the passive with the reasons for using it. Check as a class.

3 Working in pairs, students read the active sentences A–D, then answer the questions. Refer students to the **Grammar reference** on p.177 for more notes and examples of the passive. Leave this on display on eText to help students with Activity 5.

4 Give students two minutes to read *The genuine article?* without worrying about the alternatives yet. Elicit the main point that the writer is trying to make.

5 Students choose the correct alternatives in the text, then they compare answers in pairs before you check as a class.

6 Focus students' attention on the **Language tip** and read it aloud. Ask students to turn to p.167 and decide whether the actions listed are acceptable or unacceptable. Finish by asking for a show of hands to indicate opinion on each situation.

Answers

2 A 1 B 3 C 2 D 4

3 Sentences in the active sound less objective, more personal and less official.

4 The value of artwork depends more on who the artist is than the quality of the work.

5 1 is 2 have been 3 has been 4 is 5 is
6 are 7 is being 8 can be

ADDITIONAL PRACTICE | **Maximiser** p.91, Grammar 1–3 |
MyEnglishLab: Cambridge Advanced, Use of English 14: Active or passive voice

Reading focus ▶ CB p.134
Speaking

Aims

- to introduce the topic of photography
- to provide spoken practice

1 Students work in pairs to discuss the questions. Elicit a few responses to each.

Cross-text multiple matching (Part 6)

Aim

- to practise identifying differences of writer opinion in an exam-style cross-text multiple matching task (Reading and Use of English Part 6)

2 Elicit what students remember about Reading and Use of English Part 6 and how to approach the task. If necessary, refer students to the **Exam focus** on p.200 to review the task and strategies. Then read through the **Exam tip** with the class. Give students three minutes to quickly read the text for gist, then elicit the answers to the questions.

3 Ask students to answer the questions individually, then compare answers in pairs before you check as a class.

4 Allow students time to complete the questions, then go through the answers as a class.

5 Students discuss the questions in pairs. Elicit a few responses from the class.

6 Students choose the best verb to complete each sentence, then compare answers in pairs before you check as a class.

7 Elicit the noun forms of the verbs in Activity 6 and write them on the board.

8 Students discuss the questions in pairs. Ask each pair to share something interesting from their discussion.

Answers

3 1 His work continues to be very influential, 'is and will continue to be a giant in the world of photographic portraiture' and 'his relevance also endures as a fashion photographer'.

2 B ('He undoubtedly created a style that later generations of photographers have found impossible not to imitate.')

3 D ('As Penn's reputation inevitably begins to fade')

4 1 B (C: 'Penn is and will continue to be a giant in the world of photographic portraiture'; B: 'He undoubtedly created a style that later generations of photographers have found impossible not to imitate.')

2 D (A: 'From the 1940s until his last work in 2007, he remained constant in his approach, never failing to deliver anything less than utter perfection.'; D: 'Only in the last decade of his life does his work lose some of its magic')

3 A (B: 'In showing the sitters without any of the trappings of celebrity, Penn successfully reveals qualities not seen in other portraits'; A: 'The simplicity of the sets he used in all his portraits cleverly leaves his subjects nowhere to hide, exposing the individual behind the icon.')

4 C (C: 'the omission from this exhibition of some of his most iconic images for *Vogue* results in an incomplete portrayal of his achievements')

6 1 portrays 2 exposed 3 displayed 4 highlights
5 reveals 6 depict

7 portrayal, exposure/exposé, display, highlight, revelation, depiction

Additional activity

Ask students to do an internet search to see some of Irving Penn's work, e.g. on the National Portrait Gallery website, and make a few notes of their own opinions about his work. Put students in small groups to discuss their ideas.

ADDITIONAL PRACTICE | Maximiser p.92–93, Reading 1–2 | **MyEnglishLab: Cambridge Advanced**, Reading 13: Inferring meaning B, Reading 15: Following the theme B

Speaking focus ▶ CB p.136

Speaking

Aim

* to provide spoken practice

Warmer: Discussion

Focus students' attention on the pictures and elicit what each one is of (an artist touching up a waxwork of the Duchess of Cambridge, a painter copying a great master, a magician performing a trick). Elicit where each of the pictures might be taking place (a waxworks museum, an art gallery/museum, a theatre). Ask if anyone has been to any of those places. If only a few have, invite them to tell the class about their experience. If most students have, then put them in pairs to share their experiences.

1 Elicit what strategies students would use for Speaking Part 2. If necessary, refer them to the **Exam focus** on p.204. Students work in pairs and discuss the questions. Elicit some ideas for each one.

Long turn (Part 2)

expressing certainty and uncertainty

Aim

* to practise using a range of language to express certainty and uncertainty in an exam-style speaking task (Speaking Part 2)

2 Play the recording and elicit what the examiner asked. Elicit whether the students' predictions in Activity 1 were correct.

3 Students discuss in pairs which picture each statement is referring to, then check as a class. Students then underline the phrases which express certainty or uncertainty. For each one, elicit the phrase and how certain the speaker is.

4 Students discuss with their partner which of the statements they agree with and why.

5 Play the recording and elicit whether students agree with the candidate's answer to the follow-up question.

6 Play the recording again for students to listen for and note down the phrases for uses 1–3. Check as a class.

7 Read the **Exam tip** aloud, then ask students to practise the task in Activity 2.

8 Students do the tasks on p.157 and p.160, taking turns to be the examiner and the candidate. Remind them to try to use some of the phrases from Activity 3. Ask the 'examiners' to note down any good vocabulary/phrases the 'candidates' use or any vocabulary they repeat, to feed back to the student.

Answers

1 (Suggested answers)

  1 The three pictures depict people working in the arts. They all deal with the theme of real versus fake.

  2 The person in each picture is using a different medium: sculpture, paint, performance. All the pictures are taken in different settings, i.e. a waxworks museum, an art gallery, a theatre.

3 the waxworks museum: 1, 6; the art gallery: 4; the magician: 2, 3, 5

  certainty: There's no denying the fact that; I'm convinced that; There's no doubt at all that; I can say with confidence that

  uncertainty: It's doubtful that

6 1 it's quite hard to say

  2 I suppose … then that might …

  3 a high level of expertise, would take years to perfect

ADDITIONAL PRACTICE | Maximiser p.94, Speaking 1–2 | **MyEnglishLab: Cambridge Advanced**, Speaking 7: Answering the listening candidate's question

Grammar focus

▶ CB p.137

Speaking

Aims
● to present linking adverbials in context
● to provide spoken practice

1 Check students know how to pronounce *suit* correctly (rhymes with *boot*). In pairs, students discuss the questions. Elicit a few responses.

2 Students quickly read the text without worrying about the gaps, then discuss questions 1–4 with a partner. Elicit some responses to each question.

3 Elicit the answer and evidence as a class.

Answers

2 2 C

3 advantages mentioned: gain respect and credibility in public life, sign of affluence and good taste, wear a suit and you display discipline, commitment and ambition, the most effective way to win instant acceptance

3 evidence of formal written style: passive forms, no contractions, long complex sentences

abstract academic lexis (e.g. *universally recognised, attire, credibility, donning, impeccably, utter, signify, be well advised, win instant acceptance*)

Linking adverbials

Aim
● to review linking adverbials

4 Read out the **Language tip**. For a summary of linking adverbials and their uses, ask students to read **Grammar reference** 1.1 on p.170. Students read the text in Activity 2 again and cross out the linking adverbials that are *not* possible for each gap. Check answers as a class.

5 Students answer the questions, referring to the **Grammar reference** if necessary. Then check answers as a class.

6 Working in pairs, students complete the activity. Circulate, checking the linking adverbials are being used correctly. Elicit a few reasons from the class.

Answers

4 1 B 2 C 3 C 4 C 5 A 6 B

5 1 additionally, as well as this, besides this, furthermore, moreover, what's more

2 consequently, for this reason, given the fact that, in view of the fact that

3 alternatively, apart from, even so, in contrast, on the contrary, on the other hand

ADDITIONAL PRACTICE | **Maximiser** p.93, Grammar 1–2 |
Photocopiable p.168/188, 13B *Can you continue?*

Writing focus ▶ CB p.138

Speaking

Aims
● to introduce vocabulary for talking about dress codes
● to provide spoken practice

Warmer: Clothes compounds

Write the following words in two columns on the board:

high	gown
nose	flops
mini	heels
bathing	suit
flip	sweatshirt
hooded	skirt
ball	ring

Ask students to work in pairs to match the words from each column to form compound words for items of clothing and accessories. Check as a class, pointing out for each case whether it is written as one word or two. Elicit the shortened forms of *hooded sweatshirt* (*hoodie*), *miniskirt* (*mini*), *high heels* (*heels*).

Answers: high heels, nose ring, miniskirt, bathing suit, flip flops, hooded sweatshirt, ballgown

1 Students discuss the questions in pairs. Elicit some answers from the class. Point out that *dress code* is another example of a two-word compound.

Essay (Part 1)

planning your essay

Aim

- to practise planning and writing an exam-style essay (Writing Part 1)

2 Ask students to read the exam task and then ask them to make a plan including points 1–4. Students could do this in pairs if they wish. Elicit a model plan and write it on the board.

3 Set the writing task for homework. Suggest students allow 35 minutes for the writing, as 10 minutes of the allocated exam time would be used up with the planning. Remind students of the useful language for essays in the **Writing reference** on p.186. Read the **Exam tip** with students and tell them to include at least three different linking adverbials and two passive forms in their essay.

4 This could also be set for homework. Then collect the essays to provide individual feedback.

Teaching tip

Ask students to ensure their essay meets the required word count. Tell students they should practise estimating the length of their writing, to avoid wasting time counting individual words in the exam. In the Writing paper, there is 90 minutes to complete both Parts 1 and 2, with 220–260 words required for each part.

Answers

2 Sample plan:

Introduction: current situation: no clothing guidelines, currently considering dress code due to safety and image concerns

Advantage 1: improve image – scruffiness and offensive T-shirts have led to complaints from community

Advantage 2: improve safety – students wearing unsafe footwear has caused and will cause accidents

Conclusion: safety is most important reason because student safety is school's responsibility

3 Sample answer:

Introducing a dress code

We often hear that it is important for young people to be able to express themselves by what they wear. At our college, our lack of clothing guidelines has led some students to dress in a way that compromises both safety and our reputation in the community. Items of concern include ripped clothing, hoods that obscure the face, offensive T-shirts and very high platform heels. In this essay, I will discuss two advantages of introducing a dress code at our college.

The image that we present to the community is important for a number of reasons, but primarily because overly casual dress makes it more difficult to place students in homestays and on work experience. Recently, this problem seems to have escalated as we have received some phone complaints about students' scruffy appearance. Additionally, it has come to my attention that a few students have worn T-shirts with slogans that could be considered xenophobic. It seems obvious that implementing a dress code will improve the college's image.

With regard to health and safety, three students have fallen down the stairs during the last month. One of them, who had been wearing a pair of stiletto heels at the time, unfortunately broke her leg. I have grave concerns that without a dress code outlining suitable footwear choices, further accidents may be inevitable.

In my view, keeping people safe at our school is our responsibility. Consequently, this is the most pressing reason why it is time to introduce a dress code, even if it is initially unpopular with the student body.

ADDITIONAL PRACTICE | Maximiser p.95, Writing 1–4 | **MyEnglishLab: Cambridge Advanced**, Writing 20: Proofreading

Review ► CB p.139

► CB p.139

Aim

- to revise the structures, vocabulary and exam tasks covered in Unit 13

1 – **4** Ask students to complete the exercises, circulating to provide assistance. Ask students to check answers in pairs before checking as a class on eText. Alternatively, set as a homework activity and then go through the answers as a class, or on eText, to check.

Answers

1 1 is   2 for   3 were   4 without   5 before   6 A
7 only   8 ourselves

2 1 indifferent   2 discontented   3 astonishment
4 frustrating   5 relieved   6 nervousness
7 delightful   8 amusing

3 1 was to have been banned   2 is considered to have been   3 was/had been thought to have been   4 is nothing to be done/is nothing that can be done/isn't anything to be done   5 want to be seen (by others) (to be)   6 caused/provoked confusion among/in/amongst/to

4 1 Given   2 Even so   3 Despite   4 What's more

ADDITIONAL PRACTICE | Testmaster online and on **eText**, Unit 13 test |
MyEnglishLab: Cambridge Advanced, Mock Listening paper

Brilliant ideas

14

Listening and Vocabulary focus ▶ CB p.140
Sentence completion (Part 2)

Aim

- to complete an exam-style sentence completion task (Listening Part 2)

Warmer: Science

Write *science* on the board and elicit other forms of the word: *scientist, scientific/unscientific*. Write up the following areas of science on the board: *astronomy, zoology, geology, meteorology, botany, physics, neurology, chemistry*. In pairs, ask students to discuss the words for a scientist that studies each of these areas and what they specialise in. Check as a class. If anyone in the class studies or works in science, invite them to tell the class briefly what they do and what they like about it.

Ask students to share with their partner which of these areas they would most be interested in knowing a bit more about.

Answers: an *astronomer* studies stars and planets; a *zoologist* studies animals and their behaviour; a *geologist* studies rocks and the way they have changed since the earth was formed; a *meteorologist* studies the weather; a *botanist* studies plants; a *physicist* studies physical objects and substances, and natural forces such as light, heat and movement; a *neurologist* studies the brain; a *chemist* studies the structure of substances and how they combine with each other.

(Note: *chemist* is also the British English word for *pharmacist/pharmacy*.)

1 Ask students to discuss the question in pairs.

2 Play the recording and then elicit the answer.

3 Elicit what students remember about Listening Part 2 and how to approach the task. If necessary, refer them to the **Exam focus** on p.202 to review the task and strategies. Give students time to read through the text. Read the **Exam tip** aloud and play the recording twice for them to listen and complete the gaps. Go through the answers with the class.

4 Students discuss the question in pairs. Elicit a few responses.

Teaching tip

Remind students that in the exam they will need to transfer their answers to the answer sheet.

Answers

2 watching experiments, talking to the lecturer, listening to music afterwards

3 1 radio producer   2 bands   3 experiments
   4 black holes   5 questions   6 networking
   7 coffee houses   8 relevance

Multi-part verbs

science and research

Aim

- to expand students' vocabulary related to science and research

5 Students discuss the question in pairs. Elicit some ideas from a few students.

Alternative activity: Paper plane competition
For a bit of fun, students could make a paper plane each and have a quick competition with others in the class or in small groups to see whose plane goes the furthest. Then ask students to discuss what changes they would need to make to their competition to make it more scientific.

6 Tell students that they are going to read a scientific article about designing a study for paper planes, and elicit whether it should use formal or informal language (formal). Tell them that there is also some more specific vocabulary used for academic writing. Look at the first item (1) with the class and elicit the answer (*determine*). Point out that although all the alternatives fit grammatically, *determine* is a more scientific alternative than *find out* and *know*. Ask students to read the rest of the article and choose the most appropriate alternative in each case.

7 Read the **Language tip** aloud. Elicit an example of a formal single-word verb which could have a similar meaning to *put forward* (e.g. *propose*). Point out that the second example with *put forward* is more informal than the first, and that in scientific writing we can use multi-part verbs, but they must be used with the parts together (e.g. *put forward a suggestion*), not separated (e.g. *put a suggestion forward*); this is because in the second pattern, they are more informal and so not suitable.

Students replace the underlined verbs with the correct form of the multi-part verbs.

8 Students decide which other patterns can be used with the multi-part verbs, then compare answers in pairs before you check as a class.

Answers

6 1 determine   2 observed   3 arrive at   4 validate
   5 varying   6 plot   7 findings   8 initial

7 1 carried out   2 looking into   3 make clear
   4 put forward   5 take into account   6 point out
   7 set out   8 take issue with

8 1 A ✗, B ✗, C ✓   2 A ✓, B ✓, C ✗   3 A ✓, B ✓, C ✗
   4 A ✓, B ✓, C ✗   5 A ✓, B ✓, C ✗

Speaking

Aims

- to practise using scientific vocabulary
- to provide spoken practice

9 Students discuss how they would design studies to test hypotheses 1 and 2. Remind them to use some of the vocabulary from the lesson. Elicit some ideas.

Teaching tip

Irregular plural forms
Remind students that some nouns in English have irregular plural forms. Many of these nouns originally came to English from Latin or Greek (e.g. hypothesis – hypotheses; phenomenon – phenomena; analysis – analyses; thesis – theses).

ADDITIONAL PRACTICE | **Maximiser** p.96, Listening 1, Vocabulary 1–2 | **MyEnglishLab: Cambridge Advanced**, Vocabulary 9: Research and study, Vocabulary 14: Research at university, Vocabulary 15: Words relating to the concept of *idea*

Grammar focus

▶ CB p.142

Speaking

Aims

- to introduce the topic of dreams
- to provide spoken practice

1 Give students a minute to think about their answers to the questions. Then put students in pairs to discuss their answers. Elicit a few responses for each.

Cohesion

Aim

- to identify ways to make a text cohesive

2 Students read the article, then discuss the answer to the question in pairs. Elicit the answer.

3 Read the **Language tip** with the class. Elicit the meaning of *cohesion* (all the parts are connected or related in a reasonable way to form a whole). For definitions of *reference*, *substitution*, *ellipsis*, *conjunction* and *lexical cohesion*, see **Grammar reference** 3.2 on p.171. Students underline the different ways the scientists are referred to in the article. Elicit the answers from the class.

4 Students find the words and phrases. Check as a class. Tell students that this is an example of lexical cohesion.

5 Students find the examples. Check as a class.

6 Remind students that linking words are also called *conjunctions*. Students complete the paragraphs, then compare answers in pairs before you check as a class.

7 Students discuss the questions in pairs.

Answers

3 Otto Loewi: one scientist, his, Loewi, he, him
John Eccles: the other, he, his, him, Eccles, himself
Loewi and Eccles: their, Both, they

4 nap: siesta, full night's sleep
question: problem, challenges
wrote: jotted … down

5 the other (scientist), Both (scientists)

6 1 Like   2 while   3 so   4 until   5 but
6 however/though

Additional activity

For homework, assign each student a year and ask them to search the internet (in English) for some information about the person who won the Nobel Prize for Science that year. Tell them to prepare a one-minute summary for what the person's/group's main breakthrough was and how that relates to life today. Tell students that they should avoid reading/printing large sections of text. After each student has shared their summary in groups of four or five, ask each group to discuss which of the discoveries they believe is the most significant and to share this one with the class.

ADDITIONAL PRACTICE | Maximiser p.97, Grammar 1,

Use of English focus

▶ CB p.143

Key word transformations (Part 4)

Aim

- to complete an exam-style key word transformation task (Reading and Use of English Part 4)

1 Elicit what students know about Reading and Use of English Part 4 and how to approach the task. If necessary, refer them to the **Exam focus** on p.199 to review the task and strategies. Focus students' attention on the first sentence as an example. Read through the two sentences and elicit what is being tested (hypothetical meaning). Do not elicit the words in the gap and emphasise that students do not need to fill in the gaps yet. Ask students to discuss in pairs what is being tested in the rest of the examples, then check as a class.

2 Read the **Exam tip** aloud, then ask students to complete the sentences in Activity 1. Students compare answers in pairs before you check as a class.

3 Remind students that Strategies 5 and 6 in the **Exam focus** are concerned with checking answers. Tell students that the next two exercises practise checking, as the answers are not correct. Explain that in this exercise the answers don't make sense as they are each missing a word. Students add the word, then compare answers in pairs before you check as a class.

4 Explain that in this exercise the current answers make sense grammatically but do not convey the correct meaning. Students make the necessary changes, then compare answers in pairs before you check as a class.

5 Give students six minutes to complete the exercise, then check as a class.

Answers

1–2 1 only I had written down (hypothetical meaning)
2 must have been (modal verbs)   **3** was only by going (introductory *it*)   **4** was to (later) change (future in the past)

3 1 sooner had I arrived than   **2** have a terrible memory for   **3** on behalf of my daughter   **4** you are determined to remember

4 1 it is less difficult to forget   **2** take back the dress to/take the dress back to   **3** never struck me that   **4** it when people give me

5 1 wish I hadn't sent   **2** must have happened   **3** I succeeded in getting   **4** did to resolve the problem was   **5** rumoured/said to be retiring   **6** no circumstances should you say anything

Additional activity

Write *enormous chocolate cake* on the board. In pairs, refer students to the box in Activity 1. Ask them to discuss what each grammar point is and come up with an example for each of the first five points which includes the words on the board. Refer students to the **Grammar reference** for help if necessary.

Sample answers:

No sooner had I put the enormous chocolate cake on the table than it disappeared. (emphasis with inversion)

I was going to give you a piece of my enormous chocolate cake but I'm afraid it has all gone. (future in the past)

If I had an enormous chocolate cake, I'd share it with the class./If only I had an enormous chocolate cake. (hypothetical meaning)

It is widely believed that an enormous chocolate cake helps people feel better. (introductory *it*)

I could make an enormous chocolate cake for your birthday. (modal verbs)

ADDITIONAL PRACTICE | Maximiser p.97, Use of English 1 | **MyEnglishLab: Cambridge Advanced**, Use of English 16: Key word transformations

Speaking focus ▶ CB p.144
All parts
improving your performance

Aim
- to identify strategies to improve performance in the Speaking paper

Warmer: Discussion
Elicit the four parts of the Speaking paper and what they involve. To check, refer students to the **Exam focus** on p.204–205 if necessary. Ask students to discuss the following questions in pairs: *What aspects of the Speaking paper do you find easiest? What do you find challenging?* Elicit some answers. Note down any recurring themes for further practice.

1 Play the recording, then ask students to discuss the questions in pairs. Elicit the answers.

2 Ask students to turn to the strategies for Part 2 in the **Exam focus** on p.204. Get them to look at the pictures on p.144 and predict what sort of vocabulary they might hear. Play the recording, then elicit the answers.

3 In pairs, students turn to p.157 and p.160 to practise an exam Speaking task (Part 2).

4 Students look at the word map. Check they understand *telepathy* (communicating from mind to mind, without any outward communication). Play the recording, then elicit the answers.

5 Students discuss the question in pairs.

6 Students do the activity on p.154, then evaluate their performance against the **Marking guidelines** on p.207. For extra practice, ask them to swap partners and tell their new partner about their self-evaluation and identify something they would like to improve. Students repeat the task with their new partner, aiming to improve the area(s) they identified.

7 Play the recording and elicit the answers.

8 Students complete the activity in groups of three.

Answers

1 Gustave. He should give longer, more communicative answers.

2 Maria doesn't answer the first question (why people choose to do research like this). Gustave's answer is long enough but only after the examiner prompts him.

4 Both candidates use the strategies well, but Gustave is a little less inclined to involve or encourage Maria and less willing to compromise at the end of their discussion.

7 Maria performs well. Gustave should give longer, more communicative answers without having to be prompted by the examiner.

ADDITIONAL PRACTICE | Maximiser p.97–98, Speaking 1–2 | **Photocopiable** p.169/189, 14A *Over to you* | **MyEnglishLab: Cambridge Advanced**, Speaking 19: Using discourse markers

Grammar focus

▶ CB p.145

Grammar quiz

Aim

• to practise identifying and correcting grammatical errors

Warmer: Discussion

Students discuss the following questions in pairs: *What aspects of grammar do you find challenging in English? Are there any aspects which are very different from your own language?*

1 Students work in pairs. One student from each pair does the quiz on p.145 and the other does the quiz on p.168. Students then check their answers with their partner.

Alternative activity: Grammar game

Students work in pairs to complete the quiz on p.145. Give them 20 minutes. They then swap it with another pair to mark. Elicit the answers with the class or show them on eText. Pairs get one point for each correct answer and one point for saying which grammar point is involved in the incorrect sentences (a possible total of 48 points). The pair with the most points wins the game.

2 Students look back over some of their work and write a quiz with five questions. They then swap with a partner and answer each other's questions.

Answers

1 (*Below are the correct sentences and the grammar point tested in each.*)

1 I have great respect and admiration for my uncle but I don't think he understands me very well. (continuous tenses)

2 No sooner had I closed the door than I realised I had left the key in the pocket of my other pair of jeans. (emphasis with inversion)

3 In my opinion, governments should be doing a lot more to support the unemployed. (articles)

4 The person in my family with whom I have never had much rapport is my younger sister. (relative clauses)

5 I regret to inform you that all the positions have been filled and we will not be accepting any further applications. (verb patterns)

6 Sometimes life just seems so unfair. It really shouldn't be like that. (modal verbs)

7 I sometimes wish I could stop eating so many sweets. They're really bad for your teeth. (hypothetical meaning)

8 Some people say that this is the beginning of a new era of greater peace and harmony. I certainly hope so. (substitution and ellipsis)

9 She's as thin as both of her sisters. Their mother was a very slim woman too. (comparison)

10 It is completely impossible to find good sources of information on this topic online. (modifying adverbs)

11 The university would have got in touch with you by now if you had been given the scholarship. (conditionals)

12 Let's ask Kim to give us a lift. Otherwise we'll have to get a taxi. (conditionals)

13 However well you think you know someone, in some ways we are all, in fact, a mystery to one another. (-*ever* words)

14 Picking up the phone, I heard an unfamiliar voice. It said, 'Hello, dear.' (participle clauses)

15 We explained that the weather was about to improve and the man said he hoped that it would. (reported speech)

16 I had to visit some relatives in Melbourne. What this meant was I couldn't attend the meeting. (emphasis – cleft sentences)

17 She wasn't angry nor was she sad, just disappointed with their behaviour. (conjunctions)

18 Tim has a terrible loathing of jazz. He really can't stand it. (countable and uncountable nouns)

19 It's amazing how people have got so used to using smartphones in such a short time. (introductory *it*)

20 The house is said to have been built in the late fifteenth century. (the passive)

21 Given that she is very interested in art, she would certainly enjoy a holiday in Italy. (linking adverbs)

22 When I was born, it would have been impossible to predict that I would end up living here. (future in the past)

23 I was told the stopover would be just over an hour but we were stranded in the airport for a whole day. (future in the past)

24 She warned us not to go into the water because there were jellyfish. (reported speech)

ADDITIONAL PRACTICE | Maximiser p.98, Grammar 1–3

Reading focus ▶ CB p.146

Speaking

Aim

• to provide spoken practice

1 Students do the quiz on p.169, then compare answers in pairs. Tell students that they will find out some of the answers when they read the article.

Gapped text (Part 7)

Aim

• to complete an exam-style gapped text task (Reading and Use of English Part 7)

2 Elicit what students know about Reading and Use of English Part 7 and how to approach the task. If necessary, refer them to the **Exam focus** on p.200 to review the task and strategies. Students read the article and answer the questions in the quiz that they couldn't answer. See Answers below for the answer to question 6.

3 Students choose paragraphs for each gap, then compare answers in pairs. Elicit the answers and justifications for each one.

4 In pairs, students share a situation where they were not given credit for something they did, and how they felt about it.

5 Students choose the correct meanings, then compare answers in pairs before you check as a class.

Answers

2 1 Guglielmo Marconi   2 Thomas Edison   3 alternating current and direct current   4 alternating current   5 direct current   6 Heinrich Hertz, James Clerk Maxwell and Christian Hülsmeyer are all credited with the invention of radar.

3 1 G (The 'people who so rapidly answered the call' in the first paragraph were 'Tesla's hugely loyal fan-base' referred to in paragraph G.)

2 D (*one of these* (line 1, paragraph D) refers to a 'Tesla coil' mentioned in the second paragraph.)

3 A (*It*, the first word in paragraph A, refers to Marconi beating him to the radio, mentioned in the third paragraph; *this*, in the fourth paragraph, refers to the electric light bulb.)

4 F (*also*, in paragraph F, links Tesla's contribution to making the light bulb workable, in the fourth paragraph, with his making enough electricity come out of sockets in paragraph F.)

5 C (*great rival*, in paragraph C, refers to Edison and their intense antipathy, mentioned in the fifth paragraph; *though*, in the sixth paragraph, concedes that Tesla was a man of exceptional talents despite fans tending to exaggerate Tesla's inventive genius, as mentioned in paragraph C.)

6 E (*strange habits*, in the seventh paragraph, refers to sleeping only two to three hours a night and obsessions such as a loathing for round objects, as referred to in paragraph E.)

5 1 B   2 A   3 B   4 A   5 A   6 A

Vocabulary

expressions with *matter*

Aim

- to review expressions with *matter*

6 Students choose the correct alternative in each sentence. Check answers as a class.

Answers

6 1 dark **2** fact **3** principle **4** interest **5** time
 6 life and death

Additional activity: Cohesion

To extend with a strong class, see how many cohesive devices students can remember from the lesson on p.142 (reference, substitution, ellipsis, conjunctions, lexical cohesion). Ask students to find the following in the first paragraph of the article on Nikola Tesla:

1 an example of ellipsis

2 an example of substitution

3 an example of lexical cohesion

4 an example of a conjunction

Suggested answers:

1 The group (that/which was) promoting; even more (money) than they thought they needed

2 his (Tesla's) fans; the people (fans); the call (pleas to fund a museum)

3 *Plea, fund, pledge, donation, appeal, launch* and *promote* are all examples of lexicon related to fundraising.

4 until, after, But

ADDITIONAL PRACTICE | Maximiser p.100–101, Reading 1–4, Vocabulary 1 | **Photocopiable** p.170/189,14B *First to the top* | **MyEnglishLab: Cambridge Advanced**, Reading 16: Logical and cohesive development A, Reading 17: Logical and cohesive development B, Vocabulary 10: Review of activities 7–10

Writing focus ▶ CB p.148

Essay (Part 1)

using linking words and phrases

Aims

- to review features of a good essay
- to practise using linking words and phrases in an essay

1 Students complete the sentences, then compare answers in pairs before you check as a class.

2 Give students time to read the task and essay and find examples of the good pieces of advice. Elicit the answers from the class.

3 Ask students to find the four linking words and match them to uses 1–4. Check as a class.

4 Set this task as homework. Remind students to set a timer for 45 minutes. Collect in the essays and provide individual feedback.

Answers

1 1 Don't **2** Do **3** Do **4** Do **5** Do **6** Do
 7 Do **8** Don't

2 (Suggested answers)

2 'While this would almost certainly give scientific research a more positive image, it implies placing restrictions on the freedom and autonomy of the press.' (paragraph 2)

3 'In my view, the second of these two approaches should be implemented.' (paragraph 4)

4 'Nevertheless, any resistance might be overcome by' (paragraph 3)

5 'A potential difficulty here is that some adults' (paragraph 3)

6 'But how might this be achieved?' (paragraph 1)

7 (many examples) 'This lack of appreciation is the result of insufficient information about scientists and the work they do.' (paragraph 1)

3 **1** One possible approach   **2** While   **3** In my view
4 thus

4 Sample answer:

<u>Ways to encourage young people to train for careers in science</u>

Nowadays we frequently hear about the lack of students pursuing scientific careers. How can we demonstrate to the younger generation that science is a rewarding and satisfying field? In this essay I will discuss two methods that schools could employ to help persuade teenagers to consider further study in this area.

One possible approach would be to ensure that career advisors are on board by providing them with materials, training and even incentives for promoting science. While this would be fairly easy to implement superficially, a lot of information dates extremely quickly. In addition, generally speaking, career advisors have little background themselves in physics, chemistry and biology and therefore may not be able to drum up genuine enthusiasm.

A second tactic that schools might take would be to invite scientists to come to their school to talk about their work. What might prove difficult would be to secure the scientists themselves, as they are often extremely busy. It would also be crucial to enlist experts able to relate to adolescents or they might actually have an adverse effect.

Overall, I would say that the most effective measure would be to have guest speakers. Hearing an exciting story from the field is much more likely to influence career choice than some second-hand advice.

ADDITIONAL PRACTICE | **Maximiser** p.99, Writing 1–3 |
MyEnglishLab: Cambridge Advanced, Writing 3: Using linkers in an essay

Progress test 3 ▶ CB p.149

Aims

- to revise the structures and vocabulary covered in Units 11–14
- to practise Reading and Use of English Parts 1–4 type activities

1 – **7**   Ask students to complete the exercises, circulating to provide assistance, or set them as a test. Suggested time limit: 45 minutes for Activities 1–3 and 45 minutes for Activities 4–7. Ask students to check answers in pairs before you check as a class on eText. Alternatively, set as a homework activity and then go through the answers as a class.

Answers

1 **1** carried   **2** forward   **3** took   **4** into   **5** at
6 down

2 **1** A   **2** B   **3** B   **4** C   **5** B   **6** C

3 **1** She   **2** they   **3** both/the   **4** Although/Though
5 none   **6** one   **7** would   **8** to   **9** so   **10** had

4 **1** B   **2** A   **3** C   **4** D   **5** A   **6** B   **7** A   **8** C

5 **1** around   **2** out   **3** according   **4** made
5 which   **6** this   **7** where   **8** without

6 **1** indignantly   **2** abilities/ability   **3** criticism
4 demanding   **5** suspicious   **6** mismatches
7 untrustworthy   **8** responses

7 **1** suggest (that) you talk   **2** are in danger of losing
3 are sometimes prevented from entering   **4** despite being worth   **5** is to be shown/is to be put on show
6 is thought to have invented

ADDITIONAL PRACTICE | **Maximiser** p.102–103, Use of English 7 |
Testmaster online and on **eText**, Unit 14 test, Progress test 5 |
MyEnglishLab: Cambridge Advanced, Mock Speaking paper

MyEnglishLab tip

Mock Speaking paper
Students will need a partner for these activities and someone to act as 'examiner'. You can print the tasks for use in class if necessary. Before students do the task, ask them to reread the **Marking guidelines** for speaking on p.207. Students could do the mock in groups of four, with one pair completing Parts 1–4 as candidates while the other pair act as examiners, time-keeping and noting down any good vocabulary/phrases the candidates use. After pairs swap roles, give them time to discuss the feedback and what they need to improve on.

8   Students replace the underlined verbs with the correct form of the multi-part verbs.

Audio scripts

Unit 1, Speaking focus, Activity 2

 01

Examiner: Good morning. My name is Irene and this is my colleague, Deborah. And your names are?

Karl: Karl Weber.

Elena: Elena Calvi.

Examiner: Can I have your mark sheets, please? Thank you. First of all, we'd like to know something about you. Where are you from, Karl?

Karl: I'm German. I live just outside Berlin now but I grew up in the centre of the city.

Examiner: And Elena?

Elena: Italy.

Examiner: What do you do there, Elena?

Elena: I work in a hotel.

Examiner: Karl, what do you like most about the area where you grew up?

Karl: Well, there are so many things, really, but I suppose the one that really stands out for me is living so close to a great city like Berlin.

Examiner: Elena, who has more influence on your life: your friends or your family?

Elena: My family.

Examiner: Why?

Elena: I don't know, really. They just do.

Unit 1, Grammar focus, Activity 2

 02

For years I'd been telling all my friends that I wanted to get away from the hustle and bustle of London to somewhere quiet and peaceful. What I had in mind was a little cottage near the sea. Well, they do say you shouldn't wish too hard or your wish just might come true and that's exactly what happened. Out of the blue, I was offered a job managing a hotel in a remote part of Ireland. Suddenly, it seemed to me that I had, in fact, always been a real city person who could negotiate the complexities of urban life, the crowded underground trains, the roar of traffic, the millions of people – all of it – and without blinking. But the job offer was too good to turn down and a few weeks later I found myself in Castletownbere. In less than 24 hours I'd gone from a huge metropolis with a population of over 8,000,000 to a quaint fishing village with barely 800 inhabitants. It was a huge change.

By the beginning of next month I will have been living here for exactly a year. I've been looking back, retracing my steps and coming to understand just how great a change it has actually been. I've got to know almost all of those 800 people and found a real sense of belonging, though I've also occasionally longed for the anonymity of city life. I've spent hours exploring the glorious countryside by bicycle and on foot, and have discovered a taste for silence and solitude I didn't know I had. I've also had great fun managing the hotel and getting to know some of its rather eccentric regular guests. By the time the first year comes to an end, almost all my London friends will have been here to stay and they love it almost as much as I do. Of course, there are many things I miss, though in the end the crowded underground trains and the noisy London traffic I can easily do without.

Unit 1, Listening focus, Activity 3

 03

Speaker 1: When I was in the process of moving, I began to wonder if it was really feasible to live in such a small space. I mean, I've always had lots of stuff, so whittling it down has been a pretty daunting task. I'm still working on it, actually. It's hard to part with some things but the payoff is that there's less and less clutter and a lot less dusting and tidying to do than in my old flat. I spend more time outside, of course, because you can feel pretty hemmed in in such a small space and that can be too much at times. I was stuck inside for a couple of days last week in all that heavy rain and I really did begin to feel that I was going to go crazy.

Speaker 2: This was to be our dream home but in some ways it's turned out to be a complete nightmare. I'd always lived in flats where I could pretty much see into every room, so I had no idea how edgy I was going to feel in a large house like this. I have to be careful not to watch horror films on TV because I start to imagine every creak and groan from the rafters is actually someone lurking in one of the other rooms. Of course, it's glorious to have so much space after years of living in poky flats. I've finally been able to take my grandfather's grand piano and a beautiful old sideboard out of storage. I would never have got them into my old place.

Speaker 3: I used to think it would be good to move out of the centre of the city but, really, we've got it all right here. Apart from the usual shops, there's a cinema, some rather pleasant cafés and even a really great arts centre with a theatre where they show excellent movies. If we lived out of town, we'd both really miss all that. Sue is always on about how much she would love a big house with a garden but I think in her heart of hearts she would never be able to justify the expense. A nice balcony with a few pot plants is enough, though I must admit here we're walled in by other buildings on all sides and that gets to me sometimes.

Speaker 4: I tried to find something a bit bigger but everything I looked at was way outside my price range. I've had to put some of my things into storage but perhaps one day when I have my dream home I'll have space for more than a sofa bed and a desk! I tend to go out to eat – even for breakfast. The kitchenette is so tiny there's barely room to chop a carrot and it's difficult to get rid of the cooking smells afterwards. There are loads of cafés on this street anyway, so I'm spoilt for choice in terms of places to eat. A lot of my neighbours hang out there in the mornings as well, so I've got to know them. There's a real sense of community here.

Speaker 5: Where we lived before there were rooms we just never made the most of. The dining room, for example: we always ate in the kitchen, so we barely went in there. It's not at all cramped here but there's no excess either. We're in and out of all the rooms every day. We both work from home and so we've each claimed one of the spare bedrooms as an office. Mine is right next to the room our neighbour, Tom, has set up as a gym and I can hear him working out, which gets on my nerves at times. Still, at least it reminds me that I'm living in close proximity to other people. That can be quite comforting, actually.

Unit 1, Writing focus, Activity 1

 04

I like to think I know most of my neighbours but perhaps I could get to know more of them or get to know the ones I do know a bit better. There is a neighbourhood association and they hold all sorts of social events, like barbecues and picnics and even run courses of various kinds, like yoga and language classes, but I somehow haven't managed to get involved in anything they offer apart from the annual street party, which is really great.

I read something interesting the other day that made me think. I read that the average American moves more than ten times in a lifetime. That sounds like a lot to me, but I bet if you move so often, you don't have much of a chance to get to know your neighbours at all. Apparently, that's the case, so someone has come up with the bright idea of creating an online forum so that neighbours can get to know each other. The publicity says it's like a town square where people can go to voice opinions and needs and even offer things for sale. If it sounds a bit far-fetched to you for people to have to go online to get to know their neighbours, you might be surprised to hear how successful it has been. Apparently, in one small town where the forum was launched almost two thirds of the town's inhabitants had posted after the end of the first year. Perhaps if there was a forum like this for my neighbourhood, more busy people like me might get involved.

Personally, I'd like to see a local market place with stalls offering goods and services. I love markets and the idea of seeing what my neighbours have to offer really appeals to me.

Unit 2, Speaking focus, Activity 2

 05

Speaker 1: I'm not saying I'm completely addicted but I would feel anxious if I didn't get a text every couple of minutes. I'm just used to talking to my friends pretty much all the time. I mean, obviously, there are exceptions – I do turn my phone off when I'm in class and I don't text when I'm having dinner with my family. But generally speaking, I like to be in contact twenty-four seven.

Speaker 2: That totally depends on the situation – I'm sure some people would argue that not replying immediately shows a lack of interest or respect but the way I see it, there's more to life than texting. And I don't have a problem if my texts go unanswered for hours or even days.

Speaker 3: I think that goes without saying. We all know people who've been dumped by text and that's a really mean and cowardly thing to do. Only the most insensitive person would even consider doing that.

Speaker 4: I wouldn't go that far but yes, sometimes texting is preferable because you've got a bit more time to respond. I think it's fair to say that a lot of people are more outgoing and funny in their text messages than they are in a group situation.

Unit 2, Speaking focus, Activity 6

 06

In this picture I can see some people sitting in the cinema. Most people are laughing and seem to be enjoying the film but one girl in the middle of the photo isn't watching the film. She's texting, and her friend who's sitting next to her and eating popcorn is looking at her phone. Maybe he's trying to read her text. She could be texting because she's not interested in the film or perhaps she's responding to a text from a friend. Or maybe she's telling someone about the film she's watching. I think this is a strange thing to do because you can't concentrate on two things at once and she'll probably miss something important in the film. It doesn't look like the message is urgent because she doesn't look worried.

In this picture there are two people reading text messages while they're eating. I think they're probably brother and sister and they're at home. I think they must be eating lunch because the girl is eating pizza. They look very focused on their phones, so the messages are probably from friends, but they are completely ignoring each other. I don't think it's a good idea to use your phone at the table – it's better to have a conversation with the people you're with.

Unit 2, Listening focus, Activity 2

 07

1

Man: I really related to the ideas in the book. I found it quite reassuring. Before I read this, I just thought I was weird because I didn't enjoy meeting new people or going to parties. I didn't realise I was an introvert and that there was actually absolutely nothing wrong with that at all.

Woman: Of course there isn't! In fact, I actually prefer introverts to extroverts. Extroverts are so attention-seeking and are only really interested in themselves. Introverts are much nicer people. Reading this book confirmed that for me.

Man: The ideas were great but sometimes I found reading it a bit of a slog – especially all those long descriptions of studies on the brain and how that accounts for the way we behave. I found it all a bit boring, to be honest. A quick summary would have been enough. And, anyway, some of the results seemed to come to opposite conclusions.

Woman: Yeah, I'm always quite sceptical about that kind of thing. Most of those case studies are probably unreliable, so not worth devoting so many pages to them. It's a pity because she's good at making complicated scientific information quite accessible, which is a real achievement.

2

Man: I'm not saying people shouldn't use social networking sites. It's just the online relationships with casual acquaintances I have a problem with – I mean, everyone presents a certain cultivated image of themselves online, which isn't always totally accurate. You know, the way

people might admit to having a bad day in private, even if they'd never do so publicly online.

Woman: Exactly. And you can't blame them for that. I wouldn't dream of mentioning any of my insecurities online. The problem is that if all you see of someone is endless photos on Facebook of parties and exciting holidays, it can be a bit annoying. It's the same as reading about celebrity lifestyles – all you see is a carefully edited version of their lives, which gives a totally false picture.

Man: Absolutely. What gets me is people who insist on going on and on about their perfect life when they know you're going through a bad time.

Woman: Well, I suppose no one has to read anything they find boring or upsetting.

Man: But we just can't resist. Everyone, including me, is so obsessed about staying in contact. I know I'd hate not to know what people are up to more than I hate all their shameless self-promotion!

3

Woman: I decided to see what it would be like to stay offline for a month, with no internet access at all, because I thought I was becoming too dependent on the internet.

Man: Yeah, that was my motivation too. And how did you feel after the first week?

Woman: Well, I was finding it easier to distract myself with other activities, like phoning older relatives and reading. The problem was not that I was waiting to hear from anyone in particular – rather the feeling of being connected and available to the world. It was weird – almost like being invisible. I expect you'd get used to it eventually, though. But I think it's something everyone should consider trying.

Man: Yes. Actually, I'd recommend it because it made me realise how easy it is to waste time doing basically nothing. So now I limit my internet time to an hour each day. I've had to learn to be strict with myself because I do really enjoy chatting online. It's interesting because I've still managed to maintain the online relationships I care about, without having to feel I need to be available to chat twenty-four seven.

Unit 2, Vocabulary focus, Activity 4

 08

Research has shown that it's possible to identify a lot of information, such as people's socio-economic status and their emotional state from their voice alone. It's also claimed that someone's age, height and weight can also be estimated just by listening to the way they speak.

Unit 3, Speaking focus, Activity 1

 09

Examiner: Now I'd like you to talk about something together for about two minutes. Here are some things that we often think make people mature and a question for you to discuss. First you have some time to look at the task.

Now talk to each other about the extent to which these things make people consider themselves to be mature.

Daniela: Shall we make a start?

Martin: OK.

Daniela: Hmm … well, first of all, I really don't consider that we ever complete our education. What I mean is, it may be the case that you finish a university degree but nowadays a lot of people go on to do postgraduate courses or vocational training of some kind, even when they're quite old. It's more and more common for people to return to study throughout their lives.

Martin: I think that being financially independent is the key. If you are still reliant on your parents for money, you are never entirely free to make your own decisions, so in some senses you remain in the position that you were in when you were a child.

Daniela: You mean, because you're having to ask your parents for money and possibly also having to justify what you spend it on?

Martin: Yes.

Daniela: There's a lot to be said for that argument. In many cases I think it does make people less able to take responsibility for their own decisions and it often creates tensions in a family but it doesn't necessarily have to be like that. I read recently about someone who was over 40 and had to go back to live with his elderly parents. He was actually doing all sorts of things for them they needed done and couldn't do themselves, so there was a kind of balance in that case. And that brings me to another point. I don't think moving into your own flat or house necessarily makes you an adult either. A lot of people move out when they start university – I did, but although I probably thought of myself as very grown up, I wasn't, really.

Martin: Apart from earning your own living, I think the thing that really gives you adult status is having your own family. With children of your own, you grow up fast.

Daniela: Yes, you're forced to mature by having to make sacrifices and by being responsible for other people, aren't you? For me that's the crucial thing: taking responsibility or being treated as if you are capable of taking responsibility. That's why the real transition from childhood to adulthood is being treated as an adult. Do you see what I mean?

Martin: Yes.

Daniela: So, having your opinion sought by other adults is a real marker of maturity as I see it. It may be as a parent, as someone with professional skills and expertise or simply as someone who has accumulated enough knowledge of the world to justify their opinions.

Examiner: Thank you. Now you have about a minute to decide which experience has the most effect on a person's maturity.

Martin: Well, for me it's being a parent.

Daniela: I can't argue with the fact that people who are parents grow up fast – my older sister and brother-in-law certainly did – but I think having your opinions sought and respected is important too.

Martin: So which one shall we choose?

Daniela: Mmm … being a parent, I suppose, because children often seek their parents' opinions. We'll settle for that.

Unit 3, Speaking focus, Activity 4

 10

Examiner: Thank you. Can I have the booklet, please? How important is it to continue to seek advice from older people throughout our lives?

Martin: Very. I think older people have a lot to offer, particularly on family matters.

Daniela: Yes, indeed. All those years of experience of bringing up children are invaluable. But I think that there are a whole range of issues on which older people can offer advice and guidance.

Martin: Such as?

Daniela: Well, I certainly wouldn't ask my grandmother how to delete an app from my phone but I do go to her for all sorts of other practical advice. She's a wonderful cook and she knows how to make things you don't find in recipe books, for example, but I also just consider her to be a wise person in general, with insights that I perhaps don't have.

Examiner: Some people say we have stopped respecting older people. What do you think?

Martin: I think we have a bit because the world has changed so quickly and they haven't always been able to keep up with the changes – in technology, for example. This means we sometimes even make fun of them, something that certainly wouldn't have happened when they themselves were young.

Daniela: No, it wouldn't – and it doesn't happen in traditional societies even today. The idea of older people as a source of wisdom is still very strong in those contexts.

Examiner: Thank you. That is the end of the test.

Unit 3, Listening focus, Activity 2

 11

Interviewer: Thank you for joining us this morning, Dr Johnson. Both my father and my grandfather were in their 90s when they died and I like to think I've inherited their long-life genes. What are my chances of making a century?

Dr Johnson: Well, Heather, I can see that you share a tendency with many to give biology pride of place in the longevity stakes. As I see it, putting so much emphasis on genetics is just wishful thinking. People set great store by the fact that they have family members who've lived into their 80s and 90s in the vain hope that they can ignore warnings about harmful habits like smoking – a completely foolhardy attitude, as far as I'm concerned. I hate to say it, but having family members who've lived long lives doesn't mean that you will do so yourself.

Interviewer: Oh. Mind you, most people died before their 40th birthday in the old days anyway, didn't they?

Dr Johnson: In fact, the idea that they all died young is another misconception, in my view. I always tell people to take a good look at old family photographs. When they do, they see there are plenty of elderly people in them. It's true that without antibiotics, everyone was more vulnerable to diseases, particularly babies and children. Because a lot of babies and children died, the mean age at death is much lower even though those who did happen to make it into adulthood had almost as good a chance of living a long life as we do today.

Interviewer: And life was a lot less stressful then, so that would have helped too.

Dr Johnson: In fact, I think the stresses were just different, but the idea that having a stress-free life is the key to eternal youth is yet another myth. Granted, a miserable job you dislike causes the wrong kind of stress and may be a factor in your dying young but in cases where you like your job, even if it is tough and you rise to the challenges it presents, you are actually more likely to have a long life. And of course, responsible, conscientious people who look forward to going to work also achieve professional success.

Interviewer: But doesn't that contradict the idea that laid-back people live longer?

Dr Johnson: Well, they don't, necessarily. One of the most important factors is actually conscientiousness.

Conscientious people are more likely to pay attention to their health and to avoid life-threatening habits like smoking or drinking too much. They'll also be more inclined to avoid very fattening foods but they won't veer to the other extreme of starving themselves. Oh, this is another thing that I really must make clear: just because animals on a very low-calorie diet live longer, it doesn't necessarily mean that we do. Starvation dieting is disastrous for your health.

Interviewer: I seem to be getting all the factors wrong but, surely, being happily married does lead to a happier life, doesn't it?

Dr Johnson: It depends. For men, being married is closely related to being happy and healthy and if a man is happy with the relationship and healthy, his partner tends to be as well. Sadly, when the boot is on the other foot – that is, if a woman is happily married and her partner is not – then it won't have such a positive impact on the length of her life. This always strikes me as rather unfair. It doesn't matter how close they are in age, she always worries about him and feels responsible for him.

Interviewer: What about widows? I've read they often live longer than women whose partners are still alive.

Dr Johnson: Yes, that's true. Women establish and maintain strong friendship networks. Perhaps once they are on their own, they can enjoy and find support in these networks more than they could when their partners were still alive. This is just a theory, of course. There are almost certainly other explanations.

Interviewer: Indeed! Well, thank you very much for joining us, Dr Johnson. I've been keeping track of all the beneficial factors and I don't think I'm doing too badly!

Dr Johnson: That's good to hear. Thank you for having me on the programme.

Unit 4, Listening focus, Activity 3

 12

Mary Shaw: Is being a perfectionist a good thing or not? I believe that perfection is not only impossible to achieve but – rather like trying to find the mythical pot of gold at the end of a rainbow – I'd say it's nothing more than a fantasy. The closer you get to it, the further away it moves. The more you improve, the more room for improvement you'll find.

Unit 4, Listening focus, Activity 4

 13

Mary Shaw: Is being a perfectionist a good thing or not? I believe that perfection is not only impossible to achieve but – rather like trying to find the mythical pot of gold at the end of a rainbow – I'd say it's nothing more than a fantasy. The closer you get to it, the further away it moves. The more you improve, the more room for improvement you'll find. Aiming for perfection is one thing. Expecting perfection, demanding it and beating yourself up for falling short, dooms you to frustration, and diminished confidence and motivation.

Musicians are a good example of how aiming for perfection can actually harm performance. Instead of just losing themselves in the music, the more they focus on their technique while practising for a concert, the more nervous they're likely to be and won't give their best performance. Why? Because they know that the likelihood of a completely perfect performance is close to zero. Instead, what they should be focusing on is what they want to communicate to the audience and how to achieve this. I feel that the biggest problem with perfectionists is that they sometimes get so stuck in the detail that they forget the goal, which, in the case of musicians, is to move and delight an audience.

This is true for many different skills – learning a language, for example. Instead of worrying about getting the accent absolutely right or not making any grammar mistakes at all, learners should be focused on getting their message across. And I'm certain they'll find their accuracy will also gradually improve in the process.

Another problem with perfectionists, which, worryingly, is quite common among young athletes, is that they won't even take part in some competitions because their fear of failure prevents them from even trying to win. They don't consider anything less than winning an option. Their more relaxed peers, who are willing to have a go – they're the ones who are more likely to succeed as they'll learn from their experience and their mistakes.

Striving for perfection can also be harmful because perfectionists can never leave something alone. Even when they're done with a task, they can't help trying to find new things to improve on. This lingering process starts off as 10 minutes, then extends to 30 minutes, then to an hour and more. And so they become less productive as a result. The way I always recommend avoiding this is to fix a time limit and stick to it. An inevitable result of this is the realisation that good enough is usually … well, good enough.

It's not just artists and sports people who need to learn this lesson. It applies to everyday activities as well. When giving a presentation, for example, I think it's good to bear in mind that old saying: *less is more*. It's far better to try and make a few points clearly rather than lots of points in great depth, which will be lost on the audience. But many perfectionists have a tendency to include every possible piece of information so nothing gets left out.

Of course, no one is saying that you should lower your standards and be content with an average performance. The point is still to aim high and put in 100 percent effort but to be satisfied by fulfilling your potential – that's all anyone can ask. Perfectionism is most common …

Unit 4, Speaking focus, Activity 2

 14

Jan: In my opinion, the reason many people give up a sport or hobby is because of the costs involved.

Marisol: I agree. It can be very expensive to join a gym, for instance. The monthly costs can be as high as 100 euros per month, which is too much.

Jan: Yes, and then what tends to happen is that people often join with the best of intentions but then find they don't have time to go often enough to justify the membership fee.

Marisol: So you're saying lack of time and money are very significant reasons for people giving up sport?

Jan: Yes. I believe that goes a long way to explaining why people have to give up.

Marisol: What about hobbies? Playing an instrument, for example?

Jan: I could be wrong but I imagine many people get demotivated because they realise they're never going to be an amazing pianist or guitar player.

Marisol: Mmm … I know from my own experience that that's quite common. I gave up the piano after two years because I wasn't making enough progress, despite practising fairly often.

Unit 4, Speaking focus, Activity 5

 15

1

Marisol: I think there is a lot of value in having a hobby. I used to play the piano and now I've stopped, and I regret that. I used to hate practising for piano exams but, at the same time, I felt a sense of achievement. Perhaps I'll take it up again one day.

2

Jan: There's a lot of criticism of computer games but I think the people that criticise them have never played them. They're often criticised for being too violent and for stopping boys especially from doing other things, like going outside and playing football. But I think they can also develop your imagination and even social skills because often playing them is a shared experience.

Unit 5, Speaking focus, Activity 5

 16

In this part of the test I'm going to give each of you three pictures. I'd like you to talk about two of them on your own for about a minute and a half, and also to answer a question briefly about your partner's pictures.

It's your turn first. Here are your pictures. They show people who are very involved in what they are doing. I'd like you to compare two of the pictures and say why the people might be so involved in what they are doing, and how they might be feeling.

Unit 5, Speaking focus, Activity 7

 17

Which group of people do you think looks happiest? Why?

Unit 5, Listening focus, Activity 3

 18

Interviewer: My guest today is Diana McLeod, careers advisor at the University of Blackstable. She'll be talking to us about how our work can make us happy. Thank you for joining us, Diana. Isn't the key to happiness in the workplace keeping ourselves interested in what we do?

Diana: You would think so but it's actually quite hard to say whether it leads to happiness or not. A few months ago I saw some results of a survey in which graduates were asked to rate different careers in terms of how interesting they were. I was amazed to see that teaching was rated as the least boring. It came in way ahead of careers in the media or in advertising. Teachers say their work is challenging, that no

two days are the same, that they get lots of opportunities to interact with other people and that there's some scope for using their creative skills – all things that keep them engaged. But whether they were happy or not is another question.

Unit 5, Listening focus, Activity 4

 19

Interviewer: My guest today is Diana McLeod, careers advisor at the University of Blackstable. She'll be talking to us about how our work can make us happy. Thank you for joining us, Diana. Isn't the key to happiness in the workplace keeping ourselves interested in what we do?

Diana: You would think so but it's actually quite hard to say whether it leads to happiness or not. A few months ago I saw some results of a survey in which graduates were asked to rate different careers in terms of how interesting they were. I was amazed to see that teaching was rated as the least boring. It came in way ahead of careers in the media or in advertising. Teachers say their work is challenging, that no two days are the same, that they get lots of opportunities to interact with other people and that there's some scope for using their creative skills – all things that keep them engaged. But whether they were happy or not is another question.

Interviewer: So perhaps we should be asking, 'What is it that makes us unhappy at work?'

Diana: Yes, indeed. Common complaints are long hours, a long commute, unrealistic deadlines and job insecurity. You just can't feel happy if you know they're going to fire you any minute. That is definitely top of my list and it's on the increase. After that I'd put having to move away from your friends and family to take a job and contact with other people at work that is unsatisfactory in some way.

Interviewer: Are these poor relationships at work prevalent in smaller companies too?

Diana: Well, bullying, for example, happens in all sorts of organisations but it's true that the bigger the company or institution is, the more likely it is to occur. Small businesses do have a much lower incidence, which is one reason for the high levels of job satisfaction that their employees experience. In a small company, everyone is treated as if they count. There may be fewer opportunities for training and development than in the big corporations but there's more chance of your skills being appreciated. This is also because you've got fewer people above you telling you what to do. No one likes that.

Interviewer: Becoming self-employed would solve the problem, of course.

Diana: That's true but people need to bear in mind that the boundaries between work and leisure will begin to blur. As likely as not, you'll end up with your nose to the grindstone at all hours of the day, though you'll probably mind that a lot less than if someone else had coerced you into working on a long weekend. You're in control of your own destiny and that tends to make us happier.

Interviewer: I suppose money is a great source of satisfaction, though.

Diana: In fact, it doesn't make much difference once you have enough to meet all your basic needs. A bonus or pay rise might lift your spirits but not for long, especially if you suspect you didn't deserve it. In fact, if you don't see them as being related to the quality of your work or the intensity of your efforts, they'll ultimately reduce your motivation. The carrot and stick approach won't always motivate us or keep us happy.

Interviewer: But one key to happiness must surely be success.

Diana: Happy people often are successful at work but they were probably happy in the first place and that affected their behaviour in such a way that their employers noticed them and promoted them. So how do we get happy? By feeling that we matter and that our work is making a positive difference to others. There's a saying that you do a job for the money, a career for the status but a vocation because you care. So if you would do what you do even without being paid for it, then it's pretty much guaranteed to make you happy.

Interviewer: Well, I must say that's very encouraging and very good advice, especially at a time when many people find themselves starting their working lives as volunteers.

We're opening the lines to callers now, so if you would like to talk to Diana about your career plans, the number to dial is …

Unit 6, Listening focus, Activity 6

 20

1

Man: Have you been down to the archaeological site recently?

Woman: Yes, the other day. It was really fascinating to see how much the archaeologists have unearthed already. I was amazed by it, really. I mean, it's a huge site and even with a sizeable team in place, they've only uncovered a fraction of it. It's going to be absolutely enormous when they've finished. I just can't believe that something like this can remain undiscovered for hundreds of years and only now come to light. And all of us locals virtually living on top of an important ancient settlement without having a clue that it's there!

Man: I know. It makes you look at Saxton differently, doesn't it? I don't know about you but even though there are lots of more famous sites around, this feels more significant to me somehow.

Woman: I know what you mean. We're all familiar with the history of the town over the last few hundred years but this takes us back much further in time.

Man: It's like the layers of centuries have been removed and I can actually understand much better how people lived over a thousand years ago.

Woman: And in some ways our lives haven't changed that much.

2

Woman: What did you think of the dinosaur exhibition then, James?

Man: You know, I'd enjoy playing a computer game about dinosaurs more than this exhibition.

Woman: Really? All the kids around us were absolutely loving it.

Man: I know but they didn't have to pay to get in. You'd spend less on a computer game and could then relive the experience again and again. And the special effects would be far superior.

Woman: But I think you get more of an idea of the scale of dinosaurs from this exhibition and what the environment was really like.

Man: I suppose so, and the other thing is I'm not sure how historically accurate games generally are.

Woman: Well, that's quite a big consideration! The museum obviously tried hard to recreate a real dinosaur experience and some of the dinosaurs were pretty terrifying but I felt I didn't really learn enough. I gave up trying to read those little information signs because there was always a large group of people around and I couldn't see them properly.

Man: I just came away feeling confused about when the different dinosaur periods were and which dinosaurs were which.

3

Woman: That really old house in Wales is for sale – where we had that holiday – do you remember? Look, it's completely unchanged.

Man: Yes, of course. It was such a weird place, wasn't it? Great for playing hide-and-seek, though.

Woman: Yes. Brilliant, but freezing cold and Mum was always complaining there was never any hot water. But what I mainly remember is lying awake at night thinking about the people that lived there before, wondering what their lives must have been like. Dad used to make up creepy stories about the people in the old paintings.

Man: Which were quite unbelievable!

Woman: It would be awful if the person who buys it tries to modernise it. I'd hate to see it lose its character.

Man: It would be criminal to turn it into flats or a hotel but I wouldn't worry because it's bound to have a preservation order on it because it's so old.

Woman: I expect you're right. It's awful to think of all the furniture and paintings being sold off or ending up in a museum. I wish we could afford to buy it.

Man: And take our kids there on holiday. Dream on!

Unit 6, Speaking focus, Activity 1

 21

Here are your pictures. They show people finding out about the past. I'd like you to compare two of the pictures and say why the people might be interested in this kind of information about the past, and how easy it might be for them to remember it.

Unit 6, Speaking focus, Activity 2

 22

In this picture I think the children are finding out about the fairly recent past, whereas in the other picture they're learning about the ancient past. The first picture looks as if it could be in Europe and it could be a school trip for the children to learn about the lives of servants in the past. Perhaps this kitchen is in an old palace or castle, not far from where the children live. Whilst in the other picture, they look like tourists from another country who are interested in ancient cultures. I'm not sure, but this could be in South America somewhere and the tourists may have travelled a long way to get there.

I think the children look really interested in what the cook is telling them. They've probably been doing a project about this period in history at school and I imagine they'll find this information easy to remember because they can see what life was really like in those days. But I doubt whether the tourists will remember very much about the information given by the guide if they're just visiting the site for a few hours. Unless they've done a lot of reading beforehand and already know quite a lot about this site, it can be hard

to imagine what the lives of the people who lived there thousands of years ago might have been like.

Unit 7, Listening focus, Activity 3

 23

Interviewer: Welcome to the studio, Dr Patterson. There have been a number of complaints about marketing that makes use of the senses. How far do you feel the complaints are justified?

Dr Patterson: Well, there's nothing new about using the senses to sell products and services. First it was colour, then sound and now it's the sense of smell. But the use of sophisticated scent technology bothers some people. I don't think anyone has an issue with bread smelling like bread or coffee smelling like coffee. But there are occasions which do make me slightly uncomfortable with the idea.

Interviewer: Do you mean when the smell of chocolate or bread is artificially strong, for example, and it is used to trick people into coming inside a shop and spending money?

Dr Patterson: Well, if it's a place where chocolate's made, there might well be a strong smell, but if it's just a shop selling packaged chocolate, people won't be able to smell it, so the scent marketer helps things along by pumping out a chocolatey smell.

Interviewer: Ah …

Dr Patterson: That's not a problem for most of us, but the approach can backfire if people get wind of the fact that smell is being used to manipulate them. I mean, when a powerful and irresistible scent is used to entice them into a shop only to find nothing identified with that smell actually on sale.

Interviewer: What's the most unusual smell you've come across in a store?

Dr Patterson: Recently, a big toy store used scent marketing to encourage adult shoppers to spend more time looking at toys. The smell they used was piña colada – you know, the pineapple-coconut cocktail. It seems like a strange choice but it supposedly conjures up visions of holidays and tropical paradises. I guess that's why they used it but without access to the marketing company's brief, of course, we can't be sure. The store was in London, so perhaps that was it.

Interviewer: Wasn't there a complaint recently about a campaign like this?

Dr Patterson: Well, it wasn't, strictly speaking, a case of subliminal scent marketing, the kind that normally causes people to raise objections. In fact, it was the milk board in the United States that wanted to encourage people to drink more milk. The smell of milk is not one that most people like very much, so they opted, very cleverly in my opinion, for pumping out the smell of freshly baked cookies. The idea was that the cookie smell would make people want to eat some cookies and, by association, drink some milk. I think they got the idea from campaigns where the smell of coffee had been used to sell plastic kitchen products that don't have a smell.

Interviewer: So who objected and why?

Dr Patterson: The allergy lobby – and they objected very strongly. They don't like our environment being manipulated through pumping scented oils into the air – because it is potentially dangerous for this group. It's fair enough, really. If they start having breathing difficulties but can't actually smell whatever it is that is being pumped out, they won't realise they need to move away. Into the bargain, scent marketing is increasingly ubiquitous. It's being used on airlines, in hotels and even, somewhat worryingly, in casinos to encourage people to stay and keep gambling.

Interviewer: Why would a hotel or airline want to use something like this? Surely, if we're guests in the hotel or passengers on the plane already, we don't need to be persuaded to spend more time there.

Dr Patterson: Well, no, but in this case it's more a question of branding. A lot of companies are now using scents as part of an overall strategy that will include all the other senses as well. They add a kind of scent logo that identifies the company in much the same way that a print logo does. The scent marketing designers are getting lots of commissions to do this kind of work as it's highly skilled and very demanding. I really take my hat off to some of these people. Get it wrong and the company will lose customers. Get it right and they will become really competitive.

Interviewer: Well, thank you very much, Dr Patterson, for that very interesting glimpse – or should I say 'whiff' of the pros and cons of scent marketing.

Unit 7, Speaking focus, Activity 2

 24

Girl: What I think makes campaigns like these particularly effective is the fact that they're using the actual medium of advertising to attack the advertising industry.

Boy: Absolutely! It's a clever way of warning people not to be taken in by the power of advertising. Having said that, I do have some reservations. Some of these messages are a bit obvious after all. I mean, we all know the whole point of advertising is to sell us things.

Girl: I can't argue with that but, as obvious as it may seem, we are still manipulated by the whole marketing industry. What campaigns like this do is make people stop and think.

I especially like the use of humour – that's the key tool to changing hearts and minds.

Boy: Indeed it is. Poking fun at advertising robs it of some of its power. I do see that there is value in receiving an anti-advertising message from time to time but I do sometimes find things like this a bit patronising.

Girl: Patronising? I'm afraid I just don't see it like that at all. I'd really like to see at least one ad like this outside every shopping mall.

Boy: I can't think of anything worse! That would be the best way of ensuring that the message would lose its impact and its appeal.

Girl: Oh well, we'll just have to agree to differ on that one then.

Unit 7, Speaking focus, Activity 6

 25

Now I'd like you to talk about something together for about two minutes. Here are some ways of promoting fashion products and a question for you to discuss. First you have some time to look at the task.

Now talk to each other about how effective these ways of promoting fashion products would be.

Unit 7, Grammar focus, Activity 1

 26

Stealth advertising, or advertising you wouldn't even know is advertising, is coming to a living room, a college classroom or a blog near you. Here's how it works: imagine that you find your rather stylish friend is now looking more stylish than ever. Day after day she comes to college decked out in fantastic outfits that attract compliments from all and sundry. Then she lets slip that, in fact, what she is wearing is the new summer range from such and such a clothing company, available online or in-store and at the moment there happens to be a sale on, with some very attractive discounts. Would you smell a rat or would you think it was just normal chit-chat about clothes and where to get a bargain? Might it be the case that your friend is actually being paid to 'model' these fashion items and sing their praises so as to sell the brand to her classmates? I don't think anybody I know would do such a thing but if I were to learn that a friend was being paid to promote a product to me, I would be really angry.

As unlikely as this scenario might sound, this particular breed of stealth advertising is actually becoming more and more common. For the companies involved, it represents a huge saving on expensive campaigns but what's in it for people like my stylish friend? It sometimes starts with the person being offered the opportunity to trial a product – let's say a lip gloss. They get a year's supply of said lip gloss free and then, a few days later, someone contacts them to ask how they like it and then says, 'Hey, if you happen to be talking to your friends, can you just mention in passing that you use Lipluxe?' No pressure – after all, it's only if you happen to be talking to them. But you realise that you're being manipulated or your friends catch on and, outraged, contact the people who make Lipluxe to complain. In most cases they'll be fobbed off with one of those chillingly formal letters saying that it's normal practice, ending with the challenge, 'Should you wish to make a complaint, we suggest you contact the Advertising Control Board.' I say it's a challenge because nine out of ten times they know you won't.

But sometimes people do fight back. A friend of mine who is something of a fashionista has a blog where she writes about clothes and posts photos of herself wearing some of them. One day she was flicking through a magazine and she happened to see an ad for a brand of trainers in which the image was a lot of different pairs of feet wearing them … including hers! In tiny print at the bottom of the page were all the sources for the photographs, including her website. She was furious! Had the company asked my friend's permission to use her blog to promote the product, she would never have agreed to it. But a lot of bloggers wouldn't think twice about accepting money, though sometimes they're just given the clothes and encouraged to wear them. The really big bloggers demand high fees for this – sometimes as much as $50,000. I wonder what their friends would think if they knew.

Unit 8, Listening focus, Activity 3

 27

Tim Cole: I'm Tim Cole, and as an experienced travel writer, I'm here to tell you not to believe everything you read in guidebooks because following some of the recommendations they give can result in the most bizarre situations. I'll never forget the night I arrived in Sydney, for example. I'd turned up at the address of what I thought was a budget hotel given in the guidebook at 1 a.m., exhausted and looking forward to a few hours' rest, but instead found myself at a comedy club, which at the time I didn't find at all funny.

The problem is that too many travellers are too trusting of their guidebooks and don't bother to research even the most basic facts before they set off. Some guidebooks are only updated every couple of years, so it's no wonder many things have moved on by the time you get there. The most important thing when choosing a guidebook is to check the publication date; if it's not within the last 12 months, don't buy it.

Then the other thing to think about is who the guidebook is aimed at. If you're into the history and culture of a place, don't buy a guidebook full of information on the alternative nightlife scene. But my pet hate, and something I'm always extremely wary of, are the restaurant suggestions. So often I've turned up somewhere and the menu, price and décor bear no relation to the place I've been reading about – if they haven't already gone out of business and shut down, that is.

Other things to look out for in a guidebook are the maps. These need to be detailed but not so small you can't read them. You don't want to have to carry a magnifying glass around with you. Books that include unnecessary information are another thing I find annoying – like photos of famous places, for example. We already know what the Eiffel Tower looks like! Why not include more background information instead?

Of course, most guidebooks are also now available in a digital format and many travellers prefer using these because they're obviously not heavy to carry, so you can download as many as you like. But I don't find them easy to use at all because navigation is much harder than flicking through the index at the back of a book. Life's just too short and you can never guarantee you'll have wifi access anyway. Until I can get a digital travel guide which is tailor-made for my individual trip, I'm happy to stick with the traditional form of guidebook.

However, on my trip to Hawaii last summer I experimented with a new way of getting good travel advice: Twitter tourism. Instead of using a guidebook, I decided to rely on the advice of locals and visitors alike – and let them choose what I should visit, where I should stay and what I should eat. I didn't mind as long as their advice was based on a recent experience. It actually worked out really well and it felt like a real adventure. Without the Twitter travel tips, I'd never have visited the Ukulele Festival or eaten spam sushi. One thing I'd never imagined doing – and I'm so grateful for the advice – was a ten-kilometre kayak expedition along the coast for a nighttime swim with manta rays in a huge cave. A truly magnificent sight. And my top tip for anyone visiting Hawaii!

Unit 8, Grammar focus, Activity 6

 28

Matt: Mia, you went to Thailand last year, didn't you?

Mia: Yes, I did. It was amazing! You have to go there, Matt!

Matt: Well, I'm already planning to go there. In the summer, hopefully. I was wondering if you can recommend a guidebook.

Mia: Well, the guidebook I used was so out of date I really wouldn't recommend it. In fact, I don't think I'll ever use one again. I'm thinking of just relying on Twitter recommendations next time I'm travelling. I've heard that's a much more reliable way to get advice.

Matt: That sounds like a great idea.

Mia: I'll show you my photos if you like. Are you free this evening?

Unit 8, Speaking focus, Activity 3

 29

Here are your pictures. They show people on holiday buying souvenirs. I'd like you to compare two of the pictures and say why the people might want to buy these items and how useful each item might be as a reminder of their holiday.

Unit 8, Speaking focus, Activity 4

▶ 30

In both pictures the people are interested in buying local products or crafts but in one picture the woman is buying from a simple stall which doesn't look like it's in a market, whereas in the other one the people are at an expensive airport shop. Um … I would imagine that most people who travel to a new country that they may never visit again are interested in buying things that are typical of that area. But I doubt whether most tourists actually check to see if that item is actually locally made. I think some of these things are often mass-produced in countries like China. I'm pretty certain that the people in both photographs are making impulse purchases. Um … I couldn't say if they're buying presents or not. They could just be shopping for themselves. In all likelihood, the Russian dolls will be put on a shelf somewhere and forgotten about, so I'm not sure that they're a useful reminder of a trip. But I'd be surprised if the woman buying the handmade bracelet wanted it as a reminder of her trip. She probably just likes the bracelet and will wear it without thinking about where it came from. She also probably wants to give the woman selling her products some business.

Unit 8, Vocabulary focus, Activity 2

 31

New York City's population in April 2000 stood at just over eight million – the highest it had ever been since records began. However, while the city's population grew substantially in the first half of the 20th century, it dropped from nearly 7.9 million in 1950 to 7.1 million in 1980. This was despite the baby boom and the surge in immigration from Europe, which started in the 1950s and continued through the 1970s. It was during this period that many families left New York City for the suburbs. But this trend was reversed over the next two decades as parts of the city were regenerated and a rise in immigration from Asia boosted the population to a peak of eight million by the year 2000.

It is unlikely that population growth will reach the levels seen in the first part of the 20th century, when the city's population went up by 38 percent between 1900 and 1910, but sharp declines are also unlikely. A period of relative stability in population levels seems likely during the first few decades of the 21st century. Moderate growth is expected, although it will be sufficiently high to push the population up to nine million by 2030.

Unit 8, Grammar focus, Activity 4

▶ 32

1 Orla: I hate to admit it but I've got no choice. I have to leave here to find work.

2 Una: Don't worry, Mum. I'm not lonely. I've made loads of friends here already.

3 Sean: I wish I hadn't left. I think I would have had a better chance of starting my own business at home.

4 Conor: The government hasn't done enough to create jobs – that's why so many people are leaving.

5 Ryan's dad: Listen, son, I really think you should stay in Australia. You've got lots more opportunities there.

6 Keira: I don't regret emigrating for one minute. It's the best decision I've ever made.

Unit 9, Vocabulary focus, Activity 4

 33

Babies and small children pass a number of developmental milestones as they grow. Only weeks after a child is born she knows a smile for what it is and may even smile back, though she is not yet able to actually recognise the important people in her life. This comes a little later, when, at four months, the baby can identify her mother and begins to know who's who among all the people she encounters regularly. Mind you, names don't mean much to her at this stage but at ten months she will begin to recognise her own name and react to it appropriately. It's at this age also that she'll start to get a real kick out of the game of *peekaboo*. The adult hides his face behind his hands or some other object and then reveals it. This usually gets a laugh from the baby and is early evidence of a burgeoning sense of humour. She will begin to display helpful behaviour when she is little more than a year old but bear in mind that the child might actually be more of a hindrance than a help. Still, it's the thought that counts, so don't discourage her. It won't be long before she'll also get the hang of dressing herself – usually at around two. Once again, don't crush the child's enthusiasm as this may actually be slowing down her development and hanging on to an extra responsibility an adult can actually share with her.

Unit 9, Speaking focus, Activity 2

 34

In this part of the test I'm going to give each of you three pictures. I'd like you to talk about two of them on your own for about a minute and a half, and also to answer a question briefly about your partner's pictures.

It's your turn first. Here are your pictures. They show people doing things on their own. I'd like you to compare two of the pictures and say why people might be doing these things on their own and what reactions they might get from other people.

Unit 9, Speaking focus, Activity 4

35

Both these photographs show people doing things alone that we often do with others. That similarity aside, they are in some ways rather different from one another. In the first picture there is a young woman by herself watching a film in a cinema. She seems completely engrossed in whatever it is she is watching and perfectly happy to be there without anyone else. What's more, she's got a huge container of popcorn all to herself. In the second picture a woman is having a solitary meal in a restaurant and although she too seems quite engrossed in what she's doing, I have the impression that she is reading a magazine because she's feeling a bit self-conscious about being a lone diner. In another kind of restaurant it probably wouldn't seem so strange. The woman in the cinema, on the other hand, probably wouldn't attract very much attention at all. Cinemas are dark, of course, and other cinema-goers probably wouldn't even notice that she is unaccompanied. Even if they did, I don't think they would think anything of it. A lot of single people go to the movies and there's no need to talk to anyone during the film itself, anyway.

Unit 9, Speaking focus, Activity 6

 36

Examiner: Who do you think is happiest doing these things on their own? Why?

Candidate: It strikes me that the man playing chess may actually be quite content even if he's not smiling or laughing. Perhaps he would prefer not to have someone across the table playing against him.

Unit 9, Listening focus, Activity 4

37

Speaker 1: It was a really busy Saturday, so the multi-storey car park was jam-packed. I had to drive around for about 20 minutes to find a space. I was in an incredible hurry, so I locked the car, headed for the lift and got out at ground level where the shops are. It was only then that I realised I hadn't actually registered which row I'd parked in or even which floor I was on. I think I've finally got it through my own thick skull that the secret is to make a mental note of where I am. I must have looked a right idiot hanging around until most of the other cars had gone but I finally managed to find mine.

Speaker 2: I've always had trouble remembering my girlfriend's cousin's name. What pops into my head first is 'Antoinette' and then I think it's 'Brigitte'. I usually avoid calling her anything, which was what I did last time we met. I don't think she noticed but my girlfriend certainly did and she was not impressed. She was so cross she would barely speak to me for the rest of the afternoon. There's actually an old song about a girl called Bernadette and the experts say using a song or poem sometimes does the trick. I'll give it a go.

Speaker 3: I was actually really looking forward to it, but I was so busy I had to put it right out of my mind during the day. By the time I remembered, all the decent shops were closed and I ended up getting him a DVD from a petrol station. He'd bought me some pearl earrings. I could tell he was thinking I'd let our anniversary completely slip my mind and he looked so crestfallen I felt terrible. Apparently, there's some kind of anniversary alert app you can get and they'll send you messages with suggestions for gifts. I'll have to go for that next year.

Speaker 4: My sister used to put these little sticky notes all over the house with things she was trying to commit to memory. You'd find them on packets of cornflakes and on the bathroom mirror – everywhere. That's what I should have done because even if I put things down on paper, if there are lots of facts and figures and so on, I get them all muddled up. For this subject there were heaps of dates and place names. I knew that if I didn't get them straightened out in my mind, my chances of getting a good mark in the finals were out of the window, and I was right.

Speaker 5: There I was in this busy station and I needed to get some change for the ticket machine and get to the airport or I was going to miss my flight. I studied it for about seven years but my French is really rusty. I was desperately racking my brains for the phrase 'I need change' but all that came into my head were words in Spanish. Apparently, if you conjure up an image of the person who originally taught you or told you something, you sometimes remember it. So I thought of my old French teacher and suddenly a complete sentence popped into my head. I got my change.

Unit 10, Grammar focus, Activity 1

 38

Chris should start planning his future right now. There's no sense in putting it off. First he needs to prioritise his career goals. He should picture what job within his current company he'd like to aim for and he should also consider any other companies he'd ideally like to work for in the longer term and in what capacity. He should think about how it feels to be doing that job. Then he should think about the steps he needs to take in order to get there. For example, are there any training courses he needs to do? Are there any extra responsibilities he could take on now? He should set monthly targets on the road to getting promoted and achieving his goals.

Deciding when to start a family is a big decision and isn't something you should take on lightly. Chris and his wife need to have a serious discussion about this. Money is an important factor, so it makes sense to plan ahead and start saving so that one or other of them can afford to stay at home and look after the baby if they want to.

Finally, I think Chris needs to dream a little. His plans for the future aren't that well-defined and are a little unambitious.

Unit 10, Speaking focus, Activity 4

▶ 39

I'd like you to talk about something together for about two minutes. Here are some things that students can do to help them make plans for the future. First you have some time to look at the task.

Now talk to each other about how useful these experiences might be in helping students to plan for their future.

Unit 10, Speaking focus, Activity 5

▶ 40

Now you have about a minute to decide which experience would help students to make the most informed choice about their future.

Unit 10, Listening focus, Activity 3

▶ 41

Marcus King: My name's Marcus King and I've been working for Environmental Action for several years, studying ways we can encourage people to change their behaviour. A lot of things we all do, which cause serious harm to the environment, are just a habit, which we can train ourselves to change. We don't think twice about turning up the thermostat or driving to work instead of taking the train – relatively small changes that could make a big difference.

You'd think that because it wouldn't take much to change and would also bring significant benefits, it wouldn't be difficult to persuade people to do certain things. Switching the lights off when you leave the room means lower bills and more money in your pocket, as does driving a fuel-efficient car. People don't always realise that reusing plastic bags means cleaner beaches – if they did, it might be a stronger motivation for them.

But perversely, people are resistant to change, partly out of laziness – because change requires effort. It's also partly because we'll only take action if we can see a measurable benefit. For us to change our ways, we need to see the effects of our negative behaviour now and not at some distant point in the future. This is because we tend not to worry so much about things that will affect us in the long term.

Changing people's attitudes is a real challenge. One university study in Copenhagen looked at attitudes to littering and found that while the majority of people claimed to dislike litter, there was still a lot of litter about. This is a classic example of a gap in attitude between what people say they believe and what they actually do. So, to see if littering could be reduced, the researchers handed out 1,000 caramel sweets to passing pedestrians. The nearby streets and litter bins were then searched for the sweet wrappers, and they were counted.

What the researchers did next shows that making the right choice easy for people can have a big impact. So they handed the sweets out again but this time made it easier for people to find the litter bins by stencilling green footsteps on the ground. Amazingly, this led to a 46 percent decrease in the total quantity of sweet wrappers found littering the streets. This also shows that fun and imaginative solutions are usually better than the usual signs nagging people about what they should do. It also proves that people only need a gentle visual reminder not to litter – no need for fines.

These ideas have been enthusiastically taken up by some governments eager to cut energy consumption and to reach emissions targets. Known as 'nudging', the aim is to create an environment that nudges people to change their behaviour in a subtle way, without the need for regulation.

Some of these nudges have made a real difference. For example, charging drivers to bring their cars into city centres has reduced the amount of traffic congestion. But some environmentalists argue that the congestion charge hasn't led to a reduction in car ownership, nor does increased recycling at work necessarily lead to changed behaviour at home. They say they're disappointed and frustrated with the impact nudging has had, though I would say it's encouraging. While I agree that nudging isn't the solution to all our problems, it's certainly a move in the right direction.

Unit 11, Listening focus, Activity 2

 42

I did this magazine quiz called *How well does your partner know you?* You had to grade statements and then give the same quiz to your partner to answer about you. Well, there

was a huge discrepancy between my results and Charlie's, and the analysis said something like, 'You should have spent more time getting to know each other.' We started to talk about the questions and some of his answers really had me worried. He can't have been listening to half the things I've told him over the years! I did the quiz on the spur of the moment but I rather wish I hadn't now.

Unit 11, Listening focus, Activity 3

 43

Speaker 1: I did this magazine quiz called *How well does your partner know you?* You had to grade statements and then give the same quiz to your partner to answer about you. Well, there was a huge discrepancy between my results and Charlie's, and the analysis said something like, 'You should have spent more time getting to know each other.' We started to talk about the questions and some of his answers really had me worried. He can't have been listening to half the things I've told him over the years! I did the quiz on the spur of the moment but I rather wish I hadn't now.

Speaker 2: I'd already had an interview and had actually been working there for a couple of weeks. The job is perfect for me – it involves working to deadlines and I thrive on pressure. After a couple of weeks they said I had to do a personality test. They must have got my results mixed up with someone else's because they said I wasn't good at handling pressure. I've never felt so insulted in my life. Me? Not handle pressure? Well, now I think my boss sees just how wide of the mark the results were.

Speaker 3: I'm a real sucker for quizzes and personality tests. I love them! But I honestly didn't expect much from this one. I mean how could choosing colours say anything about your personality? You had to click on eight colours in order of preference, then wait a few minutes and repeat the same test. I clicked on purple first and then I can't remember but I know I put grey, blue and black last both times. When I read the results I could hardly believe it. My attitudes, my worries, my problems with my partner, my work habits – it was all absolutely spot on.

Speaker 4: The psychology department were asking for student volunteers to do a personality test. I've always wanted to get to the bottom of how these tests work, so I went along. We were asked to wait until they called us in but they put us in this really stuffy room with only three seats and there must have been at least 15 of us. We had to wait for ages! I was getting really fed up. Finally, it was my turn. They thanked me for coming and explained that they had really been looking at our behaviour in the overcrowded room and been recording it. They ought to have told us that was what was going on. It's not ethical.

Speaker 5: I've got my own translation business but I wasn't getting many commissions. I decided to see if one of those life coaches could get to the bottom of whatever was going wrong and the first thing she did was give me a personality test. I was a bit taken aback when she said my test results showed that I needed to work in collaboration with others. It's weird as I've always seen myself as a bit of a loner and as not taking too kindly to people telling me what to do. I'm not sure I'm going to like having my translations picked to pieces by others.

Unit 11, Speaking focus, Activity 1

 44

Anton: Well, shall we start?

Nadia: We may as well. I'm all in favour of personality tests myself. The key issue here is to determine whether or not a candidate has the right skills. A well-designed personality test would be likely to give you that information. Would you go along with that?

Anton: I would, up to a point. I mean, personality testing might be the best approach in some circumstances but not with something like this. I can't quite see that personality would be crucial here. For me it's a question of having good taste and being stylish yourself.

Nadia: Sure, but a stylist does need to know how to talk to people too.

Anton: Fair enough, but if it's a film, what would be vital is an ability to create the feel of the period through the right clothes and accessories.

Nadia: I suppose it would, now that you mention it. So would you be happier with some kind of interview? Do you think that would be useful?

Anton: Possibly, but I think we may well get a clear picture of their skills by looking at their portfolio. Since we want to hire them to create a visual effect, it makes sense to look at examples of the different kinds of work they've done before.

Nadia: OK. I agree that would be useful. We could also learn a lot by observing them at work. That would tell us about how they communicate with colleagues. I still think that's really important too.

Anton: Maybe, but I just wonder how practical that would be – how would you get to watch a stylist working at a fashion shoot or film set or whatever? I think looking at the way they dress themselves is a good place to start. They're often photographed and sometimes become celebrities in their own right.

Nadia: But surely, you're not saying that you could just rely on photographs of these people in the press?

Anton: No, no, no – not exclusively. But I can't help thinking that it's as good a way as any of assessing their talents.

Examiner: Thank you. Now you have about a minute to decide which methods would be the most efficient.

Nadia: Well, perhaps we could agree on what would be least efficient first. In this case, perhaps a personality test isn't really best, is it?

Anton: No, I agree. I think it would be best to have some information about how the candidate styles him- or herself, and how well he or she communicates.

Nadia: Yes, so that means observing them at work.

Anton: Well, that might be the best, but it might not be the most efficient. I mean, it might not be very practical. Apparently, these people travel all over the world, so, actually, seeing them in action could be very expensive.

Nadia: That's true. It would be more efficient to conduct an interview.

Anton: Yes, as well as seeing their portfolio. That would be important too. Don't you agree?

Nadia: Yes, I think we can agree that conducting an interview and seeing their portfolio would work best.

Unit 11, Speaking focus, Activity 4

 45

Examiner: What is the most important quality for a stylist to have?

Nadia: Well, as we were saying, they should be stylish themselves.

Anton: Though it's not just a question of being stylish themselves. Being able to empathise with the people you work with is also very important.

Nadia: And that implies being a good observer.

Examiner: Some people prefer to have someone choose their clothes and accessories for them. Why do you think this is?

Nadia: Isn't it sometimes the case that someone is so much in the public eye that they really need professional help in this area?

Anton: That may well be so, but I wonder if anyone really needs to employ someone like this. I mean, they're glorified servants to a lesser or greater extent. I would think that this is unlikely to hold true in all cases but I do think that a lot of these actors and so on are just terribly immature.

Nadia: It's a matter of opinion, really.

Anton: Yes, of course.

Examiner: Some people say that we can change our style and appearance but not our basic character. What do you think?

Anton: It's impossible to be categorical about something like this but you can work on your style. I'm not so sure about personality.

Nadia: No, neither am I. I gather it's usually fixed. But perhaps it's possible to train yourself not to reveal certain aspects of your personality. For example, if you have a tendency to be paranoid, you might be able to learn to see that pattern and somehow counteract it. How far would you regard that as feasible?

Anton: Without a specific context, it's difficult to give a *yes* or *no* answer but I must say that I find it somewhat difficult to believe that personality remains completely constant throughout our lives. Older people often show quite marked changes in character.

Nadia: Very true.

Examiner: Thank you. That is the end of the test.

Unit 12, Listening focus, Activity 2

 47

1

Man: These results of the survey on the link between music taste and personality are interesting. I mean, it's always been thought there's a strong link between these things and these results support that.

Woman: Yes. And you can't argue with the data because such a large number of people took part.

Man: Mmm … 36,000, wasn't it? The largest survey of its kind ever undertaken. And they were questioned in such detail first about their personalities.

Woman: And then they didn't just ask them about the kind of music they usually buy or listen to – they actually made them grade lots of pieces of music ranging from classical to rap. It would have been interesting to take part, I think – you know, to discover what my actual music preferences really are.

Man: Mmm … the strangest thing for me is that fans of classical music and heavy metal actually have a lot in common. Both groups are described as imaginative, gentle and introverted.

Woman: Yes. I wouldn't have expected that. And it's also contrary to the stereotype of heavy metal fans being aggressive and anti-social.

Man: Well, I never took those kinds of stereotypes seriously anyway.

2

Man: What strikes me when I play at different venues around the country is how many more families there are in the audience than there were ten years ago. You see parents with kids as young as 11 or 12 and people in their 20s with their dads.

Woman: But it usually is older men rather than women who still like live music. I like the fact that our original fans still enjoy our music and are passing it on to the next generation. I don't see why age should have anything to do with what kind of music you're into.

Man: Nor me. But what does bother me slightly is the fact that year after year it's the same bands that get booked as the main acts for the big festivals. I think they're blocking the way for younger bands who deserve to have some of the limelight.

Woman: I think the point is that that wouldn't happen if the younger bands were as good as some of the big names that have been around for 20 years or more. They attract big audiences and a lot of festivals depend on older people to buy tickets for these events.

3

Man: I used to only sing in the shower and felt embarrassed to sing in front of other people, but joining a choir at university really changed all that. The choir was for people who thought they couldn't sing, but I discovered that I'm not tone-deaf and I can actually hold a rhythm in my head.

Woman: That's pretty typical – most people underestimate their musical abilities and are, in fact, surprised to discover that they can carry a tune, even though they may only know the lyrics to the chorus.

Man: And struggle to reach the high notes. That's still sometimes a problem for me.

Woman: All you've got to do is relax and not worry about it and it doesn't become such an issue.

Man: I'd certainly recommend joining a choir to anyone. It helps you to deal with stress much better and you can really switch off while you're singing.

Woman: That's the thing – concentrating hard on music and focusing on your breathing takes your mind off everything else so that you're only aware of the present moment.

Unit 12, Speaking focus, Activity 2

 48

Examiner: Now I'd like you to talk about something together for about three minutes. Here are some ways music can benefit people when they are studying or working and a question for you to discuss. First you have some time to look at the task.

Now, talk to each other about how listening to music can help people in these ways.

Candidate 1: I think listening to music is beneficial for many kinds of jobs.

Candidate 2: Yes, so do I. Let's talk about the reasons why it's beneficial.

Candidate 3: OK. Well, music is an advantage for people who do boring jobs, like bus drivers, because it helps them to pass the time and helps them to stay awake.

Candidate 2: Yes. I think it's more interesting to listen to music when you're driving.

Candidate 1: I think it's beneficial to listen to music in jobs when you don't speak to people much.

Candidate 2: That's true. But do you think it can sometimes be a disadvantage for bus drivers to listen to music?

Candidate 3: Why?

Candidate 2: Because they need to hear if their passengers have a problem, for example. You know, if they can't open the door or something like that.

Candidate 1: Yes, that's a good point. Maybe it also helps reduce drivers' stress because it can be stressful getting stuck in traffic.

Candidate 2: I agree. I think that's the most beneficial reason for listening to music. In all kinds of stressful jobs, like being a dentist. Or even studying for an exam.

Unit 12, Speaking focus, Activity 5

▶ 49

Thank you. Now you have about a minute to decide which of these benefits of listening to music is the most important.

Unit 13, Listening focus, Activity 2

▶ 50

Presenter: Welcome to the *Review Show*. Joining me today are writers Diana Abel and Mark Shaw. The first book we'll be discussing is Robert Provine's *Laughter: a scientific investigation*. It's certainly an interesting topic, Mark. But what did you make of the idea that laughter is not primarily a response to humour but a social lubricant – something used to smooth interaction between people?

Mark: Yes. Very interesting. It's something I've come across before and I don't think Provine is the first to make this claim. But he is the first to popularise this theory. And I think a lot of people will find it really difficult to accept that we don't just laugh because we find something funny. Laughter has a much more complex role. What's really disturbing is that, according to some statistics, we're laughing much less than we used to, usually only when we're watching a comedy on TV.

Presenter: Indeed. Diana, I know you were particularly struck by the comparisons between male and female laughter in the book.

Diana: Yes, that's right. While researching the book, Provine looked at hundreds of lonely hearts ads in the newspapers and found that one of the key qualities women look for in a potential partner is a good sense of humour – something sought after much less commonly by men. That was news to me. It seems women want a man who will make them laugh, while men like women who laugh at their jokes. That might explain why until relatively recently there were so few female comedians around.

Presenter: Provine does stress the importance of increasing laughter in our lives and gives some advice on how to achieve this. Were you tempted to try out any of his suggestions, Diana?

Diana: Well, Provine thinks laughter is important for maintaining relationships but doesn't necessarily support the idea that laughter improves health or longevity. So he's not advocating attending laughter workshops or laughter yoga. His message is really quite simple. If you want to laugh more, rather than sitting in front of comedy programmes, socialise more with people whose company you enjoy – which makes sense to me. One thing I'm in favour of, which Provine doesn't mention, is that people should lighten up and laugh at themselves more.

Presenter: Did either of you find your attitude to laughter had changed after reading the book?

Mark: I certainly started noticing when people actually laughed and found it confirmed Provine's theory, that is, people were laughing at things that weren't remotely funny and also in odd places during a conversation.

Diana: The effect it had on me was to monitor my own impulses to laugh – it made me less spontaneous in a way.

Mark: … analysing what made you want to laugh instead of reacting naturally – I experienced that too.

Presenter: So did you find the book answered everything you ever wanted to know about laughter?

Mark: It was pretty comprehensive, especially the parts on how humour and comedy work. He also focuses on how humour can be abusive and cruel – anyone who's experienced this in the playground will be able to relate to that. The section on the mechanics of breathing and laughing I could have done without.

Diana: I was more interested in the social aspects of laughter. Provine argues that laughter existed before comedy and I wish he'd gone into more depth about how laughter may have begun.

Mark: That was my favourite section of the book, so more on that would have been welcome. The descriptions of how laughter may have started with chimpanzees tickling each other are wonderful.

Presenter: But, overall, would you recommend this to someone who hasn't got a professional or academic interest in laughter?

Mark: Without question, yes. There were some bits where I felt my lack of a background in neuroscience was a disadvantage but you can just skip those bits and move on to some of the lovely anecdotes about the research – some of the accounts of the contagious nature of laughter are really amazing. In some places people couldn't stop laughing for days.

Diana: Yes, incredible.

Presenter: And do you think the book will help people?

Mark: Well, if you just want to find out about the benefits of laughter, there are more appropriate self-help guides. This is more wide-ranging than that.

Presenter: I see. So, moving on to another book about comedy …

Unit 13, Listening focus, Activity 4

 51

1 Diana: So he's not advocating attending laughter workshops or laughter yoga.

2 Diana: Well, Provine thinks laughter is important for maintaining relationships but doesn't necessarily support the idea that laughter improves health or longevity.

3 Diana: The effect it had on me was to monitor my own impulses to laugh – it made me less spontaneous in a way.

4 Mark: But you can just skip those bits and move on to some of the lovely anecdotes about the research.

5 Mark: Some of the accounts of the contagious nature of laughter are really amazing. In some places, people couldn't stop laughing for days.

Unit 13, Speaking focus, Activity 2

 52

In this part of the test I'm going to give each of you three pictures. I'd like you to talk about two of them on your own for about a minute and a half, and also to answer a question briefly about your partner's pictures.

It's your turn first. Here are your pictures. They show people creating different illusions. I'd like you to compare two of the pictures and say how successful the people are at creating the illusion and why people might enjoy the experience of seeing them.

Unit 13, Speaking focus, Activity 5

 53

Examiner: Which illusion do you think requires the greatest skill to create?

Candidate: Well, it's quite hard to say because they all demand a high level of expertise and would take years to perfect but I suppose if you manage to create a copy of a masterpiece and no one can tell the difference, then that might require the greatest skill.

Unit 14, Listening focus, Activity 2

54

Max Bignall: Hi, I'm Max Bignall and I'm a physics major, so I was naturally very keen to go along to a science club I'd read about when I first arrived in New York about six months ago. It's called the Secret Science Club and it really is quite something. I knew that the club was started by two science writers, Margaret Mittelbach and Michael Crewdson, but not that the third founder was a radio producer called Dorian Devins. He did have a scientific background too, though.

The club started as a small informal gathering held in a Brooklyn bar but soon outgrew this venue and is now held at The Bell House, which is a popular Brooklyn venue for weddings and other private events. But most nights what you can see are the types of acts you would expect from a trendy New York bar, basically up and coming bands of various kinds. And somewhat bizarrely, once a month you'll find a friendly scientist lecturing in down to earth language about a topical scientific issue. The lectures often include experiments at the end, which go down well with the crowd, especially if they involve audience participation.

The talks cover all kinds of issues: they've had a climate scientist talking about super-storms, an evolutionary biologist on the elusive animals that live in our cities, an astrophysicist talking about black holes – which was the highlight for me – and last time we had a mathematical sociologist explaining how ideas spread. The lectures themselves are generally very entertaining and accessible – even for non-scientists – but where I sometimes get lost is at the end, when people ask questions which can be quite specialised. And then there's a chance for everyone to listen to music and talk about the lecture. What's really invaluable for science students like me are the networking opportunities available with some of the best experts in their field.

Nobody can agree about the precise origins of clubs like the Secret Science Club but they seem to have started in universities at the end of the 1990s. Of course, the idea itself is much older. In the 18th century people used to meet up in coffee houses in Britain and France to discuss the affairs of the day, including scientific discoveries.

I could be wrong, but I think the majority of people who attend the Secret Science Club aren't academics, just people with an interest in science. I think the appeal for people like this is that the lectures help them to understand the relevance of science to their daily lives. I like the fact that the Secret Science Club is inclusive and wants to share ideas beyond the scientific community. I think scientists have a responsibility to help people see how science continues to shape the way we see the world and the future.

Unit 14, Speaking focus, Activity 1

 55

Examiner: Good afternoon. My name is Pam and this is my colleague, Stephanie. And your names are?

Gustave: Gustave Jansen.

Maria: Maria Fernández Lourido.

Examiner: Can I have your mark sheets, please? Thank you. First of all, we'd like to know something about you. Gustave, where are you from?

Gustave: The Netherlands.

Examiner: What do you do there?

Gustave: I'm a student.

Examiner: Maria, how long have you been studying English?

Maria: Well, I started learning English in primary school, so I suppose I must have been studying it for about 15 years now.

Examiner: What do you enjoy most about learning English?

Maria: I would have to say the fact that I can watch films and TV series and understand quite a lot. That gives me a lot of satisfaction.

Examiner: Gustave, what did you like most about the area where you grew up?

Gustave: Umm … there are a lot of nice, old buildings.

Examiner: Maria, do you ever wish you were rich and famous?

Maria: To be perfectly honest, not any more, no. I used to when I was younger, of course, but I now think that there are so many responsibilities and problems that come with having money and fame and that sometimes they actually destroy the person's happiness.

Unit 14, Speaking focus, Activity 2

▶ 56

Examiner: In this part of the test I'm going to give each of you three pictures. I'd like you to talk about two of them on your own for about a minute and also to answer a question briefly about your partner's pictures.

Maria, it's your turn first. Here are your pictures. They show people doing research. I'd like you to compare two of the pictures and say why people might choose to do research like this and what problems they might have.

Maria: Both these photographs show women scientists carrying out research but they are actually quite different from one another. In the first photograph the woman seems to be doing some kind of … umm … chemistry experiment – she has a whole lot of … umm … small glass … umm … containers beside her on a bench and she is holding a plastic … umm … envelope with a slide or something inside it up to the light. The second woman is obviously doing something quite different. Instead of working in a lab she is outside doing some kind of field work at night. I think she is probably a zoologist. I imagine her work involves observing animals in their natural habitat, like the frog she's looking at. While the first woman could have the problem of an unexpected reaction of some kind, in which an explosion or perhaps some kind of poisonous gas is produced, the other woman is outside in the open air and probably has to deal with extreme temperatures. She has to wear special clothing to protect her, like gloves and a hat, whereas the chemistry researcher is wearing normal clothes and a lab coat in case she spills some of the liquids.

Examiner: Thank you. Gustave, who do you think is most involved in what they are doing?

Gustave: The woman in the laboratory.

Examiner: Why?

Gustave: She's looking at the slide very closely.

Unit 14, Speaking focus, Activity 4

 57

Examiner: Now I'd like you to talk about something together for about two minutes. Here are some ways that good ideas sometimes spread from one person to another and a question for you to discuss. First you have some time to look at the task.

Now, talk to each other about how effective these ways are for spreading good ideas.

Maria: OK, let's make a start. I actually think good ideas often spread because one person tells another person about them. Do you agree?

Gustave: I'm not sure. I mean, people do talk to each other, of course, and that plays a vital part in human communication, but unless you're referring to lectures, I think more good ideas are spread through online communication than by means of face-to-face interaction. The point I'm trying to make is that a lot of conversation is quite trivial but if someone has something important to say, they're very likely to put it in a blog or perhaps record a podcast.

Maria: It could actually just be telepathy as well, now I come to think of it. I mean, someone has an idea somewhere and then by coincidence it turns out someone else in a completely different country has the same idea.

Gustave: You may have a point there. I have heard that that happens from time to time. If you look at a lot of nineteenth and early twentieth century inventions, it's quite difficult to say who was the real originator of the idea because it often seems to have been invented by two or more people simultaneously.

Maria: Hmm … And in the past there were books and magazines, of course, but nowadays Twitter is a really important way of spreading ideas. As I see it, it's far more important than anything else, at least for young people. People are constantly tweeting things they've read or just thought about.

Gustave: Yes, it's amazing how quickly an idea or just a rumour of some kind can spread through a medium like that. I do have a few reservations about whether these things could actually be called good ideas, though.

Examiner: Thank you. Now you have about a minute to decide which method would reach the largest number of people.

Gustave: For me it would have to be online resources like blogs or even online newspapers and magazines. Wouldn't you accept that almost everyone has an internet connection and potentially has access to good new ideas because of that?

Maria: Yes and no. I still tend to think that Twitter reaches more people.

Gustave: You may be right but not everyone has a Twitter account, of course.

Maria: That's true, so perhaps we could say that the internet is our first choice because of its almost universal appeal.

Unit 14, Speaking focus, Activity 7

 58

Examiner: How important is it for people to learn about the history of science at school?

Gustave: It's very important. People should study history.

Examiner: Some people say they don't see the point of scientific research. Why do you think this is?

Maria: Well, in some cases I think it is because they don't actually know very much about it. There are reports on science research in the better newspapers but not everyone reads them and they may not be aware of the important contribution research can make to things like curing disease or warning us of dangers like global warming.

Examiner: Whose responsibility should it be to inform people about science – scientists or the media?

Gustave: Scientists.

Examiner: Why?

Gustave: They know more about it.

Maria: Yes, but they can inform the press about their work and then it can be presented to the public in an entertaining way.

Examiner: Thank you. That is the end of the test.

Contents

1 I've got a lot of bills to pay, so I won't have any money left by the end of the month.

spend

I've got a lot of bills to pay, so __ __ __ __   __²▨__ __   ⁹▨__ __ __ __ all my money by the end of the month.

2 I started searching for somewhere to live three weeks ago but I haven't found anything.

look

__ __ __ __   __ __ __ __   __⁶▨__ __ __ __ for somewhere to live for three weeks.

3 I moved to London eleven months ago.

live

Next month __ __ __ __   ¹⁵▨__ __ __   __ __¹⁸▨__   __ __ __ __ __ __ __ in London for a year.

4 It took me over two hours to walk home.

walk

By the time I got home, __ __ __   __⁴▨__ __   __ __¹¹▨__ __ __ __ for over two hours.

5 I love the countryside but I prefer the city and always have.

be

I love the countryside but __ __ __ __   __ __ __ __⁵▨__   __ __¹⁰▨__ happier in the city.

6 I haven't felt right since I had that seafood cocktail for lunch.

feel

Since I ate that seafood cocktail for lunch, __ __ __ __   __ __ __ __   ¹²▨__ __ __ __ __ __ a bit strange.

7 I haven't got any plans for the weekend but I might decorate the living room.

think

I haven't got any plans for the weekend but __ __ __   ¹⁴▨__ __ __³▨__ __ __   __ __ decorating the living room.

8 It says orange juice on the carton but anyone drinking it could easily mistake it for grapefruit juice.

taste

It says orange juice on the carton but __ __   __ __ __ __ __ __   ¹▨__⁸▨__ like grapefruit juice.

9 Tony and I spend more time together now that he lives on my street.

see

Tony and I __¹³▨__ __   __ __ __ __   __ __ __ __ __ a lot more of each other since he moved to my street.

10 I think that most of what you've said is clear.

understand

I think __ __ __ __   ⁷▨__ __ __ __ __ __¹⁶▨__ __   ¹⁷▨__ __ __ of what you've said.

1	2	3	4

5	6	7	8	9	10	11	12

13	14

15	16	17	18

Seldom	Scarcely	Rarely	Not only
Under	No sooner	At no time	Hardly
I spend time with my friends during the week.	we had got on the train than we realised it was going in the wrong direction.	any circumstances should you send personal emails on the office computers.	had the lesson just started when the fire alarm went off.
we had met than she started telling me her life history.	have I read a newspaper article that is so full of mistakes.	Veronica arrived late for class but she was also rude to her teacher.	had we got on the train and then we realised it was going in the wrong direction.
I do spend time with my friends during the week.	did Veronica arrive late for class and she was also rude to her teacher.	during the interview did I lie about my qualifications.	do I spend time with my friends during the week.
no circumstances should you send personal emails on the office computers.	the lesson had started when the fire alarm went off.	no circumstances you should send personal emails on the office computers.	had we met when she started telling me her life history.
during the interview I lied about my qualifications.	had we got on the train than we realised it was going in the wrong direction.	I have read a newspaper article that is so full of mistakes.	during the interview did I not lie about my qualifications.
had I read a newspaper article that is so full of mistakes.	had the lesson started than the fire alarm went off.	had we met that she started telling me her life history.	did Veronica arrive late for class but she was also rude to her teacher.

Team A

1 ☐ I'll never forget .... day I left home for the first time.

2 ☐ There were ten of us taking part in the debate but half of .... group didn't say anything!

3 ☐ There's .... student in my class who has never failed an exam!

4 ☐ If I worked for the government, I'd probably do more to help .... homeless.

5 ☐ My grandmother was in her thirties when she finally found .... happiness.

6 ☐ It rained all morning but later on .... sun came out and it got really hot.

7 ☐ We all need .... friends but we also need time away from them.

8 ☐ 'Look at those weird lights in .... sky!' she cried!

9 ☐ Trying to get Jo to change her mind is like banging your head against .... brick wall!

10 ☐ Do you remember .... day we were all late for class?

Your answers for Team B
1 –   2 the   3 the   4 –   5 the   6 –   7 the   8 The   9 a   10 the

✂ -

Team B

1 ☐ In my opinion, wealthy countries should do more to alleviate .... world poverty.

2 ☐ We had a very interesting chat; everyone joined in .... conversation.

3 ☐ The changes to the benefits system are not good news for .... unemployed.

4 ☐ Some people are very sociable but .... others prefer their own company.

5 ☐ She loves French food, French culture and, of course, ... French themselves.

6 ☐ 'I've had enough of this!' Sarah shouted in .... frustration.

7 ☐ As far as I'm concerned, ... world would be a nicer place if everyone learnt to get along.

8 ☐ .... students in Mrs Roberts' class say that she's a brilliant teacher.

9 ☐ I turned around to find .... man I had never seen before blocking my way.

10 ☐ I have a lot of friends but .... ones who matter the most are my oldest friends.

Your answers for Team A
1 the   2 the   3 a   4 the   5 –   6 the   7 –   8 the   9 a   10 the

1

The article says that the screen on Tekfone's new mobile isn't very sensitive and compared with some other models it can be a bit slow downloading large files.

2

The person reviewing the forthcoming CherryPhone in *Technology Today* began with an in-depth analysis of some of its good and bad points.

3

The presenter opened the programme by explaining that he was going to show the viewers how mobile phone tariffs work and why they vary so much from network to network.

4

The shop assistant was very helpful, even transferring the sim card over to my new phone.

5

The presenter gave examples of people who had received huge phone bills in spite of signing up to package deals offered by their network.

6

Many callers to the radio show complained that texting, and in particular textspeak, is killing the written language.

7

My friend Chris, who's a bit of a techie and knows about these things, gave me a few tips for maximising the battery life on my new phone.

8

The conference on the future of information technology was split into five main sections.

9

When my new phone stopped working, the man in the shop told me that I would need to restore the factory settings, which would mean losing all the apps I had downloaded.

10

When social networking websites first appeared in the 1990s, very few people thought they would catch on.

A

Somewhat surprisingly, what followed instead was a vicious exposé on the way some phone companies rip people off with hidden charges.

B

However, such is the impact they have had since then, it is almost impossible to imagine living without them.

C

The reason for this, he said, is that it's easy to accidentally end up using another network which does not honour the agreement you have signed up to.

D

This might well be true but none of them had any proof to back it up, and I think it's wrong to make claims without having all the evidence.

E

She went on to compare it with some similar models currently available, using a team of expert volunteers to test it.

F

The most interesting one was a discussion on the way in which more advanced smartphones will have a major impact on the way we do business.

G

This was not what I wanted to hear, of course, especially as I had been hoping for a solution that wouldn't inconvenience me so much.

H

Despite these shortcomings, I still think it's the one I'll go for, since it seems to be the most user-friendly one available.

I

'Shut down apps when you're not using them,' she said. 'And the same goes for 3G and 4G when you don't need them. And don't charge it to full each time.'

J

Then he demonstrated how, with just one key, I could block unwanted emails and texts with something called *SpamShield*.

Team A: Question 1 for Team B

How might these things have a negative impact on a young person? (2 minutes)

- school/college exams
- overly ambitious parents
- peer pressure to do things they might not usually do
- too much freedom to do what they want
- the environment in which they live

Which of these things would have the biggest negative impact on a young person? (1 minute)

Team B: Question 1 for Team A

How might these factors have a positive influence on a young person's sense of well-being? (2 minutes)

- having plenty of hobbies or interests
- having a large circle of friends
- getting out and about as much as possible
- spending time with their family
- balancing work/study time and leisure time

Which of these factors would have the biggest positive influence on a young person's sense of well-being? (1 minute)

Team A: Question 2 for Team B

How might these life skills help a young adult get on in life? (2 minutes)

- being able to drive
- being able to speak two or more languages
- computer literacy
- good manners
- being able to socialise easily

Which of these skills would be the most beneficial? (1 minute)

Team B: Question 2 for Team A

Which of these qualities should a young person possess if they are to succeed at work? (2 minutes)

- ambition
- the ability to learn from their mistakes
- self-discipline
- being a team player
- enjoying the work they do

Which of these qualities would be the most useful? (1 minute)

Team A: Score sheet for Team B

Did they …

	1	2
discuss all five points in the question?	☐	☐
interact with each other?	☐	☐
expand on what their partner said?	☐	☐
speak for three minutes without too much repetition or hesitation?	☐	☐
provide a satisfactory answer to the question at the end?	☐	☐

Total:

Question 1: ☐   Question 2: ☐

Team A: Score sheet for Team B

Did they …

	1	2
discuss all five points in the question?	☐	☐
interact with each other?	☐	☐
expand on what their partner said?	☐	☐
speak for three minutes without too much repetition or hesitation?	☐	☐
provide a satisfactory answer to the question at the end?	☐	☐

Total:

Question 1: ☐   Question 2: ☐

Team A

1 Little is identified about the author's early life, apart from the fact that he spent his childhood in Tanzania.

2 I demanded my tutor for more time to complete my assignment but he was adamant that I handed it in on the due date.

3 This dispute has been going on for weeks now and I personally feel it's time we concluded it once and for all.

4 Most people feel that the council has spent a considerable figure of money on promoting tourism in the city without any positive benefits.

5 The local economy has suffered a great deal since the closure of several major companies in the town and there's very little anticipation of it recovering in the near future.

6 Going to my cousin's wedding in Essex last week meant that I finally completed my ambition of visiting every county in the country!

7 Generally speaking, I get on well with the partners in my department at work, even if we don't agree on everything.

8 Incessant and noisy roadworks outside our house eventually pushed me to write a letter of complaint to my local council.

9 It is generally believed that reducing the speed limit in cities will produce to fewer accidents on the roads.

10 A proportion of students in my class have complained that they are being given too much work and not enough time to do it all.

Team B

1 My brother Tim is one of three colleagues in a law firm which specialises in company law.

2 Asked to estimate how much it now costs to bring up a child, we did our sums and the amount we arrived at was £200,000.

3 Eve wanted to become a pilot but her parents, who had other ideas for her, drove her towards a career in medicine.

4 He quickly discovered that training to become a professional musician begged a lot of dedication and hard work.

5 The director recently achieved filming his twenty-ninth feature film, probably the last in his long and illustrious career.

6 Having known the cause of the disease, scientists then set about finding a cure.

7 Research shows that people in their thirties spend a larger number of their income on entertainment than any other age group.

8 Increased investment in industry will lead a feeling of confidence in the economy.

9 After carrying out a thorough examination of the building, the investigating officer settled that the probable cause of the fire was faulty electrical wiring.

10 My cousin is coming over from the US next month to spend a couple of weeks with us, so we've decorated the spare bedroom in hope of his visit.

A

1 She's an excellent musician but she hasn't .... her full potential yet.

2 Everyone agreed that the police had .... their authority by randomly stopping and searching people in the street.

3 I really wish that I had .... the chance to travel while I was young.

4 By .... a better understanding of the cause of the disease, we may have a chance of finding a cure.

5 I'm not sure whether to study law or .... my true feelings and pursue a career in the theatre.

6 I'm prepared to .... any opportunity to help me get a good, well-paid job.

7 The expedition team .... serious problems when two of its members were injured.

8 The minister promised he would reduce crime and unemployment but we all .... his word.

9 I don't think we can .... these figures until we've done our own research.

10 Initial reports confirm that the military have .... control of the television station.

B

1 Unfortunately, Tim never .... his ambition of becoming a professional footballer.

2 James's remarkable performance in 'Romeo and Juliet' .... all our expectations.

3 When Susie asked me if I wanted to go to the concert, I naturally .... at the invitation.

4 We managed to break the user's password but .... access to his personal files was more difficult than we had anticipated.

5 I've never been much of a leader, preferring to .... the crowd and do whatever I'm told.

6 At first, we failed to .... the significance of what he was saying to us.

7 In the men's tennis final, Andy Murray .... stiff opposition from Novak Djokovic.

8 I knew that I would succeed where everyone else had failed – I never .... myself.

9 I can't tell you what to do but I think you should .... your instincts and do what you think is right.

10 If we had .... the opportunity when it was presented to us, we would have won.

1

The Dupont company thought they were on to a winner with Corfam, a synthetic leather substitute. It was cheap, easy to produce and looked exactly like the real thing. They decided it was especially well-suited to making shoes and that became the focus of their marketing campaign. Unfortunately, unlike real leather, Corfam wasn't flexible and didn't stretch, making it less than ideal for the product that was showcasing the material. Meanwhile, in response to the perceived threat from Corfam, real leather companies began reducing their prices. Corfam was never a commercial success and very few people today have even heard of it.

Message:
Make sure your product is fit for purpose. (**YES / NO**)

2

In 1976 Clairol introduced a new brand of shampoo called Look of Buttermilk. Test markets gave it a big thumbs-down. Everyone agreed there was nothing wrong with the product itself but Clairol found themselves continually answering the same two questions from their test consumers: 'What exactly is the 'look of buttermilk?' and 'Why should I want it?' Consumer brows were furrowed again a few years later when the company introduced Touch of Yoghurt shampoo. Nobody liked the idea of washing their hair with yoghurt and there were rumours that some people had even mistaken it for food and eaten it.

Message:
The name of a product can sometimes cause confusion. (**YES / NO**)

3

Wall's make sausages and ice cream, and Rolls Royce make cars and aircraft engines. So if diversification works for them, why didn't it work for potato crisp producers Frito Lay when they introduced a new lemonade onto the market? It probably made sense at the time: when you eat our salty crisps, you get thirsty, so why not quench your thirst with our lemonade? Unfortunately, it never caught on, thanks to the simple reason that 'thirst-quenching' is not something people think of when they think of Frito Lay.

Message:
A company that is well-known for one type of product shouldn't make other products. (**YES / NO**)

4

Some people are prepared to spend a fortune on their cats and dogs. Thanks to them, millions around the world are kept in employment grooming, boarding and providing food, healthcare and a myriad of other products and services for pampered pets. Unfortunately, the producers of Thirsty Dog! and Thirsty Cat!, bottled water for cats and dogs, failed to benefit from our love of animals. Inexplicably, although the drink came in mouth-watering flavours like tangy fish and crispy beef, it never caught on with pet owners or their feline and canine charges.

Message:
People are unwilling to spend money on unnecessary things. (**YES / NO**)

5

Ready meals are big business today. After all, why go to all the trouble of preparing a delicious, home-cooked curry or lasagne when you can buy one that's been made for you and all you need to do is pop it into the microwave for a few minutes? And if it works for food, why not for hot drinks? The creative team at Maxwell House may have been thinking that when they came up with the idea of Ready-to-drink coffee – a carton of prepared coffee with milk and sugar that you could put into the microwave. There was just one problem: it wasn't possible to microwave the coffee in its original container, which meant pouring the drink into a cup first. Customers found it just as easy to prepare their coffee the old-fashioned way.

Message:
Convenience food is not always so convenient. (**YES / NO**)

6

In 1975 Sony introduced the first mass-market video recorder, using a format known as Betamax. The following year one of their main competitors, JVC, introduced their own recorder, utilising a different video format called VHS. Since the two formats were incompatible with each other, consumers had to choose between the two. Within a few months there was a fierce format war, with both companies trying to persuade the public that their version was the best. However, while JVC shared their technology with others, Sony refused to license Betamax technology. Consequently, with a far greater choice of models available, the public opted for VCRs, condemning Betamax to technological history.

Message:
Don't let other companies copy your technology. (**YES / NO**)

1 Write the missing first sentence.

Charlie: ....

Clarice: I know. It hasn't let up for days.

Oliver: Do you remember what it was like this time last year?

Clarice: I do. Glorious wall-to-wall sunshine for weeks!

Charlie: Oh well, I must go. Where's my umbrella?

Brian: Forget the umbrella. You'll need a boat out there!

2 Match the first half of the sentences (1–6) with the second (A–F).

1	I wish our teacher	**A**	listened to music instead of watching TV?
2	If only I	**B**	smoke in here.
3	I'd rather you didn't	**C**	wouldn't give us so much homework.
4	I wish I'd	**D**	had more money!
5	It's high time we	**E**	gone to the party – it sounds fun!
6	Would you rather we	**F**	left – it's getting late.

3 Complete the sentences with your own ideas.

1 I wish ....

2 If only I ....

3 I'd rather you didn't ....

4 I wish I'd ....

5 It's high time we ....

6 Would you rather we .... ?

4 Listen to the conversations and write the missing first sentences.

Team ....

1 ....

2 ....

3 ....

Team ....

1 ....

2 ....

3 ....

Team ....

1 ....

2 ....

3 ....

Team A

Your sentences

1 I'm extremely _____ of internet banking, so, _____ , when my bank asked me if I wanted to sign up for their online services, I refused.

2 I wrote to the magazine explaining that parts of the article were a bit _____ , so, _____ , they'll publish a correction in their next edition.

3 _____ , for a book about the importance of good spelling, there are a lot of _____ .

4 The minister's comments about immigration could easily have been open to _____ but _____ enough, this was completely overlooked in the newspaper article.

Your hits and misses

	A	B	C	D
1				
2				
3				
4				
5				
6				
7				
8				
9				

Your words for Team B

	A	B	C	D
1			misgivings	
2				misunderstanding
3		surprisingly		
4				
5				
6	unfortunately			understandably
7			thankfully	
8			misconception	
9		misguided		

✂ -

Team B

Your sentences

1 _____ , given everything we know about the health benefits of regular exercise, there is still a popular _____ that too much exercise is bad for you.

2 _____ , there appears to have been some sort of _____ : I booked a ticket to Budapest and they've sent me a ticket to Bucharest.

3 There have been several reported cases of accidents at nuclear power stations, so, _____ , people have serious _____ about nuclear power.

4 The tourist board's decision to run a 'murder sites' tour of the city was somewhat _____ but, _____ , they changed their mind before it was implemented.

Your hits and misses

	A	B	C	D
1				
2				
3				
4				
5				
6				
7				
8				
9				

Your words for Team B

	A	B	C	D
1		naturally		
2				
3				
4	mistrustful		misleading	misprints
5				
6				oddly
7		hopefully		
8	misinterpretation			ironically
9				

---

analyse   astonish   complete   consider   discover   effect   final   hunt   refer   remain

---

1 The two .... in the tennis match were known to have a long-standing rivalry.

2 Our science professor likes to be .... to by his title, *Dr* Sarkissian.

3 After several delays, the flight .... left at half past nine.

4 When we conduct an investigation into the incident, we need to take a number of facts into ....

5 We've got a plan but we just need to .... the details.

6 I thought the project would be easy but I was .... wrong, as usual.

7 The pit was found to contain pieces of broken pottery along with some animal ....

8 What .... me is that so much information is available online.

9 The lecture was so boring that most of the audience left and only a handful ....

10 There were thousands of these animals on the island until .... arrived in the early eighteenth century.

11 You must pay half the fee by 1 April and the .... at least two weeks before the course begins.

12 Over the course of 200 years, the birds were .... almost to the point of extinction.

13 This new hay fever inhaler is completely .... I might as well put water up my nose!

14 The animals' .... ground is limited to the coast, where they feed on insects and small mammals.

15 Footballers are often tempted to argue with the ....

16 Recent archaeological .... in the valley have shed more light on this ancient civilisation.

17 I think I did extremely well in the exam, ... I didn't do much revising.

18 The city remained .... by European travellers until 1817.

19 The project has a(n) .... date of 1 May, although there may be one or two delays.

20 Marie and Pierre Curie are best known for .... radium in 1898.

21 Going through some old boxes in the attic, we made a(n) .... discovery.

22 It was extremely .... of her to arrange a meeting without telling us beforehand.

23 Once we had downloaded and .... the data, we were able to start work on the report.

24 I'm afraid I think your essay is .... , as you haven't discussed all of the main points.

25 Blood samples were sent to the laboratory for ....

26 'I can't believe you spoke to her like that!' he said, looking at me in ....

27 Economic .... were consulted to see if they could understand how the economy was doing.

28 It's not possible to communicate .... in another language with just a few basic words.

29 During his talk, he made continual .... to the royal family.

30 The film wasn't very good but the special .... were excellent.

✂ --

absolutely bitterly deeply disappointed emotional enormous exceptional fairly furious
highly impossible perfect plausible practically predictable quite seriously somewhat
surprised unremarkable worried

1 The spider in their living room last night was …

2 The meal they had last night was …

3 The film they saw at the weekend was …

4 They find getting up early in the morning …

5 They were … to discover that the museum they went to charged an entry fee.

6 They were … with their exam results.

7 They were … when they found that their email accounts had been hacked.

8 Their new English teacher is …

9 Their best friend was … when his pet goldfish died.

10 The storyline in the book they have just read was …

11 The latest album by their favourite group is …

12 They are … about the rising crime rate in their neighbourhood.

Mystery word

The advertising company you work for has been asked to promote a new brand of potato crisps and you have come up with four mottos. You must now choose one of these. Which one would you choose? Alternatively, think of your own.

- Add some crunch to your lunch.
- Taste the fun.
- Bet you can't stop at just one.
- Real potatoes, real flavour, real good.

Your motto:

....

The advertising company you work for has been asked to promote a new airline and you have come up with four mottos. You must now choose one of these. Which one would you choose? Alternatively, think of your own.

- Faster, cheaper, better.
- We'll give you the world without charging the earth.
- To us, you're more than just a piece of human luggage.
- Nobody gives you quality air time like us.

Your motto:

....

The advertising company you work for has been asked to promote a new supermarket and you have come up with four mottos. You must now choose one of these. Which one would you choose? Alternatively, think of your own.

- Eat to live, live to eat.
- Tip-top food at rock-bottom prices.
- Fill your trolley without emptying your purse.
- We put the fun back into shopping.

Your motto:

....

The advertising company you work for has been asked to promote a new smartphone and you have come up with four mottos. You must now choose one of these. Which one would you choose? Alternatively, think of your own.

- Get yourself connected.
- The whole world in the palm of your hand.
- It's much more than just another phone.
- The shape of things to come.

Your motto:

....

The advertising company you work for has been asked to promote a new sports car and you have come up with four mottos. You must now choose one of these. Which one would you choose? Alternatively, think of your own.

- It's not just a car – it's a whole new lifestyle.
- Love at first sight.
- Get in, start up, pull out and take off.
- Turning your fantasy into reality.

Your motto:

....

The advertising company you work for has been asked to promote a new hotel chain and you have come up with four mottos. You must now choose one of these. Which one would you choose? Alternatively, think of your own.

- Make yourself at home.
- Five star luxury at two star prices
- Where every guest is a VIP.
- Whether it's for work or play, we're the place to stay!

Your motto:

....

You have a meal in a restaurant and then leave. Halfway home, you realise you didn't pay for the meal. Do you return to the restaurant and pay?

A group of friends is coming over to your house to have one of your famous vegetable curries. You remember at the last minute that one of them is a vegetarian and you have used meat stock in the curry. Do you tell him/her?

You have an important test tomorrow. Worried about it, you decide to go to the classroom to talk to your teacher. She is not there but you see the test paper lying on your teacher's desk. Do you have a quick look?

You find a wallet on the bus. It has clearly been dropped by the man you saw getting off a few stops back. As there is no address in it, the only way you can return it is by getting off the bus and walking back a few stops. Do you?

While the waiter in the restaurant where you are having dinner is being very polite and helpful to you, he is being extremely rude to a couple at the next table. You suspect that this is because of their skin colour. Do you say something to the waiter?

You see a woman shoplifting in a supermarket. She is clearly quite poor and has three small children with her. Do you report her to a shop assistant?

An unemployed friend has had a successful job interview and asks you for a reference. You know from past experience that your friend is not a good worker. Do you provide a reference for her?

While cycling down the street, you accidentally hit a parked car, leaving a long scratch down the side. Do you leave a note on the windscreen explaining what you have done and offering to pay for the damage?

You want a copy of the *Gold Advanced Exam Maximiser* but don't have much money. A friend tells you about a website where you can download a free copy. You know that this is illegal and is effectively stealing from the publisher and author. Do you download the book?

You are using your friend's computer without her permission and you accidentally erase some important files. Do you tell your friend what you have done?

You are using a cash machine to withdraw cash. You want to take out £100 but the machine gives you £150. The receipt says you have only withdrawn the £100 you wanted. Do you return the money to the bank?

A friend has bought a new dress and wants to know what you think of it. You think it looks terrible on her. Do you say so?

While walking down the street, you see a paper bag on the pavement. Looking inside, you find £500 in £20 notes. There is no indication who the money belongs to. Do you hand it in to the police?

The only parking space available outside the supermarket is for disabled drivers. You are only going into the shop for some milk, so won't be more than a few minutes. Do you park there?

Andy Watson

A The important thing is to not make comparisons with the way things are done in your own country. If something is different, it isn't necessarily worse.

B You've 'gone native', as the expression goes but in the best way possible.

C It's perfectly normal to feel disoriented during your first few days in a foreign country but as long as you accept from the beginning that this is all part of the experience, you should get along just fine.

D Eventually, you'll start thinking and behaving just like your hosts.

E You should also remind yourself that you won't integrate overnight – that's something you need to work at and not give up if it all becomes challenging.

1 A feeling of confusion is natural at first.

2 It's common to have some negative feelings.

3 You can quickly become part of your new community.

Alice Griffin

A They accept others and, in turn, they are accepted as one of them.

B When they arrive in their host country, many people have problems adapting.

C It can be three or four months before they tell themselves that they either have to accept the way things are or leave.

D Assuming they make the former choice – and it's much easier to do this when they start living and behaving like the locals – that is when things start changing for the better.

E The initial thrill of being somewhere different doesn't last long and they find themselves really missing their friends and family back home.

1 The excitement of moving abroad is short-lived.

2 Most people leave again after a short time.

3 Integration is easier if you adapt to local ways of life.

Olivia Jenkins

A Providing they can maintain this momentum, they are certain to last the course and begin playing an active role in their community, even if they never fully become as much a part of it as they would like.

B What's more, they refuse to seek out the company of their compatriots or scour the streets looking for food from their own country.

C As soon as they arrive in a new country, many people make an active decision to make the most of their new situation.

D Instead, they throw themselves into the deep end, going places, making new friends, joining clubs.

E They tell themselves from the start that they aren't going to sit around feeling homesick, avoiding strangers and complaining that 'they don't do things the same here'.

1 Feelings of homesickness are common.

2 Involvement in the community helps you to integrate.

3 People who make an effort are able to integrate.

Peter Carter

A Then they start finding themselves getting irritated with little things, saying, 'We don't do things like this at home, so why do they?' and that's when homesickness sets in.

B Eventually, there comes that wonderful moment when they really feel that they are a part of things and they can say, 'I'm one of you now.'

C This doesn't happen straight away, of course, but perseverance and determination will ensure that it eventually does happen.

D However, they gradually began to embrace their new surroundings, meet people, get involved in the local social scene and so on, and that's when they began to feel a part of things.

E At first, people moving abroad experience a 'honeymoon' phase: everything is new and exciting.

1 Making comparisons with home isn't a good idea.

2 People become homesick when they can't integrate.

3 Integration cannot always be achieved.

Questions

Which person ...

1 has a similar view to Peter Carter about the process people go through as they assimilate into a new life abroad?

2 shares Olivia Jenkins' view that a positive attitude from the start can help someone moving to another country?

3 has the same opinion as Andy Watson that becoming a part of a new community requires time and effort?

4 expresses a different view from the others regarding the extent to which people can integrate into their community?

> accused   admitted   announced   asked   blamed
> claimed   doubted   invited   objected   permitted
> regretted   said   suggested   told   warned

1 He/She _____ that his/her _____ _____ _____ _____

_____ .

2 He/She _____ me _____ he/she _____ _____ my _____ for

a _____ _____ .

3 He/She _____ us _____ _____ _____

_____ .

4 He/She _____ us _____ _____ his/her _____ _____

_____ .

5 He/She _____ _____ _____ _____ .

6 He/She _____ John _____ _____ _____ .

7 He/She _____ that he/she _____ _____ _____ _____

_____ _____ _____ .

8 He/She _____ us _____ _____ _____ .

9 He/She _____ us _____ his/her _____ _____ _____ .

10 He/She _____ _____ my _____ .

11 He/She _____ us _____ _____ _____ _____ _____

_____ _____ the _____ .

12 He /She _____ we _____ _____ _____ a _____ .

13 He/She _____ _____ _____ .

14 He/ She _____ that Alice _____ _____ _____ .

15 He/She _____ that _____ _____ _____ _____ at

_____ .

Team A

Read these sentences to Team B.

1 I failed my driving test yesterday.
2 I think that new restaurant on George Street is a bit expensive.
3 This new camera is absolutely fantastic!
4 I really fancy a coffee and a piece of carrot cake.
5 Can I help? You look like you've lost something.
6 I don't understand why some people complain all the time.
7 I've booked a holiday to the Parakeet Islands.
8 I sometimes find it hard to concentrate when watching a film.
9 I hate revising for exams. I can never seem to remember anything.
10 The doctor told me the headaches I was getting were nothing serious – just a result of stress.
11 I was going to study Medicine at university but then I decided Law would be a better option.
12 You aren't interested in history, are you?

Complete these sentences with the phrases in the box and match them with Team B's sentences.

> bear that in mind   bored out of my mind
> has something on his mind   have a mind of its own
> mind your language   make up your mind
> mind boggling   mind how you go   mind went blank
> never you mind   have half a mind   wouldn't mind

A I agree. I _____ to leave without paying.
B Thanks, I _____ . It's really nice.
C Awful. I was _____ .
D Not well. When I was asked what my strengths were, my _____ .
E Very polite and proper, so _____ when she's around.
F Yes. Perhaps he _____ .
G Oh, right. I'll _____ next time.
H Amazing! That's a _____ amount of money.
I I know. It seems to _____ .
J Well, _____ . The pavements are really icy.
K _____ . It was strictly between her and me.
L Well, _____ . The waiter's coming over.

Team B

Read these sentences to Team A.

1 What's your sister like?
2 Apparently, the movie *Avatar* cost $500 million to make.
3 Your talk was great but I thought you spoke a bit too quickly.
4 Would you like another slice of cake?
5 I can't decide whether to have the soup or the seafood for a starter.
6 What were you and Claudia talking about earlier?
7 I think I'll go for a walk.
8 How was that play you saw last night?
9 Sam seemed a bit distracted, didn't he?
10 This is one of the worst meals I've ever had.
11 This new computer doesn't seem to do what you want it to do.
12 How did your interview go yesterday?

Complete these sentences with the phrases in the box and match them with Team A's sentences.

> change your mind   don't mind me   mind reader
> get my mind round   have a mind like a sieve
> if you don't mind my asking   of the same mind
> in the right frame of mind   mind you
> never mind   out of your mind   set your mind at rest

A Same here. I _____ .
B Oh, _____ . I've just misplaced that cheque I was supposed to post.
C I agree. _____ , it's worth it.
D Really? What made you _____ ?
E Oh well, _____ . Better luck next time.
F Me too. I have to be _____ , otherwise I just don't get into it.
G Good, that must have _____ . But you need to relax a bit more.
H How much did it cost, _____ ?
I Are you _____ ? There's a full-blown revolution going on over there!
J It's not that. It's just that I can't _____ all those dates and events.
K In that respect, you and I are _____ . Stop moaning, that's what I say!
L Wow, you must be a _____ ! That's just what I was thinking!

Sentence beginnings	Sentence endings
1 What makes us happy is … *Our answer:* ☐ *Other pair's answer:* ☐	**A** ....
2 What we like about weekends is … *Our answer:* ☐ *Other pair's answer:* ☐	**B** ....
3 What makes us angry is … *Our answer:* ☐ *Other pair's answer:* ☐	**C** ....
4 What we'd like to do this evening is … *Our answer:* ☐ *Other pair's answer:* ☐	**D** ....
5 What we would like for dinner tonight is … *Our answer:* ☐ *Other pair's answer:* ☐	**E** ....
6 What annoys us about some people is … *Our answer:* ☐ *Other pair's answer:* ☐	**F** ....
7 What we'd most like to do for a living is … *Our answer:* ☐ *Other pair's answer:* ☐	**G** ....
8 What makes us sad is … *Our answer:* ☐ *Other pair's answer:* ☐	**H** ....
9 What we like/dislike about the internet is … *Our answer:* ☐ *Other pair's answer:* ☐	**I** ....
10 What we need right now is … *Our answer:* ☐ *Other pair's answer:* ☐	**J** ....

1 When my classmates first established a litter patrol in my town, many people laughed at us. Our local newspaper, which seems to take delight in making people look stupid, even ran an article in which we were referred to as 'the Dirty Dozen'. I guess we were a bit discouraged at first but we decided to ignore the jokes and just got on with it. Gradually, as we began making a difference, ridicule turned to respect. That, I guess, is the secret to life: don't give up and lose heart just because others poke fun at you.

2 With crime becoming a big problem in my town, I decided it might be a good idea to set up a neighbourhood watch scheme on my street. The idea was that the residents would all keep an eye on one another's properties and report anyone behaving suspiciously to the police. I put the idea forward at our annual residents' meeting but my initial enthusiasm was replaced by a sense of disappointment at their lack of interest.

3 The environment is in big trouble, and has been for many years. What worries me is that so few of us seem to have any concern about things like global warming, pollution and all the other environmental problems that are damaging our plant. I believe that people are aware of these problems but need to be encouraged to actually do something about it. It's all too easy to do nothing in the belief that others will take care of it for you.

4 When it came to homelessness in my city, I was a bit apathetic. I felt sorry for homeless people, of course, but I didn't feel there was anything I could do to help. However, visiting London one evening, I came across a group of volunteers who spend their nights roaming the city streets giving food, help and support to those unfortunate enough to live rough. The inspiration they gave me to do something was remarkable, so I when I returned home, I set about starting up a similar organisation.

5 The other day I saw a young man drop an empty bag of crisps on the street. I hate litter, so I politely asked him to pick it up and put it in the bin. The rebuke I received was alarming but not altogether unexpected. 'Mind your own business!' he said and then, somewhat illogically, 'Show me some respect!' I explained that I couldn't do the former because his littering was everybody's business and I could only do the latter once he had done something to deserve it – like using a litter bin, for example. This merely earned me more abuse and the feeling that some people just don't care about their environment.

6 When I suggested to my local council that the town set up a public bicycle-sharing scheme similar to those in places like Paris and London, I came up against a lot of opposition. The main argument was the cost and the belief that it would be money wasted. Using data obtained from public research into the viability of these schemes, I was able to prove to the council that not only would it cost less than they thought but, in the long run, it would actually make them money. And, of course, it would help to cut down on motor traffic in the town, making it a more desirable place to live in, work in and visit. That seemed to work and so far the scheme has been a great success.

7 When congestion charges for privately owned vehicles were first introduced to my city, many people complained that the system was rather confusing. It didn't matter to me at first, since I took the bus into the city. However, when I was promoted, I was given a company car, which meant I would have to drive. I quickly found out that the system was in fact pretty straightforward. Drivers of private vehicles had to pay £10 to drive into the city centre, unless they were carrying two or more passengers or if their vehicle was an electric-hybrid one, and charges weren't applied at the weekend. Very simple, really.

✂ -

1 The speaker thinks that you shouldn't be .... when people fail to take you seriously.
(letters 1 and 10)

2 The speaker expresses his/her .... at the apathy of others.
(letters 1 and 8)

3 The speaker thinks that when it comes to the state of the environment, people's lack of ....
needs to be addressed.
(letter 4)

4 The speaker found a great deal of .... in the people he/she met.
(letter 7)

5 The speaker says the man dropping litter wanted .... that he hadn't earned.
(letter 7)

6 By persuading the council of the benefits of his/her plan, the speaker managed to overcome his/her

....
(letter 6)

7 The speaker found the congestion charge scheme less .... than he had heard.
(letters 2 and 8)

Mystery word

If you want to succeed in something, what you need above all is …

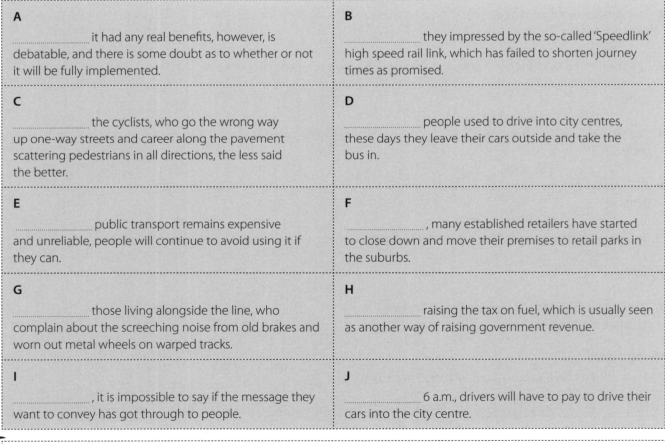

1
Encouraging people to take buses and trains into urban centres seems to have little effect.

2
The urban congestion charge comes into effect this Monday.

3
The Environment Agency has been running an advertising campaign encouraging people to use public transport more.

4
Many of the country's main urban areas now have Park and Ride schemes in place.

5
The public bicycle sharing scheme, trialled last year, was hailed by the papers as a major step towards reducing traffic in city centres.

6
Increasing the cost of vehicle licences has had little, if no, effect on the number of vehicles on our roads.

7
Traffic congestion and increasingly high levels of pollution have done nothing to encourage new shops to set up in business in the city centre.

8
Commuters are complaining that train and bus services into the city are becoming increasingly expensive and unreliable.

9
People using the town's dated trams say that they are in serious need of repair.

10
The drivers in my city are terrible, ignoring road signs, pedestrian crossings and red lights.

A
.... it had any real benefits, however, is debatable, and there is some doubt as to whether or not it will be fully implemented.

B
.... they impressed by the so-called 'Speedlink' high speed rail link, which has failed to shorten journey times as promised.

C
.... the cyclists, who go the wrong way up one-way streets and career along the pavement scattering pedestrians in all directions, the less said the better.

D
.... people used to drive into city centres, these days they leave their cars outside and take the bus in.

E
.... public transport remains expensive and unreliable, people will continue to avoid using it if they can.

F
.... , many established retailers have started to close down and move their premises to retail parks in the suburbs.

G
.... those living alongside the line, who complain about the screeching noise from old brakes and worn out metal wheels on warped tracks.

H
.... raising the tax on fuel, which is usually seen as another way of raising government revenue.

I
.... , it is impossible to say if the message they want to convey has got through to people.

J
.... 6 a.m., drivers will have to pay to drive their cars into the city centre.

| as do | as for | as from | as it is | as long as | as yet | nor are | nor has | whereas | whether |

Ron

I like a challenge. In fact, the greater the challenge, the more I enjoy it. My motto is 'I don't do can't', which basically means that I'll do anything I'm asked to do. This can be exhausting, of course, and I've lost several nights' sleep working on things that are particularly difficult.

John

Many people go to pieces when they're working to a tight deadline but not me. In fact, quite the opposite. That's when I'm at my best. My brain becomes more focused and I'm less easily distracted. The best essay I ever wrote I did three hours before it was due in.

Roberta

I'm not a solitary person, either in my personal or my professional life. I prefer being part of a team, especially when a job is particularly demanding or when I'm being put under a lot of pressure. I get on well with my colleagues, so this helps a lot when we're told to work together on something.

Amelia

I'm quite an imaginative person and I love inventing things. I recently designed a cover that protects my e-reader from damage, so now I can drop it on the ground or in a swimming pool and it's still OK. I'm also working on a device that waters your plants when you're away.

Jo

I think that people look up to me, respect me. It's nice to know that you're helping someone, even if you're just setting an example. One of the nicest things anyone has ever told me was that when they were given a difficult or challenging job to do, they wondered how I would do it. I must confess that made feel really good about myself!

Teresa

My boss is always looking over my shoulder, breathing down my neck, asking me where my report is or if I've sorted out the accounts yet. This would put a lot of people off but, to be honest, I quite enjoy being pushed like that and I must admit it helps me to get the job done more effectively.

Jane

In a game or competition, I'm not happy unless I win. Second place just isn't good enough. After all, being second just makes you the first of the losers, doesn't it? I'll do absolutely anything to ensure I win; anything. Would I cheat? Probably not but perhaps if I was seriously pushed, I might.

Mark

I don't like it when someone gives me a difficult job to do and I'm left to struggle through it alone. However, put me with others and that's a different story. There's something about being in a group that helps you to focus more on the job at hand, exchange ideas, allocate tasks and so on. There's an English phrase that says, 'Many hands make light work,' and I think that's very true.

Alan

I don't think I'm any better or worse than my work colleagues but I seem to be alone on this one. It seems that I'm always being approached by one of them saying, 'You're always making good sales. How do you do it?' or 'What's the secret of your success?' I usually just tell them that it's not so much hard work as having confidence in yourself. I believe that's true. I really do.

Ollie

If you have a problem and want a solution, I'm your person! I'm especially good when it comes to improvising when you need something but haven't got it. The other day I went to a barbecue at my friend's and he didn't have any firelighters. I found the solution in his kitchen: a packet of Brazil nuts – they did the job perfectly!

1 I offered to look after my friend's flat while she was away and then decided that I could use her sunbed in her absence.

.... to look after my friend's flat while she was away, I then decided that I could use her sunbed in her absence.

2 I needed to leave work early and asked my boss if I could finish my report on at home.

.... to leave work early, I asked my boss if I could finish my report at home.

3 I wasn't expecting any visitors last night, so was surprised when the doorbell rang.

.... any visitors last night, I was surprised when the doorbell rang.

4 I hadn't seen my friend Keith for ages, so I was really pleased when he suddenly paid me a visit.

.... my friend Keith for ages, I was really pleased when he suddenly paid me a visit.

5 Since I was a nervous flyer, I wasn't looking forward to the ten-hour flight to San Francisco.

.... a nervous flyer, I wasn't looking forward to the ten-hour flight to San Francisco.

6 Because I wanted to text a few friends during my lesson, I decided to sit at the back of the class.

.... to text a few friends during my lesson, I decided to sit at the back of the class.

7 As I was walking home the other day, I saw a large brown envelope lying in the road.

.... home the other day, I saw a large brown envelope lying in the road.

8 Because I was convinced that my boss was up to no good, I hid a video camera in the office.

.... that my boss was up to no good, I hid a video camera in the office.

9 I hadn't asked my brother if I could borrow his car, so knew that I would have to drive it extra carefully.

.... my brother if I could borrow his car, I knew that I would have to drive it extra carefully.

10 I knew that my sister was frightened of spiders, so I decided to play a little trick on her.

.... that my sister was frightened of spiders, I decided to play a little trick on her.

11 I hadn't had time for breakfast, so I decided to pick up something to eat on my way into town.

.... time for breakfast, I decided to pick up something to eat on my way into town.

12 As I didn't want to forget my laptop when I went to work the next morning, I left it by the front door.

.... to forget my laptop when I went to work the next morning, I left it by the front door.

13 I thought that the flat next door was empty, so I was alarmed to hear strange noises coming from it.

.... that the flat next door was empty, I was alarmed to hear strange noises coming from it.

14 Because I had heard that my favourite group were giving a concert, I went online to look for tickets.

.... that my favourite group were giving a concert, I went online to look for tickets.

15 I badly wanted to attend a football match, so decided to phone my boss and pretend I was ill.

.... to attend a major football match, I decided to phone my boss and pretend I was ill.

A

buzz	chatter	click	creak	croak	drip	gurgle
hiss	hoot	hum	patter	pop	roar	rustle
shuffle	sigh	snap	splash	whisper	whoosh

If you think that a tropical rainforest is somewhere you'll get some peace and quiet, then you should think again. The whole place is ¹_____ (B11) with animal and insect activity, and even the trees themselves refuse to remain quiet. Listen carefully. Can you hear the ²_____ (B3) of the branches as they bend slightly in the breeze ³_____ (B2) and ⁴_____ (B15) through the leaves? And that loud ⁵_____ (B12) noise is probably a branch breaking off under the weight of its foliage.

Alright, let's walk further into the forest and see what we find. I don't know about you but I love the sound of dead leaves ⁶_____ (B14) underfoot. It reminds me of autumn back home. That ⁷_____ (B10) noise you can hear in the distance is probably a big cat. A leopard, maybe, or a panther. Let's hope it doesn't come too close! The same goes for the bees ⁸_____ (B4) around the flowers collecting pollen – they can get quite aggressive if they're disturbed – and the monkeys ⁹_____ (B8) in the branches above us. In fact, it's probably best to avoid close contact with any of the wildlife – you never know when it might turn on you. Uh oh, what's that ¹⁰_____ (B16) noise? It could be a snake. Watch where you put your feet!

OK, now we've come to a clearing with a pond. That ¹¹_____ (B6) noise you can hear is the stream that feeds it. Can you hear the frogs ¹²_____ (B9)? At night they're so loud you can't hear yourself think! In fact, night in the rainforest is an amazing auditory experience, what with the frogs, insects and ¹³_____ (B13) owls all competing to make themselves heard.

Oh dear, it's started raining! Well, this is a rainforest, I suppose, what else did we expect? And that brings more noise, of course, with rain ¹⁴_____ (B7) on the leaves and ¹⁵_____ (B5) down the back of our necks. Let's turn back. In fact, let's turn back quickly: I really don't like the sound of whatever large animal is ¹⁶_____ (B1) towards us through the undergrowth!

B

buzz	chatter	click	creak	croak	drip	gurgle
hiss	hoot	hum	patter	pop	roar	rustle
shuffle	sigh	snap	splash	whisper	whoosh

Well, here we are at the theatre. Have you got the tickets? Great, let's go in. Past the box office with a long line of people waiting to buy tickets, ¹_____ (A16) their feet and ²_____ (A3) with impatience, through the ³_____ (A2) doors (the hinges could really do with a bit of oil!) and into the foyer. It's certainly ⁴_____ (A8) with activity in here, isn't it? There are so many people. Look at that lady over there – she's absolutely ⁵_____ (A15) with jewellery. I don't think I've ever seen so much gold and silver on one person! Oh dear, someone's brought a baby with them! I hope it doesn't spoil the show with its crying and ⁶_____ (A11). Oh, it's OK, they're leaving. That's a relief!

Alright, we've got a bit of time before the show begins, so let's go to the theatre café for a drink. Up the stairs, our feet ⁷_____ (A14) on the marble steps, and into the café. It's busy in here as well: a couple of friends ⁸_____ (A9) over their drinks, a man with a sore throat ⁹_____ (A12) at his wife, a loud group ¹⁰_____ (A7) with laughter at a joke one of them has just told, the waitress ¹¹_____ (A1) a tune to herself as she collects empty glasses and a man ¹²_____ (A5) his fingers to get her attention. How rude of him!

OK, there's the bell. Time to go in for the show. It's much quieter here in the auditorium. You can hear the occasional ¹³_____ (A13) of car horns in the street outside but it's barely audible through the soundproof walls. The lights dim and the curtain goes up. The only sounds now are those of people ¹⁴_____ (A6) their programmes, a couple ¹⁵_____ (A4) to each other about where to go for dinner after the show and an angry man behind them, ¹⁶_____ (A10) at them to be quiet. The actors are appearing on stage and it's show time!

A It set the tone for the rest of the album, with subsequent tracks cranking up the anger factor even more.

B The music world suddenly roused itself from its collective lethargy and went, 'Woah! Hang on a moment – what is *that*?'

C However, *Heat Rash* did it so well, with razor-sharp lyrics, catchy tunes and a healthy splash of humour, that it was able to appeal to a much wider demographic.

D At the beginning of the twenty-first century, British rock music was a bit of a lost cause.

E Some, like *Let Me Be*, even became unofficial anthems for disenfranchised youth around the country

F **Review: Turnip Surprise – *Heat Rash***

G Consequently, it was a huge hit and should surely go down as one of the all-time greats.

H And while the album did allow the listener a bit of breathing space from time to time, even the cooling breeze provided by more pop-oriented songs such as *Birds of a Feather* seemed tainted.

I Most artists seemed content to follow in the weary footsteps of the so-called Britpop bands of the 1990s, and there seemed little desire to change.

J From the very first song, the upbeat and angry *Low Self-esteem*, *Heat Rash* left you reeling like a man who had just done ten rounds with Floyd Mayweather.

K Angry and cynical albums like this frequently fail to find an audience outside of those who are equally angry and cynical.

L Then in 2005 along came *Heat Rash*, an eclectic collection of original songs by Newcastle-based indie rockers Turnip Surprise.

Review: Turnip Surprise – *Heat Rash*

At the beginning of the twenty-first century, British rock music was a bit of a lost cause. Most artists seemed content to follow in the weary footsteps of the so-called Britpop bands of the 1990s, and there seemed little desire to change. Then in 2005 along came *Heat Rash*, an eclectic collection of original songs by Newcastle-based indie rockers Turnip Surprise. The music world suddenly roused itself from its collective lethargy and went, 'Woah! Hang on a moment – what is *that*?'

From the very first song, the upbeat and angry *Low Self-esteem*, *Heat Rash* left you reeling like a man who had just done ten rounds with Floyd Mayweather. It set the tone for the rest of the album, with subsequent tracks cranking up the anger factor even more. Some, like *Let Me Be*, even became unofficial anthems for disenfranchised youth around the country. And while the album did allow the listener a bit of breathing space from time to time, even the cooling breeze provided by more pop-oriented songs such as *Birds of a Feather* seemed tainted.

Angry and cynical albums like this frequently fail to find an audience outside of those who are equally angry and cynical. However, *Heat Rash* did it so well, with razor-sharp lyrics, catchy tunes and a healthy splash of humour, that it was able to appeal to a much wider demographic. Consequently, it was a huge hit and should surely go down as one of the all-time greats.

Student A cards

	1	20	6
START ⇨	When his chair collapsed under him, he went bright red with	You didn't do any revision. That's absolutely ....!' he said.	Judy gave a deep sigh of .... 'This weather is just perfect.
21 'I am so ....!'	**17** The .... welled up inside me until I started screaming and crying.	**13** 'I don't do it for your ....!' I said angrily. 'I do it so we can eat.'	**18** There seems to be some .... about the new dress code rules.

Student B cards

14	11	15	2
In fact, I don't think I've ever seen him look so	'It's so .... trying to make you see sense!'	'You should hang your head in ....!'	My maths teacher at school was a really .... man.
12 'Whether he fires me or keeps me on is a matter of complete .... to me,' he said.	**8** 'I find it really .... watching you try to cook. You haven't got a clue, have you?' said Julie.	**9** People are .... as to whether or not they can wear casual clothes like jeans.	**FINISH**

Student C cards

16	7	10	5
… she shouted, storming out of the room and slamming the door in	He looked at me in utter .... 'How on earth did you get an A in the exam?	I would be .... to just sit here all day and soak up the sun.'	'Talking to your grandmother in such a rude way was really ....,' my sister said to me.
4 His perpetual .... was reflected in his face, giving you the impression he had just been sucking on a lemon.	**19** Imogen sighed with .... 'Thank goodness the test has been cancelled!' she said.	**22** 'Oh, for goodness sake, don't be so ....!' my mother said. 'It's only a little spider!'	**3** Don felt completely .... about his boss's threats.

Alternatively, …	Apart from …	As well as this, …	Besides this, …
Consequently, …	Despite this, …	Even so, …	For this reason, …
Furthermore, …	Given …,	In contrast, …	In view of …,
Moreover, …	On the contrary, …	On the other hand, …	What's more, …

Some teachers wear a suit and tie to work to confer authority.	Wearing socks with sandals looks really silly.	I usually dress very casually at the weekend.	Wearing smart, well-tailored clothes makes you feel good.
Wearing trainers with a suit is never a good idea.	Jolokia shoes are beautiful but unbelievably expensive.	I almost never wear a suit.	It's bad form to wear too much jewellery.
Wearing an ill-fitting or badly pressed suit does not make you look smart.	I think that some of the latest fashion designs are really over the top.	For quality clothes, you should go to Smart's on the High Street.	I believe that the secret of success is to always dress smartly, no matter what the occasion.
My brother has absolutely no taste when it comes to clothes.	I never have much money to spend on the latest fashions.	People who dress smartly for work are taken more seriously than those who dress casually.	The new sportswear shop on Rose Street is really good.
Buying designer clothes on the internet is cheaper than going to a department store.	Dressing well these days can be quite expensive.	They say that you shouldn't judge someone by the clothes they wear.	That shirt you're wearing really suits you.

What would you both look for in a good job and why?

- colleagues
- prospects
- employer
- responsibility
- (working) environment
- salary/wage(s)
- (paid) holiday(s)
- (job) satisfaction
- promotion
- (job) security

Do you think that the next 100 years will be better or worse than the last 100?

- (the) Earth
- pollution
- natural disaster(s)
- (over)population
- environment
- natural resources
- famine
- technology
- peace
- war

What steps could we as individuals take to help improve the environment?

- conserve
- recycle
- cut down on
- reduce
- dependence
- natural resources
- energy
- public transport
- pollution
- turn down

How important is it that we develop a greater awareness of the kinds of food we eat?

- balanced (diet)
- healthy
- cut down on
- obesity/obese
- fast/junk food
- meat
- fat
- organic
- fruit/vegetables
- variety

Some people say that we have become too reliant on technology. Would you agree?

- advances
- internet
- complicated
- smartphones
- computers
- (over) reliant
- depend
- science
- develop/development(s)
- social networking

What role should media such as newspapers and the internet play in our lives and to what extent do you think they do this?

- advice
- news
- educate
- current affairs
- entertain
- report
- inform
- resource
- interesting
- truth(ful)

centimetres complicate courtesy dark different drop fact fall grey hand hands have help
honour interest laughing life and death make mince mind opinion organic personal raise
routine similar small subject taste time urgency waiting

Student A	Student B	Student C
9 I'm not scared of heights. It's just a case of _____ over matter.	**9** The internet connection is very slow and to _____ matters further, my computer keeps crashing.	**9** The programme was good but I thought that some of the _____ matter was inappropriate for children.
8 I didn't need to ask his permission to leave but did so as a matter of _____ .	**8** New employers usually ask your previous employers for a reference as a matter of _____ .	**8** My tutor asked to see me to discuss the _____ matter of my exams next month.
7 The machine converts _____ matter such as vegetable peelings into usable energy.	**7** Everyone was in a bad mood and the temperature in the room certainly didn't _____ matters.	**7** The need to find a cure for the virus has now become a matter of great _____ .
6 Whether or not she is a good boss is a matter of _____ .	**6** Some people like modern art while others prefer something more traditional. It's a matter of _____ .	**6** The car drove onto the pavement and missed me by a matter of _____ .
5 She told me exactly what she thought of me, and certainly didn't _____ matters!	**5** At today's meeting, I'd like to _____ the matter of competition and falling sales.	**5** You've made your point several times. Now can you let the matter _____ ?
4 This problem is serious. It's no _____ matter.	**4** He's OK when you meet him in a group but meeting him alone is a(n) _____ matter.	**4** I want your full attention. We really need to concentrate on the matter in _____ .
3 Can I leave work early today? It's a(n) _____ matter.	**3** We can't wait for him to help us. We need to take matters into our own _____ .	**3** I haven't heard from him today. As a matter of _____ , I haven't heard from him all week.
2 We're not yet sure if the new drug will work. Now it's a matter of _____ to see if it has any effect.	**2** I love solving complicated mathematical problems. Besides, it's good exercise for the old _____ matter.	**2** Scientists are looking for a cure for the illness. It can only be a matter of _____ before they find one.
1 I don't mind if your assignment is a little late. It's not exactly a matter of _____ .	**1** We're determined to prove ourselves innocent of the crime. It's a matter of _____ .	**1** Just as a matter of _____ , where did you go to school?
Student A Start ⇧	**Student B Start** ⇧	**Student C Start** ⇧

Teaching notes

1A   Find the phrase

Aim

To review perfect and continuous tenses

Exam link

Reading and Use of English Part 4 (Key word transformations)

Activity type

Completing gapped sentences to reveal a hidden English phrase

Classroom dynamics

Pairs or groups of three

Time taken

20 minutes

When to use

After Grammar Focus Activity 7 on page 8

Preparation

Make one copy of the activity for each pair or group of three students.

Procedure

1   Divide your class into pairs or groups of three and give each pair/group a copy of the activity.

2   Explain that the second sentence in each pair should be completed with a form of the word in bold. Students should write the missing words on the lines provided (one letter on each line; note that apostrophes also count as characters, so should also be written on one of the lines). In some cases, there may be more than one way of transforming the sentence but only one will fit into the spaces provided, so a certain amount of trial and error will be involved.

3   Some of the lines are shaded in grey and preceded by a number. Students should write the letters from these lines into the appropriate numbered boxes at the bottom of the activity. If they do this correctly, they will reveal a common English phrase.

4   The first pair or group to reveal the phrase is the winner.

5   (Optional) The phrase students should reveal is *make yourself at home*, which is a phrase used to welcome visitors to your home and help them relax and feel comfortable. If you have a multilingual class, you could ask students what they say to visitors in their country and ask them how the phrase translates into English.

Answer key

1 I'll have spent   **2** I've been looking   **3** I'll have been living   **4** I'd been walking   **5** I've always been **6** I've been feeling   **7** I'm thinking of   **8** it tastes more **9** have been seeing   **10** I've understood most
The phrase students should reveal is *Make yourself at home.*

1B   Choose carefully

Aim

To review and practise language of emphasis with inversion

Exam link

None, but useful for Reading and Use of English Part 4 (Key word transformations)

Activity type

Listening to sentences and then identifying their correct inverted forms

Classroom dynamics

Groups of four or five

Time taken

20 minutes

When to use

After Grammar Focus Activity 6 on page 13

Preparation

Make one copy of the activity for each group of four or five students and cut into cards. (You do not need to shuffle them.)

Procedure

1 Divide your class into groups of four or five and give each group a set of cards. They should spread them out on the desk.

2 Explain that they are going to hear eight sentences. After each sentence, they should choose one of the shaded cards and one of the white cards to form an inverted version of the sentence they have just heard. In some cases more than one shaded card may be possible but they should only choose one in each case.

3 Read out the following sentences, pausing for about 1–2 minutes between sentences so that students have time to discuss the best card for their answer.

 1 *We had only just met when she started telling me her life history.*

 2 *The lesson had just started when the fire alarm went off.*

 3 *I did not lie about my qualifications during the interview.*

 4 *Veronica arrived late for class and she was also rude to her teacher.*

 5 *I have hardly ever read a newspaper article that is so full of mistakes.*

 6 *We got on the train and then immediately realised it was going in the wrong direction.*

 7 *I hardly ever spend time with my friends during the week.*

 8 *You should not send personal emails on the office computers under any circumstances.*

4 Review students' answers carefully, making sure they have chosen the correct inverted sentence in each case. Award one point for each correct sentence. The winning group is the group with the most points.

2A Let's risk it!

Aim

To review the use of definite and indefinite articles

Exam link

None

Activity type

Identifying where articles are needed in a 'casino'-style activity

Classroom dynamics

Groups of four, divided into pairs

Time taken

20 minutes

When to use

After Grammar Focus Activity 5 on page 19

Preparation

Make one copy of the activity for each group of four students and cut into two sections.

Procedure

1 Divide your class into groups of four and ask each group to divide into pairs (Team A and Team B). Give each team a *Team A* or *Team B* section of the activity.

2 Explain that each team has ten gapped sentences. The gaps can either be completed with *the* or *a*, or left blank if no article is needed. The aim of the activity is to decide what is needed in each gap and win or lose points in the process.

3 Both teams choose a sentence on their paper (they do not need to work through them in order) and then decide whether or not an article is needed. They write the answer in the gap (or leave it blank if no article is needed).

4 They then decide how certain they are that their answer is correct and how many points (1–5) they are prepared to risk. They write this number in the box for each sentence. The more certain they are of their answer, the more points they can risk.

5 Each team then tells the other which sentence they chose, what their answer is and how many points they are risking.

6 The opposing team tells them if their answer is correct. If it is correct, they win the points that they risked; if it is wrong, they lose those points.

7 Steps 3–6 are repeated for the remaining sentences. The winning team in each group is the team with the most points.

2B Ten perfect pairs

Aim
To identify 'follow-on' sentences using reference words and context

Exam link
Reading and Use of English Part 7 (Gapped text)

Activity type
Matching pairs of sentences

Classroom dynamics
Groups of four or five

Time taken
30 minutes

When to use
After Reading Focus Activity 7 on page 20

Preparation
Make one copy of the activity for each group of four or five students and cut into cards. Keep the numbered and lettered cards in two separate sets.

Procedure

1 Divide your class into groups of four or five and give each group a set of numbered cards (1–10).

2 Ask students to work in their groups and predict the sentence that follows each of the numbered sentences. Allow about ten minutes for this.

3 Hand out the lettered sentences (A–J). Ask students to match each lettered sentence with one of the numbered sentences. Allow about 10 minutes for this, then tell students to stop and review their answers. The winning group is the group with the most correct matches.

4 Ask students how they knew which lettered sentences followed on from which numbered sentences. They should have done this using a combination of reference pronouns (e.g., *this*, *these*) and the context of the sentences. Ask students if any of their predicted sentences were similar to the lettered sentences.

Answer key
1 H   2 E   3 A   4 J   5 C   6 D   7 I   8 F   9 G   10 B

3A A good answer

Aim
To practise collaborative speaking

Exam link
Speaking Part 3 (Collaborative task)

Activity type
Answering CAE-style Speaking questions while being assessed by other students

Classroom dynamics
Groups of four, divided into pairs

Time taken
20 minutes

When to use

After Speaking Focus Activity 5 on page 31

Preparation

Make one copy of the activity for each group of four students and cut into cards.

Procedure

1 Divide your class into groups of four and ask each group to divide into pairs (Team A and Team B). Give each team a *Team A* or *Team B* set of cards.

2 Explain that in their teams, students are going to do a collaborative speaking activity and their responses are going to be analysed by the other team in their group.

3 Team A begins by giving Team B their Question 1. The students in Team B should take a few seconds to read the question and then answer it. They should make sure they:

- discuss all five points in the question and the summary question at the end.
- interact with each other.
- expand on what their partner says.
- speak for the allocated time (3 minutes), without too much repetition or hesitation.

4 The students in Team A time the Team B students and use the checklist on their score sheet to tick the things the Team B students do. When the Team B students finish speaking, Team A should give them feedback based on how they did. They should then award them points based on their answer.

5 Team B then gives their Question 1 to Team A and follows the same procedure.

6 The process is repeated with the Question 2 cards. The winning team is the team with the most points.

3B   Word exchange

Aim

To identify incorrect words in sentences

Exam link

Reading and Use of English Part 1 (Multiple-choice cloze)

Activity type

Identifying incorrect words in sentences and exchanging the wrong words with other students

Classroom dynamics

Groups of four, divided into pairs

Time taken

20–25 minutes

When to use

After Use of English Focus Activity 6 on page 32

Preparation

Make one copy of the activity for each group of four students and cut into two sections.

Procedure

1 Divide your class into groups of four and ask each group to divide into pairs (Team A and Team B). Give each team a *Team A* or *Team B* section of the activity. They should not show this to the other team in their group.

2 Explain that each of the ten sentences on each team's sheet contains *one* wrong word (one that does not collocate with other words in the sentence or does work in the context of the sentence). Students work in their pairs and try to identify incorrect words. They should delete these words from their sentences and write them on a separate sheet of paper. Set a time limit of about 10 minutes for this.

3 Tell students to pass their written list of words to the other team in their group. That team should then try to use those words to replace the words they have deleted from their own sentences. Allow them about 5–10 minutes for this.

4 Tell students to stop and review all the answers. Groups award themselves one point for each word correctly placed in their sentences (maximum 20 points). The group with the most points wins.

Answer key

A1, B6: identified, known   **A2, B4:** demanded, begged
A3, B9: concluded, settled   **A4, B2:** figure, amount
A5, B10: anticipation, hope   **A6, B5:** completed, achieved   **A7, B1:** partners, colleagues
A8, B3: pushed, drove   **A9, B8:** produce, lead
A10, B7: proportion, number

4A Same word, different sentences

Aim
To review verbs and collocations

Exam link
None

Activity type
Collaborative crossword

Classroom dynamics
Pairs

Time taken
15–25 minutes

When to use
After Use of English Focus Activity 7 on page 38

Preparation
Make one copy of the activity for each pair of three students and cut into three sections.

Procedure
1 Divide the class into A and B students and give each student their A or B sheet. Do not give out the crossword yet. Put students into AA and BB pairs. Explain that they have a set of gapped sentences. They must look at their sentences and think of all the verbs that could go in the gaps. Allow around 5–10 minutes for this.

2 Put students into A/B pairs and give them a copy of the crossword. Students now work together to look at their sentences together and complete the crossword. Each verb in the crossword must fit the sentence with that number on both sheets. For example, answer 1 in the crossword (*realised/ achieved*) fits in the gap in sentence 1 on sheet A and sentence 1 on sheet B.

3 Let students continue until one group has completed their crossword or set a time limit of about 10 minutes, then review their answers. The winning pair is either the first pair to finish or the pair with the most correct answers when the time is up.

Answer key
1 realised/achieved   **2** exceeded   **3** grabbed
4 gaining   **5** follow   **6** grasp   **7** encountered
8 doubted   **9** trust   **10** seized

4B Get the message?

Aim
To practise reading for gist or the author's implied message

Exam link
Reading and Use of English (especially but not confined to) Part 5 (Multiple choice)

Activity type
Identifying the gist or main message on a set of cards

Classroom dynamics
Groups of three or four

Time taken
20 minutes

When to use
After Reading Focus Activity 6 on page 40

Preparation
Make one copy of the activity for each group of three/four students and cut into cards.

Procedure
1 Divide your class into groups of three or four and give each group a set of cards.

2 Explain that each card contains a short paragraph about a product that has failed. The paragraph is followed by a sentence that either conveys the message being implied by the writer of the paragraph or gives the gist of that paragraph. Three of the sentences are an accurate reflection of the message implied in the paragraph but three of them are not.

3 Working in their groups, students read the paragraphs and decide which sentences are correct and which are not. They should then decide what the message *should* be for the paragraphs where the sentence is incorrect.

4 Let students do the activity for about 15 minutes, then review their answers. Award the groups one point for each message identified as being correct or incorrect and up to three points for the message they think *should* be there (see suggested messages below).

5A You wish!

Aim
To review hypothetical structures

Exam link
None

Activity type
Performing/Listening to short conversations and deciding what the 'prompt' sentences were

Classroom dynamics
Four groups

Time taken
25–30 minutes

When to use
After Grammar Focus Activity 5 on page 49

Preparation
Make one copy of the activity for each student in the class.

Procedure

1 Divide your class into four groups (Teams A–D) and give each student a copy of the activity.

2 Ask students to do Activity 1. Ask them what clues helped them identify Charlie's first line.

3 Students do Activity 2. Check answers and review the tense uses in the sentences if necessary.

4 Students do Activity 3.

5 Students now choose three of the sentences from Activity 3 and use them as the opening lines of a conversation. They prepare and practise their conversations but should not say the opening lines.

6 Teams take turns to perform their conversations, making sure they don't include the opening lines. The other teams should write the letter (A–D) of the team performing and, for each conversation, write down what they think the opening line was.

7 When each team has completed its conversations, ask the other teams what they thought the opening line was in each one. They get one point if they correctly identify the main idea and two points if they get the exact sentence. The winning team is the team with the most points.

5B Hit and *mis-*

Aim
To review the prefix *mis-* and sentence adverbs

Exam link
None

Activity type
Completing sentences in a *Battleships*-style game

Classroom dynamics
Groups of four, divided into pairs

Time taken
15–20 minutes

When to use
After Writing Focus Activity 2 on page 54

Preparation
Make one copy of the activity for each group of four students and cut into two sections.

Procedure

1 Divide your class into groups of four and ask each group to divide into pairs (Team A and Team B). Give each team a *Team A* or *Team B* section of the activity. They should not show these to each other.

2 Explain that each team has four sentences and each sentence has two words missing. One of these is a word beginning with the prefix *mis-* and the other is an adverb. Their opposing team has the words they need to complete their sentences and they need to obtain these words from them.

3 Team A begins by giving Team B a letter/number reference from their left-hand grid (e.g. *C7*). They tick off this space on their left-hand grid so they don't repeat it. Team B looks at that space in their right-hand grid and tells Team A if there is a word there and what that word is.

4 If there is a word in that space, Team A decides which sentence that word goes into and writes it in the gap in the sentence. Play then passes to Team B, who repeat steps 3–4.

5 Steps 3–4 are repeated until one team in each group has completed all their sentences.

Answer key

Team A

1 mistrustful, naturally   2 misleading, hopefully
3 Ironically, misprints   4 misinterpretation, oddly

Team B

1 Surprisingly, misconception   2 Unfortunately, misunderstanding   3 understandably, misgivings
4 misguided, thankfully

6A   Three in a row

Aim

To review modified word forms (including prefixes and suffixes)

Exam link

Reading and Use of English Part 3 (Word formation)

Activity type

Completing gapped sentences with correct word forms while playing a board game

Classroom dynamics

Groups of four, divided into pairs

Time taken

20–25 minutes

When to use

After Use of English and Listening Focus Activity 5 on page 58

Preparation

Make one copy of the activity for each pair of students and separate the sentences from the grid.

Procedure

1 Divide your class into groups of four and ask each group to divide into A and B pairs.

2 Give each pair a copy of the sentences. Explain that for each word in the box, there are three sentences that can be completed with a different form of the word (e.g. *analyse, analysis, analysts*. Allow pairs time to complete as many sentences as they can (allow 5–10 minutes for this).

3 Hand out a grid to each group of four students. Tell them that they are now going to play a game using the words in their sentences and the grid.

4 Team A begins by choosing one of the base forms from the word box. They write a sentence number and one of the words from that base form (e.g. *3 finally*) in one of the spaces on their grid. This is then repeated by Team B, who choose a different base word and write a sentence number and word (e.g. *30 effects*) in another space on the grid.

5 Team A then write another sentence number and word formed from their base form (e.g. *1 finalists*) in the space to the left, right, above or below their previous answer. The aim of the activity is to collect a row of three answers, with each answer being a different form of the same word. Not only should they try to collect rows for themselves but they should prevent the other team from doing so (similar to *noughts and crosses*). Tell them that they will have to plan their strategy with their partner and decide if they are going to concentrate primarily on forming rows for themselves or preventing their partner from forming rows!

6 Let the activity continue for about 15 minutes, then tell them to stop and review their answers. Teams get one point for each correct word form and three points for each row of three, provided all of their answers in that row are correct. The winning team is the one with the most points.

Answer key

analyse: 23 analysed, 25 analysis, 27 analysts

astonish: 8 astonishes, 21 astonishing, 26 astonishment

complete: 6 completely, 19 completion, 24 incomplete

consider: 4 consideration, 17 considering, 22 inconsiderate

discover: 16 discoveries, 18 undiscovered, 20 discovering

effect: 13 ineffective, 28 effectively, 30 effects

final: 1 finalists, 3 finally, 5 finalise

hunt: 10 hunters, 12 hunted, 14 hunting

refer: 2 referred, 15 referee, 29 reference

remain: 7 remains, 9 remained, 11 remainder

6B   Absolutely right

Aim

To review modifying adverbs

Exam link

None

Activity type

Completing sentences to reveal a missing word

Classroom dynamics

Groups of three or four

Time taken

25 minutes

When to use

After Grammar Focus Activity 5 on page 65

Preparation

Make one copy of the activity for each group of three or four students.

Procedure

1 Divide your class into groups, and give each group a copy of the activity.

2 Explain that each sentence can be completed with a modifying adverb and adjective from the box, and these words should be written into the grids underneath each sentence (one letter per space). Point out that one of the adverbs will be used twice and one will be used three times. In some cases, more than one answer may be possible but only one combination of words will fit into each grid. When completed, the letters in the shaded spaces will spell out another modifying adverb.

3 Invite one student from each group to the front of the class and show them the answer to the first sentence (*absolutely enormous*). They should read this to themselves, then return to their desk.

4 They then convey the meaning of the adverb and adjective to their group but *without* using the words. The other members of their group must guess the correct adverb and adjective. When they have guessed the answer, they can write it in their grid, and another student from their group comes to you for the next answer.

5 The activity continues until one group has completed all the sentences. Check answers and ask students to use the letters in the shaded boxes to form the mystery word.

Answer key

1 absolutely enormous   **2** quite unremarkable
3 fairly predictable   **4** practically impossible
5 somewhat surprised   **6** bitterly disappointed
7 absolutely furious   **8** quite exceptional
9 deeply emotional   **10** highly plausible
11 absolutely perfect   **12** seriously worried
mystery word: surprisingly

7A   Make your pitch

Aim

To practise using language of agreement and disagreement in a collaborative/decision-making task

Exam link

Speaking Part 3 (Collaborative task)

Activity type

Choosing a motto for a new product and promoting that product to the class

Classroom dynamics

Six groups

Time taken

25–30 minutes

When to use

After Speaking Focus Activity 5 on page 74

Preparation

Make one copy of the activity and cut into cards.

Procedure

1 Divide your class into six groups and give each group a card. Explain that they work for an advertising company and have been asked to come up with an advertising campaign for a new product or service. So far, their company has come up with four possible mottos for this product, which they will see on their card.

2 In their teams, they should think of a name for their product or service, then choose their motto. They should discuss the advantages and disadvantages of each motto on their card, using language of agreement and disagreement where relevant. If they are not happy with any of the mottos, they can make up their own. Allow about 10 minutes for this, monitoring the groups to make sure that everybody is participating and that no students are dominating the discussion.

3 When the time is up, tell them that they are going to promote their product/service to the rest of the class. In their groups, they should decide what they are going to say and how they are going to say it. They shouldn't write this down but they should have a clear idea of the main message they want to convey. Their presentation should end with their motto.

4 Students decide who in their group is going to give the presentation to the class.

5 One student from each group then gives the presentation. When all the groups have finished, groups should award points to each presentation, based on how persuasive they thought the advertising pitch was (5 = very persuasive, 1 = not at all persuasive), Ask groups to explain why they awarded the points they did. The winning group is the group with the most points.

7B   Just supposing

Aim

To practise different forms of conditionals

Exam link

None

Activity type

Making decisions based on moral dilemmas

Classroom dynamics

Groups of three or four

Time taken

30–40 minutes

When to use

After Grammar Focus Activity 5 on page 75

Preparation

Make one copy of the activity for each group of three or four students, cut into cards and shuffle.

Procedure

1 Tell your class that you are going to give them a dilemma to think about. The dilemma is this: *It is dark, and you are driving home from work along a lonely stretch of road. You see a desperate-looking man hitch-hiking by the side of the road. Do you stop to pick him up?* Ask students if they would stop for him. They can give three answers: *Yes*, *No* or *It depends*.

2 Now ask students to qualify their answers using a conditional sentence. For example: *Yes, I'd stop, otherwise he might freeze to death.* Or *It depends; were there someone else in the car with me, I probably would but if I were on my own, I wouldn't.*

3 Give each group a set of cards, which they should place face down on the desk. Students take it in turns to pick up a card. They read out the dilemma on the card, then all the students in the group say what they would do and qualify their answer with a conditional sentence. One student in each group should write their answers down on a separate sheet of paper.

4 Let this continue for about 20 minutes, then ask students to stop. Ask each group to tell the class about the dilemmas they had and the responses they gave, then award each group 1 point for each correct conditional sentence. The winning group is the group with the most points.

8A   Four texts

Aim
To practise cross-text multiple matching

Exam link
Reading and Use of English Part 6 (Cross-text multiple matching); also useful for Part 7 (Gapped text)

Activity type
Arranging sentences to form complete texts, then answering questions about the texts

Classroom dynamics
Groups of four

Time taken
20 minutes

When to use
After Reading Focus Activity 5 on page 82

Preparation
Make one copy of the activity for each group of four students. Cut into cards.

Procedure
1 Divide your class into groups of four and ask each group to divide into pairs. Give one pair the cards for Andy Watson and Alice Griffin, and the other pair the cards for Olivia Jenkins and Peter Carter. Give them the Question cards but ask them to put these face down on the table until later.

2 Explain that each card contains a short text in which someone gives their opinion on moving or living abroad. The text has been broken up into five sections and these sections have been put in the wrong order. Working in their pairs, they should number the text sections for each of their texts 1–5. They should then decide if the three statements which follow each text are true or false, or if the information is not given in the text.

3 When they have done this, they should read out their texts (in the correct order) to the others in their group, who should decide if they sound right.

4 Once the group have all agreed that their text sections are in the correct order, they then look at the Question card and answer the questions. At this stage they can look at all the text cards together.

5 The first group to correctly answer all of their questions is the winner.

Answer key
Andy Watson: C, A, E, D, B (**1** true, **2** not given, **3** false)
Alice Griffin: B, E, C, D, A (**1** true, **2** not given, **3** true)
Olivia Jenkins: C, E, B, D, A (**1** not given, **2** true, **3** not given)
Peter Carter: E, A, D, B, C (**1** true, **2** not given, **3** false)
Questions
1 Alice Griffin   **2** Andy Watson   **3** Peter Carter
4 Olivia Jenkins

8B   The whole sentence

Aim
To review reporting verbs and structures

Exam link
None, but useful for Reading and Use of English Part 4 (Key word transformations)

Activity type
Listening to direct speech sentences and converting them to reported speech

Classroom dynamics
Five groups and whole class

Time taken
20–25 minutes

When to use
After Grammar Focus Activity 4 on page 85

Preparation
Make one copy of the activity per student.

Procedure

1 Divide your class into five teams of roughly equal size and give each student a copy of the activity. Ask each group to nominate a team captain.

2 Explain that they are going to hear fifteen direct speech sentences and they are going to report what was said. For each direct speech sentence they hear, they will complete the gapped sentences on their activity sheet using a verb from the top of the sheet and other words.

3 One student from each team comes to the front and writes down the first sentence from the list below. They go back to their seats and read the sentence to their team. They must not show the sentence, only read it. The students in their team listen carefully and work together to decide how it should be transformed into reported speech You could do this first sentence as an example. Note that the student who reads out the sentence cannot help his/her team mates. Also note that in some cases, more than one reporting verb may be possible but each verb should be used once only. The team captain has the final say if there is any disagreement.

4 Step 3 is repeated for the other sentences, team members taking it in turns to come to the front of the class to collect the next sentence. When one team has finished all the sentences, stop the activity and review the answers. Teams receive 1 point for each correctly completed sentence.

Sentences:

1 My camping holiday was terrible.

2 Can I borrow your bike for a few hours?

3 Don't touch the red wire.

4 You borrowed my camera without asking first!

5 I'm really sorry I was so rude.

6 It was John who was responsible for making the mess.

7 I was at the theatre on Friday evening.

8 You can leave early.

9 Would you like to come to my place for lunch?

10 It was me who broke your mobile.

11 Don't believe everything you read in the papers.

12 Why don't we go into town for a meal?

13 I don't see why I should work on Saturday.

14 I don't think Alice is telling the truth.

15 The next flight will leave at half past ten.

Answer key

1 He/She said that his/her camping holiday had been terrible.

2 He/She asked me if/whether he/she could borrow bike for a few hours.

3 He/She told/warned us not to touch the red wire.

4 He/She accused us of borrowing his/her camera without asking first.

5 He/She regretted being so rude.

6 He/She blamed John for making the mess.

7 He/She claimed/said that he/she had been at the theatre on Friday evening.

8 He/She permitted us to leave early.

9 He/She invited us to his/her place for lunch.

10 He/She admitted breaking my mobile.

11 He/She told/warned us not to/we shouldn't believe everything we read in the papers.

12 He/She suggested we go/went into town for a meal.

13 He/She objected to working on Saturday.

14 He/She doubted that Alice was telling the truth.

15 He/She announced/said that the next flight will/would leave at half past ten.

9A   As quick as you can

Aim

To review expressions with *mind* and introduce new expressions

Exam link

None

Activity type

Matching and completion game

Classroom dynamics

Whole class, divided into two teams

Time taken

20 minutes

When to use

After Use of English and Vocabulary Focus Activity 8 on page 89

Preparation

Make one copy of the activity per two students, and cut into cards

Procedure

1   Divide your class into two teams, A and B. Ask students to move so that the members of each team are all sitting together.

2   Give each student a *Team A* or *Team B* card. Explain that each team has twelve prompt sentences (1–12) and twelve responses to the other team's prompts (A–L). Each response is missing an expression with *mind*, which can be found in the word box. The aim is for teams to match their responses with the other team's prompt sentences using one of the expressions with *mind*.

3   Students in Team A take it in turns to read out one of their prompt sentences. Team B must listen and work together to identify the correct response and correct expression with *mind*. They write their answers down on the sheet, e.g.*1 E never mind*.

4   When they have finished, the roles are reversed, with Team B giving the prompt sentences and Team A choosing the responses and the correct expressions with *mind*.

5   Review all the answers and award points. Teams get one point for each correct response and one point for each correct expression with *mind*. The winning team is the team with the most points.

6   (Optional) How much can your students remember? Ask them to put their cards away, then give them definitions of the expressions with *mind* and ask if they can remember what the expressions were. For example: *If you forget things very easily, we can say that you …* (have a mind like a sieve). You could also award students points for this to add to their total from the main part of the activity.

Answer key

Team A

1   E mind your language
2   H mind boggling
3   G bear that in mind
4   B wouldn't mind
5   L make up your mind
6   K Never you mind
7   J mind how you go
8   C bored out of my mind
9   F has something on his mind
10   A have half a mind
11   I have a mind of its own
12   D mind went blank

Team B

1   E never mind
2   C Mind you
3   H if you don't mind my asking
4   L mind reader
5   B don't mind me
6   K of the same mind
7   I out of your mind
8   F in the right frame of mind
9   A have a mind like a sieve
10   G set your mind at rest
11   D change your mind
12   J get my mind round

9B   Beginnings and endings

Aim

To practise cleft sentences beginning with *what*

Exam link

None, but useful for Speaking Parts 3 and 4 (Collaborative task and follow-up discussion)

Activity type

Discussing likes, dislikes, ambitions, etc, with the aim of finding something in common.

Classroom dynamics

Pairs and groups of four

Time taken

20–25 minutes

When to use

After Grammar Focus Activity 5 on page 95

Preparation

Make one copy of the activity for each pair and cut into two parts.

Procedure

1 Divide the class into pairs. Give each pair a copy of the two parts of the activity. Explain that they have a series of sentence beginnings starting with *what*. Working in their pairs, they should think of an ending for each sentence. They should write their endings only in the *Sentence endings* grid (gaps A–J), but in a jumbled order. They should write the correct letter (A–J) for each answer in the *Our answer* box for the appropriate sentence beginning. For example, if they finish sentence 1 with *sitting on the beach* (*What makes us happy is sitting on the beach*), they write *sitting on the beach'* next to letter D, for example, and write *D* in the *Our answer* box under sentence beginning 1. Allow about 10 minutes for this.

2 Put pairs together into groups of four. Students exchange their sentence endings and try to match the other pair's jumbled sentence endings with the sentence beginnings. They should write the answers in the *Other pair's answer* box for each sentence beginning. Allow about 5–10 minutes for this.

3 Students compare answers. They get a point for each sentence ending they matched correctly. The winning pair is the pair with the most points.

10A That's what you need

Aim

To practise listening for specific information

Exam link

Listening Part 2 (Sentence completion)

Activity type

Listening to monologues and completing sentences with the correct word to reveal a 'mystery' word

Classroom dynamics

Groups and whole class

Time taken

20 minutes

When to use

After Listening Focus Activity 3 on page 104

Preparation

Make one copy of the first page of the activity and cut into cards. Make seven copies of the second page of the activity.

Procedure

1 Divide your class into seven groups. Give one student in each group one of the cards. They should not show this card to the others in their group. Also give each group a copy of the second page of the activity.

2 Explain to the class that they are going to hear seven short monologues read by a student from each group. They should listen carefully and complete each sentence with one word, which they will hear in the monologue. They should then look at the words they have written and take the letters indicated by the numbers after each sentence. They should use these letters to complete the final sentence with the mystery word.

3 The student with card number 1 comes to the front of the class and reads out their monologue twice. They then rejoin their group. The groups decide what the answer is for sentence 1 (note that the student who read out the monologue cannot help their team).

4 Step 3 is repeated for monologues 2–7.

5 Review the answers. Groups get one point for each correct answer and three points for revealing the mystery word in the final sentence.

Answer key

1 discouraged   **2** disappointment   **3** concern
4 inspiration   **5** respect   **6** opposition   **7** confusing
mystery word: dedication

10B Transport links

Aim
To review conjunctions

Exam link
None, but useful for Reading and Use of English Part 7 (Gapped text) and Writing

Activity type
Matching and completing sentence pairs/parts

Classroom dynamics
Pairwork

Time taken
15–20 minutes

When to use
After Grammar Focus Activity 4 on page 105

Preparation
Make one copy of the activity for each pair and cut into cards. Keep the two sets of cards and the list of conjunctions separate.

Procedure
1 Divide your class into pairs. Give each pair a copy of each set of cards and the list of conjunctions.

2 Explain that students should put the shaded cards (A–J) face down in a pile on the desk. They should share out the numbered cards (1–10) between them and hold these cards in their hands. Explain that the numbered sentences (1–10) have a follow-on sentence or part in the lettered sentences (A–J). The aim of the activity is to match the sentence pairs and complete the lettered sentences with one of the conjunctions in the box.

3 Students take turns to turn over one of the shaded cards from the pile on the table. If they think the shaded card matches one of the cards they are holding, they can complete it using one of the conjunctions and then claim it. They must show their partner the sentence they are holding, to confirm the match.

4 Let play continue for about 10 minutes or until some students have matched all their sentences. Check answers. The player with the most correct matches wins.

Answer key
1 E as long as   2 J As from   3 I As yet   4 D Whereas
5 A Whether   6 H Nor has   7 F As it is   8 B Nor are
9 G as do   10 C As for

11A Compatibility

Aim
To practise reading for general meaning

Exam link
None, but useful for Reading and Use of English Part 8 (Multiple matching)

Activity type
Reading to find pairs of people who have something in common

Classroom dynamics
Groups of four or five

Time taken
20–25 minutes

When to use
After Listening Focus Activity 5 on page 115

Preparation
Make one copy of the activity for each group of four or five students and cut into cards.

Procedure
1 Divide your class into groups of four or five and give each group a set of cards.

2 Explain that the cards contain short monologues by ten people, each one on the theme of work. Each person has something in common with another person in the set. The aim of the activity is to match these people with a compatible partner.

3 Allow your groups about ten minutes to read through their cards, discuss and identify the people who have something in common.

4 When the time is up, read out the following questions, pausing between each one. On a separate sheet of paper, students write down the names of the people.

 1 *Can you name two people who place great demands on themselves?*

 2 *Can you name two people who always come up with great ideas?*

 3 *Can you name two people who work well under pressure?*

 4 *Can you name two people who work well in collaboration with others?*

 5 *Can you name two people who are an inspiration to others?*

5 Review students' answers and award one point for each correctly matched pair. The winning group is the group with the most points.

Answer key

1 Ron + Jane   **2** Amelia + Ollie   **3** John + Teresa
4 Roberta + Mark   **5** Jo + Alan

11B   Participle clause bingo

Aim
To review participle clauses and past forms

Exam link
None

Activity type
Changing sentences using participle clauses and using the clauses in a game of *Bingo*

Classroom dynamics
Pairs or small groups

Time taken
25 minutes

When to use
After Grammar Focus Activity 6 on page 116

Preparation
Make one copy of the activity for each pair or small group of students.

Procedure

1 Divide your class into pairs or small groups and give each pair/group a copy of the activity.

2 Explain that students should complete the second sentence in each item so that it has a similar meaning to the first. In each case, they will need a participle clause. When they have done this, they should choose any nine of the participle clauses in their answers and transfer the missing words to the grid at the bottom of the sheet (e.g. *needing*, from sentence 2).

3 Explain that they are now going to play a game of *Bingo*. You are going to read out the missing words and they are going to tick them off in their grid. The first pair/group to tick off all the words in their grid calls out *Bingo!* and wins the game.

4 Read out the missing words below at random, pausing briefly between each one. Do not read out the numbers – these are for your reference only and refer to the sentences they are used in.

 1 *Having offered*   9 *Not having asked*

 2 *Needing*   10 *Knowing*

 3 *Not expecting*   11 *Not having had*

 4 *Not having seen*   12 *Not wanting*

 5 *Being*   13 *Thinking*

 6 *Wanting*   14 *Having heard*

 7 *Walking*   15 *Badly wanting*

 8 *Being convinced*
    (or *Convinced*)

5 It is possible (albeit unlikely) that all of the pairs/groups in the class will get one or more answers wrong, in which case nobody will win. However, even if they get one answer wrong, they should continue playing. In the event that all of the other pairs/groups make a mistake, the winning pair/group will be the one with the most correct answers when you have read out all of the words.

12A   It sounds right to me

Aim
To review onomatopoeic words

Exam link
None

Activity type
Completing two texts with the same words

Classroom dynamics
Groups of four, divided into pairs

Time taken
15–20 minutes

When to use
After Vocabulary Focus Activity 5 on page 124

Preparation
Make one copy of the activity for each group of four students and cut into two sections.

Procedure
1 Divide your class into groups of four and ask each group to divide into pairs. Give each of the pairs one section of the activity (A or B). They should not show this to the other pair.

2 Explain that both pairs have different texts which can be completed with the same words. These words are continuous forms of the verbs in the word box. Allow students a couple of minutes to read through their texts but explain that they should not start filling in any of the gaps.

3 Next, explain that the numbers in brackets after each gap refer to the numbered gap in the other pair's text. These gaps should both be completed with the same word (e.g. gap A1 uses the same word as B11 and gap B1 uses the same word as gap A16). Tell students that there are four words in the word box that they do not need to use.

4 Working together but without looking at the other pair's text, students should fill in the gaps in the texts. They should do this by looking at the gaps in turn and discussing which word can be used to complete both the relevant gaps. The first group to complete both their texts is the winner. Alternatively, you could set a time limit of 15 minutes. The winning group is the one that has correctly filled in the most gaps after this time.

Answer key
A1/B11 humming   **A2/B3** creaking
A3/B2 sighing   **A4/B15** whispering
A5/B12 snapping   **A6/B14** rustling
A7/B10 roaring   **A8/B4** buzzing
A9/B8 chattering   **A10/B16** hissing
A11/B6 gurgling   **A12/B9** croaking
A13/B13 hooting   **A14/B7** pattering
A15/B5 dripping   **A16/B1** shuffling
Click, *pop*, *splash* and *whoosh* are not used.

12B   A great album

Aim
To prepare students for writing a review

Exam link
Writing Part 2 (Review)

Activity type
Arranging sentences to make a complete review

Classroom dynamics
Pairs

Time taken
20–25 minutes

When to use
After Writing Focus Activity 3 on page 128

Preparation
Make one copy of the activity for each pair and cut into two parts. Cut the top part into cards.

Procedure

1 Divide your class into pairs and give each pair a set of cards.

2 Explain that their cards contain a review of a music album. The review consists of the title and three paragraphs of four, four and three sentences respectively. The aim of the first part of this activity is to arrange the sentences to form the complete review. Let students do this for about 10 minutes, then give them the complete review (the bottom part of the activity sheet) so that they can check their answers. Note that this review uses the past tense as it makes an historical reference to a song's relevance at the time. If this was not included, the review could have used the present tense.

3 Students then interview each other to find out about their favourite album. Alternatively, they could talk about a song or collection of songs by one artist that they have downloaded, or a concert they have been to. They should ask each other objective questions such as the name of the album or song(s) and artist, the genre of music, etc. before focusing on more subjective matters such as what it is about the album, song(s) or concert that their partners liked and who they think it would appeal to. They should write their answers down.

4 (Optional) If you have time, your students could tell the rest of the class about their partner's album, song, etc.

5 Students then pass their notes to their partner, who can use these as a plan for the review they now have to write (Activity 4 on page 128 of their coursebook). When they have written their review, you could ask them how useful their notes were. (Hopefully, this will emphasise the importance of making a plan before writing an essay.)

Answer key
F, D, I, L, B, J, A, E, H, K, C, G

13A The right word, the right form

Aim
To review words to describe emotions

Exam link
None, but useful for Reading and Use of English Part 3 (Word formation)

Activity type
Dominoes-style sentence matching and completion activity

Classroom dynamics
Groups of three

Time taken
15–20 minutes

When to use
After Vocabulary and Use of English Focus Activity 3 on page 130

Preparation
Make one copy of the activity for each group of three students. Cut into cards along the dotted lines (do *not* cut along the solid lines) and keep in three separate sets (Student A, Student B and Student C).

Procedure

1 Divide your class into groups of three and give each student in the group a *Student A*, *Student B* or *Student C* set of cards. They should not show their cards to one another.

2 Explain that their cards contain eleven short situations or conversations, broken into two sections. The aim of the activity is to match the sections together (the left-hand sections of each card follow on from the right-hand section of a different card). At the same time, students must also complete the sentences with the words to describe emotions in Activity 2 on page 130 of their coursebook. The same word must be used in both sections of a situation but in a different form (e.g. a noun + an adjective). Students should note that they will not need all of the words from their coursebook and that the numbers on the cards are only for checking and reference at the end of the activity. They should do the activity as follows:

3 Student A has the *Start* card. He/She reads out the sentence on the right-hand side of that card (*When his chair collapsed under him, he went bright red with …*). As a group, the three students discuss which word might be missing. Student A writes this word in the gap and puts the card down on the desk.

4 The other two students decide who has the follow-on sentence for Student A's sentence (in this case, it is student B's number 14). Student B reads this out, then together they decide if it is the correct follow-on sentence and agree on the word form. Student B places his/her card alongside the first card.

5 Students repeat Steps 3 and 4 with the other cards. The winning group is the group that correctly match all of their cards and complete all of the sentences.

Answer key

1 + 14 embarrassment/embarrassed
11 + 16 frustrating/frustration
7 + 20 astonishment/astonishing
6 + 10 contentment/content
5 + 15 shameful/shame
2 + 4 bitter/bitterness
19 + 21 relief/relieved
17 + 22 hysteria/hysterical
3 + 12 indifferent/indifference
8 + 13 amusing/amusement
18 + 9 confusion/confused

13B Can you continue?

Aim
To review linking adverbials

Exam link
None, but useful for Speaking Parts 2–4 (Individual long turn, collaborative task and follow-up discussion)

Activity type
Card game requiring students to continue sentences using linking adverbials

Classroom dynamics
Groups of four divided into pairs

Time taken
20–25 minutes

When to use
After Grammar Focus Activity 6 on page 137

Preparation
Make one copy of the activity for each group of four students and cut into two sets of cards.

Procedure

1 Divide your class into groups of four and give each group two sets of cards: the shaded (adverbial) cards and the white (sentence) cards. They should spread these out face down on their desk. Ask the groups to split into pairs.

2 Explain that the aim of the activity is to be the first pair to collect ten of the sentence (white) cards.

3 One pair turns over one of the sentence cards, and reads the sentence on it. They then turn over one of the adverbial cards and decide if they can use the linking adverbial on it to add another sentence that is relevant to the one on their sentence card. For example: *I usually dress very casually at the weekend. + On the other hand, I like to dress smartly when I'm at work.* In some cases, it may not be possible to add another relevant sentence with the adverbial they pick.

4 The other pair decide if the follow-on sentence works in that context. If they decide it does, the first pair keep their sentence card and return the adverbial card to the desk (face down). Both pairs should try to remember what is on that card, as it may be used again. You might want to make a rule that adverbials can only be used a certain number of times so that they are not overused. If the first student pair are unable to give a follow-on sentence, *both* cards are returned to the desk. Note that in any dispute as to the relevance and grammatical accuracy of the follow-on sentence, students should consult you.

5 Steps 3 and 4 are repeated, with the second pair of students picking a sentence card and an adverbial card and seeing if they can add a follow-on sentence.

6 The activity continues until one pair has ten sentence cards and so becomes the winner.

14A Over to you

Aim

To practise talking together about different subjects

Exam link

Paper 4 Speaking Part 4 (Follow-up discussion)

Activity type

Collaborative speaking in a game of skill and chance

Classroom dynamics

Groups of four, divided into pairs

Time taken

30 minutes

When to use

After Speaking Focus Activity 8 on page 144

Preparation

Make one copy of the activity for each group of four students and cut into cards.

Procedure

1 Divide your class into groups of four and ask each group to divide into pairs. Give each pair three cards. They should make sure the other pair in their group do not see what is on them.

2 Explain that each of their cards contains a question, which they are going to ask their opposing pair. That pair will then have three minutes to answer it. Their cards also contain ten key words or phrases which are relevant to the topic of the question. Students must try to predict these words and use them when they speak.

3 One pair reads out the question on one of their cards to the other pair, who then work together to answer it (similar to Part 4 of the CAE Speaking test). The other pair have two minutes to think of key vocabulary related to the topic and note it down. They then have three minutes to complete the speaking task, using the key vocabulary they have thought of (see *Note* below). The pair who asked the question will listen out for the words or phrases which accompany the question. Each time one of these is used by the answering pair, they tick it off on their card.

4 When the three minutes are up, the first pair tell the answering pair how many words/phrases they used that matched those on their card and award them one point for each one. They should also award them between one and three points for *how* they answered the question. For example, did they work together or did one student dominate the conversation? Was their answer relevant or did they stray from the subject? Were there too many pauses?

5 Steps 3 and 4 are repeated but with the roles reversed: the pair which just answered a question give *their* question to the other pair.

6 Steps 3–5 are then repeated until all of the cards are used up. They then add up all of their points. The pair with the most points in each group is the winner. Point out to students that thinking of key vocabulary before you start speaking is a useful strategy for the speaking exam.

> **Note:** In the exam, Part 4 of the Speaking Paper lasts for five minutes. However, in the exam, students would normally be asked two or more questions rather than just the one, as is the case here.

14B First to the top

Aim

To review/extend expressions with *matter*

Exam link

None

Activity type

Completing gapped sentences with correct words while playing a board game

Classroom dynamics

Groups of three

Time taken

15–20 minutes

When to use

After Reading Focus Activity 6 on page 146

Preparation

Make one copy of the activity for each group of three students.

Procedure

1   Divide your class into groups of three and give each group a copy of the activity. Explain that the aim of the activity is to be the first student to reach the top of the grid.

2   Student A starts by looking at their sentence 1 in the grid and deciding which word(s) from the word box can be used to complete it. Students B and C should act as 'referees' and decide if the answer is correct. If it is correct, Student A can complete their sentence and play passes to Student B. If the answer is incorrect, play passes to Student B.

3   Students continue taking turns to try to complete their next sentence and move up the grid. They should note that not all the words in the box will be used.

4   The winner is the first student to correctly complete all of their sentences and reach the top of their grid.

Answer key

Student A
1 life and death   2 waiting   3 personal   4 laughing
5 mince   6 opinion   7 organic   8 courtesy   9 mind

Student B
1 honour   2 grey   3 hands   4 different   5 raise
6 taste   7 help   8 routine   9 complicate

Student C
1 interest   2 time   3 fact   4 hand   5 drop
6 centimetres   7 urgency   8 small   9 subject

Dark, fall, have, make and *similar* are not used.

Recommended Pearson products for use with Gold Advanced

Longman Exams Dictionary

With expert guidance on vocabulary building and writing skills, plus hours of interactive exam practice on the CD-ROM, the *Longman Exams Dictionary* is a must-have for all serious students preparing for examinations. Definitions in the *Gold Advanced Teacher's Book* have been taken from the *Longman Exams Dictionary*.

- Covers key academic study areas such as computing and medicine
- 10,000 synonyms, antonyms and word families
- Over 1,000 Study Notes on vocabulary, grammar and common errors
- Academic Word List highlighted
- Topic Activator section focuses on vocabulary for common exam topics
- Essay Activator section focuses on key vocabulary for writing tasks

The *Longman Exams Coach CD-ROM* improves exam performance with hours of interactive practice, with feedback including practical strategies to improve academic essay writing and listening practice.

Practice Tests Plus *Cambridge* Advanced 2 New Edition

Practice Tests Plus Cambridge Advanced 2 offers comprehensive practice for each exam paper and includes:

- eight complete practice tests, two with exam guidance and question-specific tips
- audio and colour visual materials allowing students to practise for the Speaking and Listening papers at home
- a guide to the exam so your students know what to expect
- answer key and audio script to support teachers doing exam practice in class.

Practice Tests Plus Cambridge Advanced 2 includes online support including:

- authentic examples of the Speaking exam
- writing samples
- teaching tips and activity ideas
- interactive phonetics chart

Pearson Education Limited
Edinburgh Gate
Harlow
Essex CM20 2JE
England
and Associated Companies throughout the world.

www.pearsonelt.com/examsplace

Teaching notes by Clementine Annabell
Photocopiable activities by Rawdon Wyatt

First published 2014
Second impression 2014

ISBN: 978-1-4479-0709-1

Set in Myriad Pro
Printed by Neografia

Acknowledgements
Illustrated by Oxford Designers & Illustrators